ITALIAN AMERICANS
Into the Twilight
of Ethnicity

RICHARD D. ALBA

Department of Sociology
State University of New York at Albany

With a Foreword by Milton M. Gordon

PRENTICE-HALL, INC., Englewood Cliffs, New Jersey 07632

Library of Congress Cataloging in Publication Data

Alba, Richard D.
  Italian Americans.

  Includes bibliographical references and index.
  1. Italian Americans–Cultural assimilation. 2. Italian
Americans–Ethnic identity. I. Title.
E184.I8A47 1985   305.8'51'073   84-6885
ISBN 0-13-506676-X
ISBN 0-13-506668-9 (pbk.)

For Michael

*so that he may know what he could never learn
on his grandfather's knee*

Prentice-Hall Ethnic Groups in American Life
Milton M. Gordon, Editor

Printed in the United States of America

10 9 8 7 6 5 4 3 2 1

ISBN 0-13-506676-X   01
ISBN 0-13-506668-9 {pbk}

Prentice-Hall International, Inc., *London*
Prentice-Hall of Australia Pty. Limited, *Sydney*
Editora Prentice-Hall do Brasil, Ltda., *Rio de Janeiro*
Prentice-Hall Canada Inc., *Toronto*
Prentice-Hall of India Private Limited, *New Delhi*
Prentice-Hall of Japan, Inc., *Tokyo*
Prentice-Hall of Southeast Asia Pte. Ltd., *Singapore*
Whitehall Books Limited, *Wellington, New Zealand*

CONTENTS

FOREWORD

As the United States, with its racially and ethnically variegated population, moves through the last two decades of the 20th century, the myths of the melting pot and complete assimilation recede farther and farther into the distance, both in this country and abroad. Contrary to the expectations and pronouncements of many social scientists, industrialization and urbanization have not reduced the salience of ethnicity in the modern world, nor is there substantial evidence that ethnicity as a critical issue subsides because it happens to exist within the borders of a particular social system: capitalist, socialist, communist, or some mixture in between. The stubborn persistence of the racial and ethnic factor as a source of ethnic communality, and the conflict of ethnic collectivities as interest groups seeking by various means their (frequently previously withheld) fair share of material and status rewards make it all the more imperative that the resources of the sociologist, the political scientist, the historian, the psychologist, the anthropologist, and other practitioners of the art and science of understanding human behavior be brought to bear on the problem. Such application should produce both the theoretical knowledge and the practical measures that would help create a state of affairs where the positive potentialities of ethnic pluralism can be effectively realized while the negative results of unlimited ethnic conflict can be minimized and kept within tolerable bounds.

Thus, the ethnic problem before the American people today is what shape the new pluralism shall take. Will it be cultural pluralism, with its emphasis on a broad kaleidoscope of ethnic patterns and peoples, reaching the point of conscious promotion of sustained bilingualism? Or will structural pluralism, with its social separation in primary-group relationships, be the dominant mode, with differing cultural heritages to be recognized and maintained by symbolic appropriations and reinterpretations of one's ethnic past? What form and resolution will be taken by the political contests that will be brought on by the Black revolt and newly emphasized, ethnic consciousness and sense of pride among Hispanic Americans, Native Americans, and Asian Americans? And will the traditional white ethnic groups of European national origin follow this pluralistic trend, reviving the collective consciousness of their immigrant forebears, or increasingly develop primary group relations, including intermarriage across ethnic and religious lines, thus entering a period of "twilight of ethnicity," to use a phrase coined by one of the authors in the series?

The issues around which this new pluralism will form have such names as affirmative action, de jure and de facto segregation, school busing to achieve racial integration, cultural nationalism, community control of local institutions, housing desegregation, ethnic voting, and confrontation politics; and they are all intimately related to the overriding question of how present-day America deals with the problems of inflation, unemployment, and recession, which fall with particularly heavy impact on its racial minorities.

In order to make the best decisions on these issues, the American of the late 20th century needs to be well informed not only on the history, contributions, and current problems of the racial and ethnic groups that make up the American people but also on how the issues highlighted above are affected by, and in turn affect, the nature of the emerging pluralism. The books in this series are designed to provide this information in a scholarly, yet highly accessible, manner. Each book on a particular ethnic group (and we include the white Protestants as such a sociologically definable entity) is written by an expert in the field of intergroup relations and the social life of the group about which he or she writes. In many cases the author derives ethnically himself or herself from that group. I hope that the publication of this series will aid substantially in the process of enabling Americans to understand more fully what it means to live in a multiethnic society and, concomitantly, what we must do in the future to eliminate the corrosive and devastating phenomena of prejudice and discrimination and to ensure that a pluralistic society can at the same time fulfill its promised destiny of being truly "one nation indivisible."

MILTON M. GORDON

PREFACE

Only a few decades ago, the dominant voice in discussions of ethnicity's role in American life was that arguing the case for the imminence of assimilation and the transience of ethnic subcultures and distinctions. But in a very short span of time, this has been replaced by a near consensus on the permanence of ethnic pluralism and the irrevocable importance of ethnic groups. While this conversion was taking place among social scientists, ethnic conflicts seemed to intensify worldwide, from Northern Ireland to the Middle East, from Biafra to Southeast Asia, as if to provide living proof of the vitality of ancestral claims on the present. Even in the comparatively sedate United States, recently prosperous white ethnics were discovering again pride in their origins and proclaiming their refusal to assimilate. In the twinkling of a historian's eye, the "ethnic mosaic" replaced the "melting pot" as the prevailing image of American society, and the very concept of assimilation fell into disrepute.

Italian Americans provide a natural vantage point from which to assess the adequacy of these alternative views of ethnic experience. They are, comparatively speaking, a large group, about 5 percent of the population, and among the most recently arrived of the European ancestry groups; data presented in Chapter 5 will show that even in the late 1970s, nearly a full century after the beginnings of mass immigration from Italy to the United States, the majority of adult Italian Americans were either immigrants or the children of immigrants. Perhaps because of this recency, they have left a definite imprint on the American consciousness—of close-knit families, tidy and stable working-class neighborhoods, tasty food, and sadly, also of organized crime. Indeed, the prevalent image of Italian Americans is of a cohesive group that has retained its cultural viability, which on the one hand provides members of the group with a cushioning matrix for social life and on the other retards their entry into the mainstream. This image and the theoretical views of ethnicity that lie behind it will be thoroughly scrutinized in the chapters that follow.

My argument will be, as the book's title deliberately telegraphs, that the conventional imagery notwithstanding, Italian Americans (and indeed other white ethnic groups) are rapidly converging with majority Americans. This means, first of all, that both are becoming alike in the important matters of social standing as well as those of culture. It means also that different ethnic origins no longer provide any very serious impediment to social relations, including those of the most intimate and enduring kind, as the rising tide of intermarriage will indicate. To be sure, ethnic differences have not altogether disappeared among those of European heritages in the United States, and it is unlikely that they will do so, at any rate for the near future. But they have become so mild as to constitute a barrier neither to achievement nor to extensive contact with individuals from diverse backgrounds.

One intention I had in writing the book was once again to place assimilation in the inner circle of concern for the study of ethnicity. In my view, it was pushed too hastily to the periphery. I am convinced this happened in part because of a faulty conception of assimilation, which placed too much emphasis on social psychological matters, such as the motivations of a majority group's members to accept those of a minority and of the minority group's members to merge with the majority. This conception made it seem as if assimilation could be banished merely by enough people proclaiming their refusal to assimilate. But as I try to argue throughout this volume, the key forces that have propelled the process of convergence are *structural* and include the transformation of the occupational structure in the urban North, the residential dispersion to the suburbs, and the timely demographic shift to the second and now to the third generation. Paradoxically, it is precisely because of these forces and the convergence they have wrought that ethnic pride is now possible on a mass scale. This argument, it should also be noted, does not imply that assimilation is everywhere and for every group inevitable, but rather that it is brought about by a particular conjunction of forces.

On one point I do not wish to be misunderstood: that I argue on behalf of assimilation does not imply that I believe assimilation to be good and ethnic pluralism to be bad. My position is truly more neutral: that fading of ethnicity that I see demands to be documented and to be understood. When it comes to pride in one's origins, I concede first place to no one. Accepting and understanding who one is and where one came from is, I believe, an important goal to be reached along the route to the fullest realization of one's human potential. But with respect to ethnic origins, the profound changes that have occurred among Italians and other white ethnic groups place definite limits on where this process can lead and what its social significance can be. That is the ultimate message of this book.

This is an appropriate point to acknowledge my long-standing debt to Robert K. Merton. Without his generous assistance at a critical juncture in my career, this book might never have been written. I owe a considerable intellectual debt to Milton M. Gordon, whose work has long influenced me. I am also grateful to him and to Susan Taylor of Prentice-Hall, Inc. for providing me with the opportunity to write this book and their guidance along the way. As always, I have been happily surprised at the number of colleagues, even those who have never met an author, who are willing to take the time to read and critique a manuscript. Those who read most or all of this manuscript and gave me insightful counsel include Paul DiMaggio, John Farley, Herbert Gans, Milton Gordon, Jerre Mangione, Stephen Steinberg, and Walter Zenner. Helpful advice on specific chapters was provided by Thomas Kessner and Jane and Peter Schneider. I was assisted in obtaining valuable census data by Michael Batutis, Leonard Gaines, and Robert Scardamalia of the New York State Data Center. Barbara Hale typed the manuscript. But my greatest debt is to my family, who endured with little complaint my midnight sessions at the computer terminal and weekend afternoon brainstorms, which demanded to be set on paper there and then.

RICHARD D. ALBA

CHAPTER ONE
ETHNICITY: ICONS AND INTERPRETATIONS

Everyone knows something about ethnicity. Nearly every American has met some-one who was ethnically different and wondered, Just how different from me is that person? Those who have had little of such experiences directly have had them vicariously, through the mass media. Ethnicity has become a staple of television, a sort of electronic shorthand, telescoped bundles of symbols that can be let loose by the mention of a last name or the sight of a patch of skin to suggest social differ-ences. Some years back, Columbo and Kojak, to take two prominent examples, were depicted as tough cops, whose ethnic, working-class roots helped them to puncture the mannered gentility of middle-class suspects; more recently, Hill Street's Captain Frank Furillo is portrayed as exercising power in a humane and decent way that seems somehow connected with his ethnic background.

Most Americans also have some direct experience of their own ethnicity; at its heart, ethnicity is just a sense of having certain origins, of coming from a group with a definite history and culture.[1] For some, that experience is a part of child-hood, perhaps sitting at a grandmother's table on a Sunday afternoon, surrounded by cousins, aunts, and uncles and the aromas of grated cheese and garlicky tomato sauce. For others, ethnicity is not something glimpsed nostalgically in the past, but a living, breathing reality of everyday life. For others still, it is not something posi-tive, but negative. Awareness of ethnicity comes in rude fashion, when playmates suddenly turn away, hurling a name such as "dago" or "kike" over their shoulders.

In recent years, Americans have renewed their interest in the intricate ethnic differences visible in their society, differences in which Italian Americans figure prominently. Several decades ago, ethnicity had seemed of little consequence, something that was certain to dissipate under the heat of the "melting pot." There is little of certainty in the present interest, and running through it is the question, What is to be the fate of ethnic groups—will they endure as permanent features of the American landscape, or will they fade gradually into the background as a result of assimilation? The present book addresses this question, at least for the groups whose ancestors came from Europe in the 19th and 20th centuries, by examining the Italian Americans.

Italian Americans hold a place of strategic importance for questions of ethnicity because of the widely accepted images that swirl around this group. In the popular iconography of ethnicity, by which I mean the conventional and highly stylized representations of it, Italian Americans are depicted as resiliently ethnic and working class. The centerpiece of this description is the presumed family solidarity of Italians, the supposed fruit of a Mediterranean peasant culture that placed a supreme value on loyalty to the family. The image of the strength of the family group makes Italian-American culture attractive to other Americans, concerned about high divorce rates and unsure of the meaning of familial ties. It is also reflected in another image of the Italian group: that of "urban villagers," who have created vibrant urban communities that resist the social and physical decay to be found elsewhere in the inner city, and that remain places dominated by neatness and order, as symbolized by well-kept, tiny yards and prolific vegetable gardens. It is no doubt these images of authentic ethnicity that explain the new admiration for things Italian-American. This has been joined by a new pride felt by many Italians, which seems to defy the power of the "melting pot" to boil away ethnic differences.[2]

There is another side to this description, however. It lies in a view that the cultural value attached to family solidarity constitutes the heart of a resistance to social mobility and entry into the American mainstream. Intense loyalty to the family is seen as preventing many Italian-American sons and daughters from breaking out of the parochial worlds of family and neighborhood to achieve greater educational and occupational success and a less narrowly ethnic way of life.[3]

This ambivalent iconographic representation of Italian-American life can be seen in many strands of popular American culture, from such minor and slightly comical ones as the television ads for spaghetti sauce that feature tastings in the family kitchen, to the major films and novels that portray Italian Americans. The film *The Godfather,* with its underlying theme that the iconoclastic son, Michael Corleone, cannot escape his cultural and family destiny, captures the essence of the portrait.

The Italian-American experience, then, can serve as a litmus test for the persistence of ethnicity in American society. But before we can examine this experience in detail, it is essential to stand back from the popular imagery of ethnicity and clarify the ideas we have about it, since these form a prism through which the realities are refracted and, indeed, without which they cannot be perceived. This requires some review of the attention that ethnicity has received from social theorists. Curiously, although the salience of national, religious, and racial differences has always provoked speculation about their origins and meaning, our ideas about ethnicity derive to a surprising degree from the social thought of the 19th and early 20th centuries. It is here that we begin.

THE HERITAGE OF CLASSICAL SOCIAL THEORY

The heritage from the European social theorists of the 19th and early 20th centuries has left a profound imprint on thinking about ethnicity, but not so much by their intent. These thinkers, including Karl Marx, Émile Durkheim, Ferdinand Tönnies, and Max Weber, were concerned with the ramifications of the earth-shuddering transformation of European society wrought by the Industrial Revolution. One of their chief interests was to identify the principal directions of the transformation. Paramount in this respect was their view of it as destroying or casting to the periphery old modes of thoughts and venerable forms of relationship. This view was formulated in the terms of sociology's most famous dichotomies, which identify the polarities of change: feudalism and capitalism; mechanical and organic solidarity; *Gemeinschaft* and *Gesellschaft*; tradition and rationality. Ethnicity was not an important focus for these formulations, but by implication or by explicit reference, it was among the old forms to be cast onto the rubbish heap of history. The master trait that would shape an individual's social being was to be his or her place in the industrial or economic order. Work, not family and ethnic origins, was destiny.

The thought of Karl Marx and his collaborator, Friedrich Engels, provides an extreme case in point, but one that is critical, since, as one commentator has perceptively observed, much of sociology is a debate with the ghost of Karl Marx.[4] The master social trait in Marx's thought was social class, an individual's place in the social order of production and, specifically, his or her relation to the so-called means of production—the instruments for the production of economic wealth. Broadly speaking, Marx and Engels saw the other aspects of social life as subordinate to social class (although there is still debate about their exact views on this point). By implication, class-linked experiences should overshadow those associated with ethnicity: Individuals belonging to the same social class shared experiences whose similarity *should* outweigh whatever ethnic differences might exist between them. (Of course, Marx and Engels were sufficiently realistic to recognize that considerations of ethnicity could be salient enough to be an obstacle to the emergence of class awareness, as Marx indicated in a famous discussion of English and Irish workers.) Likewise, individuals of the same ethnicity would see each other as enemies if they belonged to different, and hostile, social classes.

For Marx and Engels, the driving force of history would demolish traditional social forms and, with them, the importance of the ethnic tie. These thinkers delineated clearly a mechanism that would have this effect as one of its by-products. During their lifetimes, the ground swell of history was a movement from feudalism to capitalism; but the capitalism coming into being already contained the seeds of its own destruction and the transition to communism. These historical processes would be accomplished through the emergence of class consciousness, a unification of workers of all nationalities that was an inevitable product of capitalist development. Class consciousness would arise naturally as the scale of industry increased, because the structure of dominance would be revealed in a naked form when workers were massed together in factories. It would also be promoted by the capitalist drive for a world market, since national boundaries would break down under the infiltration of modern communications and transportation, making all nations vulnerable to capitalist predations. In the long run, workers were bound to see that their common class situation overrode whatever differences might exist among them.[5]

Other classical theorists did not speak so much about social class. The terms in which they expressed the notion of transformation were very different; the key point is that their theories generally left little place for ethnicity. This is true even for the one theorist who is often cited as an exception—Max Weber. His well-known essay on three principal forms of stratification—class, status, and party (or political power)—identified one of these forms, status, as a dimension that includes ethnicity. But elsewhere his emphases were different. For instance, his analysis of bureaucratic organization as a characteristic form in modern society stressed its impersonal character, insisting that the imperatives of organizational structure and process take precedence over the personal traits and preferences of an organization's incumbents. Implied in this analysis is the view that organizational functioning stays largely the same, regardless of the ethnicities of the individuals involved. In this respect, moreover, Weber's analysis of bureaucracy was quite representative of his vision of modern Western society, in which increasing rationalization was portrayed as its master trend.[6]

Despite the diversity of their formulations, the classical European social theorists left a definite heritage, a reflex tendency that is deeply engrained in sociology as a discipline. This tendency is to see the essential development in an industrial society as being a shift in the criteria for the allocation of individuals to social roles—away from particularism, which is keyed to aspects of birth such as kinship and ethnicity, and toward universalism, keyed to meritocratic standards that in principle can be satisfied by anyone, regardless of social origin. From this perspective, ethnicity seems destined to wither away. Ethnic groups may survive for a long time at the periphery of an industrial society, but the irreversible dynamic of development is to assimilate these marginal groups to the culture of the modern core, the majority culture, and to loosen individuals' ties to these groups by means of mobility. The ultimate result of the classical sociological heritage, then, is a theoretical bias against ethnicity, a discounting of its potential as a basic social force, even in the face of evidence of its persistence.

THE UNITED STATES DURING
AND AFTER MASS IMMIGRATION

American social theory of the early 20th century does not have such a clear thrust, even though ethnicity lay in the foreground of American concerns. Issues surrounding ethnicity have been forced into the American consciousness as a result of the confrontations between peoples that have occurred throughout American history. These episodes, which extend like an unbroken chain through the American experience, include the conquest of the indigenous peoples by the European colonizers and the enslavement of Africans, as well as the more or less voluntary immigration of millions from many lands, but chiefly from Europe. A consequence of these events, which engendered dilemmas felt acutely by many, has been to stimulate thought about ethnicity in relation to American society. What concern us here are the reactions to immigration, particularly during the century of mass immigration, running roughly from 1830 to 1930.

Matters concerning immigration still provoke heated debate, but even so, it is difficult for the contemporary observer to imagine the depth of feelings and the sense of crisis provoked by the immigration of the 19th and early 20th centuries. It was enormous in magnitude, the largest population movement ever known: In a span of 100 years, 38 million people arrived, entering a nation that had a population of only 13 million at the period's opening. At moments in particular places, the foreign-born and their children made up astoundingly large proportions of the population; for example they were nearly 70 percent of Chicago's population in 1910.[7] Not only was this immigration large in numbers, but its ethnic character was different from that of "old stock" Americans. Early in the century of mass immigration, the arrival of hundreds of thousands of Irish Catholics fleeing famine-stricken Ireland introduced the first large group of Catholics and led to intense religious conflict. Nonetheless, its significance seems to pale before the sense of crisis brought on by changes in the immigrant stream later in the century, when the sources of immigration shifted from northern and western Europe to the south and east, provoking profound anxieties about the future of America. Many Americans envisioned their nation as sinking under a flood of different, and inferior, peoples.

These anxieties, which were heightened during World War I, led to the hopeful expectation that the immigrants and their descendants would assimilate. Both in theory and in practice, the expectation concerned first and foremost the external signs of ethnic difference—immigrant language, customs, clothes and behavior. Relevant here was the view—frequently labeled today as *Anglo-conformity*—that recently arrived ethnic groups should accept without alteration the culture and institutions, derived largely from English models, that dominated American society at the time of their arrival. The immigrants and their children were expected thereby to throw off the cultures of their homelands, as so much old clothing that would no longer be needed in the benign environment of the New World. The

Anglo-conformity view was probably held by a majority of Americans, since it was a popular viewpoint reflecting no particular systematic theory about ethnicity. It is also especially appropriate for characterizing the frenzied xenophobia of the World War I years, when demands were voiced loudly for the "pressure-cooker assimilation" and "100 percent Americanization" of the immigrants.[8]

There was another view of assimilation, that of the "melting pot." It was more intellectually elaborated and possessed deep roots in American soil, with adherents such as Ralph Waldo Emerson. But it, too, drew its inspiration not from a theory of ethnicity but rather from a particular vision of America. This was a vision of America as a pristine world, where a new society could develop free of the social shackles, the political and religious despotisms of the Old World. This faith in the cleansing power of the New World is visible in a famous passage from J. Hector St. John Crèvecoeur's *Letters from an American Farmer* (1782):

> What is the American, this new man? He is either an European, or the descendant of an European, hence that strange mixture of blood, which you will find in no other country. I could point out to you a family whose grandfather was an Englishman, whose wife was Dutch, whose son married a French woman, and whose present four sons have now four wives of four different nations. *He* is an American, who leaving behind him all his ancient prejudices and manners, receives new ones from the new mode of life he has embraced, the new government he obeys, and the new rank he holds. He becomes an American by being received in the broad lap of our great *Alma Mater.* Here individuals of all nations are melted into a new race of men, whose labours and posterity will one day cause great changes in the world.[9]

Not merely limited to the early history of immigration, the melting-pot view was a regular presence among reactions to it. During the massive influx from southern and eastern Europe in the early 20th century, it was popularized by Israel Zangwill's play *The Melting Pot,* whose central image was America as "God's crucible." Distinctive of the melting-pot ideology was the emphasis, evident in the passage quoted above, on a fusion of cultures, rather than the wholesale acceptance by many different nationalities of the culture of a single one of them. But still the basic idea of assimilation remained: There was to be an *American* culture, however it came about, and immigrants and their children were to accept it, even if they also made some contribution to it.[10]

Thus, the American reactions to immigration kept the notion of assimilation in the foreground, blocking out other conceptions of ethnicity that might have granted it a more durable place. The same point holds for the writings of American social scientists during the early part of this century. Like other Americans, sociologists were concerned with the ultimate implications of the ethnic tumult they saw before them, but their work does not lead (as European social theory by contrast does) to a clear prediction about the future of ethnic groups. Nonetheless, since American sociologists were preoccupied by what happens when peoples of different cultures come into contact, notions of ethnic change occupy an important place in their writings, making American social theory at least compatible with a view that assimilation would ultimately win out, even if not unambiguously endorsing it.

One eminent sociologist whose work bears this out was Robert Ezra Park, who formulated the "race relations cycle" of "contact, competition, accommodation, and eventual assimilation."[11] Park sometimes wrote as if the stages of the cycle formed an inevitable progression leading to assimilation, and at other times as if the cycle were an ideal type, from which there were exceptions, groups that would not assimilate. But even if he recognized that there were exceptions and that the long-run outcome was unclear, the race relations cycle presumed change, not fixity, and it thus suggested the transience of ethnicity. The same point applies to W. Lloyd Warner, who gave prominent attention to ethnicity in his well-known study of "Yankee City." Warner saw the mobility of American society as undermining the solidarity of ethnic groups and hence promoting their assimilation. Nonetheless, he recognized that some groups, especially nonwhites, might be exceptions because of the difficulties they faced in gaining full acceptance by American core groups. But his basic model remained one of assimilation, so that despite the explicitly acknowledged exceptions, his thought directs attention towards assimilation processes, rather than toward the possibility that ethnicity would prove to be an enduring feature of social life.[12]

THE RENEWAL OF INTEREST IN ETHNICITY

A sea change in thinking about ethnicity, to which many streams contributed, occurred around 1960; and ethnicity became a topic of serious investigation for social scientists and discussion in the popular media. One current that contributed to the new tide was the Civil Rights movement, which forced Americans to recognize the continuing racial and ethnic diversity of American society, and which, by giving legitimacy to the demands of Blacks for an acknowledgement of their separate realities, unintentionally gave legitimacy to the demands of non-Black ethnics. Perhaps a more important reason for the ferment over ethnicity among whites lay in the coming of age of the white ethnic groups themselves. By the 1960s, a third generation—a second native-born generation—was emerging even among the most recently arrived European groups, such as the Poles, Italians, and Jews. This third generation felt secure in its Americanness and, for that reason perhaps, was able to assert its ethnicity more confidently. It was in fact sufficiently American in its behavior and values that its ethnic assertions were not threatening and divisive, as those of earlier generations might have been perceived. Moreover, the mobility of the white ethnic groups had carried substantial numbers of their members into places of prominence in American life. From there, they were able to draw attention to ethnic sentiments and diversity to an extent that would not have been possible otherwise.

The election of John F. Kennedy in 1960 set the seal on this coming of age of the ethnics. In the 1960s, for the first time generally in American society, it seemed acceptable, even good, to be "ethnic," to hold on self-consciously to an ethnic heritage and to forswear assimilation. Journalists and social scientists proclaimed an "ethnic revival," looked for its causes, and announced that ethnicity was a fixture of American life. If there was anything strange about this, it was that the vitality of ethnicity was discovered at the very point when massive chunks of ethnic cultures had dropped away.

To be sure, there were precursors for the position that ethnicity would persist. One lay in the ideal of *cultural pluralism* as expounded by Horace Kallen. Kallen began writing during World War I, the period of the most intense anti-immigrant sentiments. In opposition to the then popular demands for the immediate Americanization of the immigrants and their children, he argued that equality of ethnic cultures is more consistent with democratic ideals than a cultural uniformity imposed from without. He believed, moreover, that the development of American society would reach farther if pluralism were respected and ethnic groups were allowed to make contributions from what was uniquely valuable in their cultural heritages. As Kallen put it,

> The American way is the way of orchestration. As in an orchestra, the different instruments, each with its own characteristic timbre and theme, contribute distinct and recognizable parts to the composition, so in the life and culture of a nation, the different regional, ethnic, occupational, religious and other communities compound their different activities to make up the national spirit.[13]

But Kallen's notion of cultural pluralism remained an ideal; he provided no analysis to indicate how this ideal would be attained. A second precursor of the renewal of interest in ethnicity made its contribution by describing how ethnicity would re-emerge. Marcus Hansen's famous essay *The Problem of the Third Generation Immigrant* was written in the late 1930s. Hansen, a Swedish-American historian, started from the observation of a renewal of interest in ethnicity among third-generation Swedish Americans in the Midwest. He fit this observation into a sense of the psychological dynamics affecting the generations after immigration. In his eyes, the second generation, the children of the immigrants, was obsessed by its difference from other Americans and attempted frantically to throw off the remaining traces of ethnicity to become just like other Americans. But the third generation, secure in its place in America, sought to recover what its parents had lost. In Hansen's pithy formulation, "what the son wishes to forget, the grandson wishes to remember."[14]

Neither Hansen's Law, as it came to be called, nor Kallen's ideal of cultural pluralism was forgotten by the ethnic writers of the 1960s. But both were woven together with broader interpretive strands in an attempt to provide a fully developed sociological demonstration of the enduring place of ethnicity, one that would solve the theoretical problem of how ethnicity was to survive while ethnic groups accommodated themselves to American society.

One of the interwoven strands, the less compelling from the sociological point of view, is stated in terms of deep-seated human needs. It assumes that humans need to be able to answer for themselves the question, Who am I? and the most satisfying answer, so it is argued, involves a connection to their origins. This is a *primordial* need, one that is not fundamentally altered by the overlay of civilization. Ethnicity is an important point of self-reference in the answer, especially since in contemporary society, the powers of kinship and geographical place, two traditional reference points, have been diminished by widespread mobility. Ethnicity is satisfying also because it psychologically links the individual to a large social grouping with a mythology, a pantheon of imagery that can be used to make sense of the world. Thus, it provides a rich soil to nourish the individual's identity, compensating for the thin psychological depth of modern life. In other words, ethnicity is held, despite the implications of classical social theory, to be inseparable from an industrial order because it provides the basis for an enduring personal identity amid the social flux of a rapidly changing society. This hypothesis is supported by the apparent worldwide renaissance of ethnicity, disproving the leveling power of industrial society.[15]

But the image of primitive sentiments that break through the veneer of modern society gives the primordial interpretation an irrational cast. More satisfying in this respect is the *ethnogenesis* interpretation, which stresses that ethnicity is not some fixed form handed down by tradition, but that it is continuously regenerated, and hence altered, in the process of adjustment to American society. The first persuasive attempt along these lines was by Nathan Glazer and Daniel Patrick Moynihan in their now classic book, *Beyond the Melting Pot*. Since their pioneering argument, the interpretation has been widely accepted.[16]

The essence of the ethnogenesis position can be summarized by three linked statements. First, the original form of ethnicity, brought by the immigrants, does not survive for long in America, because it is generally not compatible with American life. This obviously applies to such externals as language and clothing, but it applies as well to the values in the immigrants' culture, which are finely attuned to the exigencies of life in the Old World but may clash with those of the New World. These values need not disappear altogether, but generally speaking, they must be transformed to survive. Second, the immigrants from any group, along with their children and grandchildren, come to share many commonalities of *American* experience that set them apart from other groups. These arise partly from the simple facts that the immigrants come at the same time, settle in the same places, and work at the same jobs, those that are open at the time and in the place of arrival. The commonalities, then, are forged from the structure of opportunity that exists in the new society, but they are also molded indirectly from the cultural materials the immigrants bring with them. The immigrants and their children choose certain possibilities over others that are open to them because of the propensities inherent in their values; this too contributes to a distinctive, shared American experience. Third and finally, this common American experience provides a basis for a *transformed* ethnicity, one that is not a simple derivative of the society from which the immigrants came. The group's culture is filtered through this experience; many elements are rejected, while others must be reshaped in order to fit. Moreover, the American experience provides a fertile ground from which new cultural elements arise. It provides as well the foundation for an ethnic identity, a shared sense by the members of the group that "we are alike."[17]

A fourth statement is sometimes added: The regeneration of ethnicity out of American experience is strengthened by a function that ethnicity can play in American society—namely, as a vehicle for *political* interests. Ethnic groups are particularly suitable for such a role, because in American society, which lacks sharp class cleavages, ethnic groups correspond with social differences as they are actually perceived. In *Beyond the Melting Pot,* Glazer and Moynihan noted some features shared by many of New York City's Italian Americans, such as their concentration in the city's working class and among its homeowners. The coincidence of such politically relevant facts is presumed to bring ethnicity to the foreground of political consciousness.[18] It also leads to the emergence of ethnically based organizations to promote common interests, and these organizations provide the ground for a new level of group-sustaining contacts among ethnics. In the eyes of some social scientists, the political aspect of ethnicity was reinforced by governmental support for affirmative action in the 1970s. These writers held up a vision of what America was becoming as a result of the push for affirmative action: a nation of contending ethnic blocs, each demanding proportional representation in important spheres.[19]

One aspect of the ethnogenesis thesis that resonates with important sociological themes lies in the role attributed to culture. Despite the short life assumed for Old World cultural traits, they play a crucial role in defining the initial place in American society of an immigrant group. Since this initial place in turn provides a basis for the shared experiences of the group, the imprint of the Old World culture can be seen long after its vitality had faded. The cultural traits imported by the immigrants help to determine what sorts of jobs they take, what advantage their children take of American schools, what sort of family and community life the group establishes—in a word, what niche the group is able to carve out in the new society.

In this way, the ethnogenesis interpretation echoes a key thesis of American sociology, that culture affects the socioeconomic success of a group. During the 1950s, social scientists investigated the social psychological prerequisites of social mobility and identified a configuration of attitudes, values, and motivations that appeared a virtual necessity—the "achievement syndrome." In a famous paper, "Race, Ethnicity, and the Achievement Syndrome," Bernard Rosen described the value components of the syndrome as an orientation to the future rather than the present, an emphasis on the needs of the individual over those of the group, and encouragement for the individual to believe in the possibility of manipulating the world to his or her advantage. The opposite to the second value is the subordination of the individual's needs to those of the group, and to the third value, fatalism— traits, incidentally, that are often ascribed to Italian Americans. Rosen traced racial and ethnic differences in socioeconomic success to subcultural differences in these key values. His research lent support to the view that ethnic groups become concentrated in different social strata, as they sort themselves out according to the advantages and disabilities inherent in their ethnic subcultures.[20]

The thesis that culture determines mobility has lost in recent years the universal acceptance it once had (although it still has wide acceptance); but the view that has risen up in opposition to it remains compatible with the ethnogenesis interpretation. In contrast to the earlier view of ethnic inequality as arising out of the natural propensities of a group's culture, the newer view sees inequality as imposed from without by the institutions of a society, which sort individuals and groups on the basis of cultural symbols. This view of inequality as imposed has achieved great depth in the study of educational institutions. Critical theorists of education view inequality as created in part by the sorting of students into different educational tracks, such as vocational and academic, on the basis of cultural cues, such as accent and dress, that distinguish between ethnic groups. The outcome of this sorting process, which happens in many other institutions as well, is a "cultural division of labor," in which different cultural groups are concentrated in different social strata, just as in the earlier view.[21]

Either view of culture's role could be used to argue that initial cultural differences between ethnic groups lead to rough congruence between ethnicity and social position, and that this in turn lends strength to ethnicity. This congruence, by the way, does not mean that pluralist writers deny the evident possibilities for mobility in American society, possibilities that many ethnics have used to move ahead. But in their view, occupational similarities hold for a sufficient number, and ethnic groups thus retain their critical mass. And even the mobile may continue to identify with the group because the memory of the ethnic pattern remains strong and is perhaps part of the story of their own success.

Culture is important in another respect: It continues to serve as a badge of group membership. Cultural differences continue to exist among groups; however, they no longer bear much resemblance to the cultural baggage of the immigrants but, instead, have been rebuilt, partly out of American materials. Andrew Greeley has emphasized this aspect of the ethnogenesis argument and has furnished a good deal of evidence in support of it. In book after book, he has documented that cultural differences, for example in the sphere of moral values, remain visible in data collected by public-opinion surveys.[22] These cultural differences, it should be noted, coexist with a public American culture, which all groups acquire within a few generations. Coexistence is possible because the two cultures are confined largely to different realms. The public American culture bears on the behavior involved in contact in public places between persons from different ethnic groups, such as that which occurs on the job or in school. The realms of ethnic subcultures are more private ones; ethnic subcultures receive their chief expression in terms of the values concerned with home, family, and community.

Finally, the ethnogenesis interpretation is satisfying from a sociological point of view because it does not insist on the importance of ethnicity in and of itself. Rather, ethnicity remains salient because it coincides with other social differences, particularly those of income, wealth, and power. Ethnicity, in other words, does not stand on its own but stands because it is draped over the skeletal structure of inequality. In attaching ethnicity's persistence to the inequalities among groups, the ethnogenesis interpretation seems consistent with much of American history.

ASSIMILATION THEORY AFTER 1960

Enduring pluralism, captured in the image of an ethnic mosaic, has been the dominant theme of the study of ethnicity in recent years, and during this period an equally developed counterinterpretation, arguing the weakening of ethnicity, has not been articulated. But the materials for such an interpretation are near at hand, for theories of assimilation have not lain dormant since 1960.

The premier event was the publication of Milton Gordon's influential *Assimilation in American Life* in 1964. Gordon's book was not an attempt to argue the disappearance of ethnicity through assimilation; rather, it offered a theoretically precise dissection of assimilation in order to make possible a more accurate description of the state of ethnicity in America. Gordon distinguished seven dimensions of assimilation, but the crucial distinction lay between two of these: acculturation, the acquisition by the individual or the group of the culture of the host society; and structural assimilation, the entry by the individual or group into primary relations (those involving affect, such as friendship or marriage) across ethnic boundaries. These dimensions are not dichotomous but continuous, and hence there are degrees of both. The acculturation of a group (or individual) is complete when it has acquired the language, dress, manners, and values of the host society. Structural assimilation is complete when a group's members no longer exhibit any tendency to prefer their co-ethnics as neighbors, friends, and spouses.

The perception at the heart of Gordon's analysis was the recognition that assimilation does not unfold along all dimensions at once, but that it proceeds at different rates along each and that, even, it may happen in some ways but not at all in others. Specifically, in Gordon's words, "cultural assimilation, or acculturation, is likely to be the first of the types of assimilation to occur when a minority group arrives on the scene"; and "cultural assimilation . . . may take place even when none of the other types of assimilation occurs simultaneously or later, and this condition of 'acculturation only' may continue indefinitely."[23] But structural assimilation is the key that unlocks the door to complete assimilation. Again in Gordon's words, "once structural assimilation has occurred, either simultaneously with or subsequent to acculturation, all of the other types of assimilation will naturally follow."[24] One type that naturally follows in the wake of structural assimilation is psychological assimilation, the loss of a distinctive ethnic identity.

Gordon did not present a complete description of the state of ethnicity in the United States at the time that he wrote, nor did he give a prognosis for its future. But he did say enough to make his basic views clear. First of all, he believed that the acculturation of most groups was fairly complete. Moreover, in contrast to the emphasis in the melting-pot credo, acculturation generally meant taking on a culture derived from English models and abandoning the culture of one's own group; there was no fusion, except in minor ways. In a much-cited passage, Gordon asked if acculturation was largely a one-way process and answered his own question with a qualified yes. Aside from the area of institutionalized religion, the influence of ethnic cultures appears chiefly on the cultural periphery: in such areas as place names, cuisine, and words borrowed by the English language. Thus, the culture acquired by ethnic groups through acculturation remains essentially Anglo-Saxon in its inspiration.[25]

But if cultural pluralism is not characteristic of the United States, structural pluralism is. Gordon saw ethnic groups as self-contained entities, each with its own structure of cliques and institutions, within which an individual may choose to spend an entire lifetime. The nature of American society requires some intergroup contact because such institutions as the school and the workplace are integrated ethnically. But for the individuals involved, this contact can remain fragmentary and partial; it does not have to grow into relationships of intimacy and affect— primary relationships, in other words. According to *Assimilation in American Life,* there is considerable separation among ethnic groups in primary relations.

Gordon's thesis of structural pluralism without a cultural foundation is summarized well in his concept of the *ethclass.* The ethclass represents the inter-section of social class and ethnicity and corresponds with the social differentia-tion Americans perceive. Personal identity is rooted in the ethclass, which is made up of "people like me." Consequently, individuals tend to confine their primary relationships to others of the same ethclass, that is, who belong to the same social class *and* ethnic group. With respect to behavior or culture, however, only the social class aspect of the ethclass is important. In other words, people of the same social class tend to behave alike, regardless of their ethnic backgrounds.[26]

Gordon's analysis of assimilation is taken one step further by Peter Blau's macrosociological theorizing, published in his 1977 book, *Inequality and Hetero-geneity: A Primitive Theory of Social Structure.*[27] Gordon's analysis leaves ample room for ethnicity to persist, although in an attenuated way, without a cultural base. But Blau's theory suggests strongly that the presumed remaining fortress of ethnicity, widespread structural pluralism, is likely to crumble under the conditions that hold in American society.

Blau's theory is very general. He is not concerned explicitly with ethnicity and assimilation, but with how a society's social structure impinges on its social integration. He defines *social structure* as the distribution of persons among the combinations of meaningful social positions (for example, ethnicity, occupation, and age) and defines *social integration* as extensive social association among the occupants of different social positions.[28] Blau attempts to describe theoretically how social structure constrains as well as promotes social relations across group boundaries, and since ethnicity is one of the positions that form social structure, his theory has an immediate bearing on structural assimilation.

The theory is a deductive one. From definitions and a few self-evident or plausible axioms, Blau derives theorems about the rate of intergroup association. Frequently in fact, these theorems are derivable from very simple group properties, especially size. The simplest of these theorems is that "in the relation between any two groups, the rate of intergroup association of the smaller group exceeds that of the larger."[29] This theorem is a tautological consequence of the fact that any intergroup relation must be between one member from the smaller group and one from the larger; hence, since the number of such relations is the same for both groups, they involve a larger proportion of the smaller group's members. This theorem, it will be noted, applies with absolute determinism to relations that are exclusive—i.e., that can involve only one partner, such as marriage (friendship, however, is not an exclusive relation). Therefore, it and the theorems that follow from it apply directly to intermarriage, a paramount indicator of structural assimilation.

Although the theorem just mentioned is tautological, from it and others flow significant insights into the structural constraints on in-group associations. Essentially, these reveal the forces in American society that promote structural assimilation. For example, "the probability of extensive intergroup relations increases with decreasing size."[30] Small groups—and most American ethnic groups represent only small fractions of the population—have difficulty maintaining high rates of in-group association and high rates of endogamous, or in-group, marriage. There are, of course, exceptions—groups that enforce a rigid segregation, such as the Amish, or that suffer from a high degree of segregation enforced by the majority, such as Black Americans.

An interesting light is cast on the difficulties small groups face in maintaining their solidarity when group membership is considered in relation to other dimensions of social structure. Blau refers to the various dimensions, such as ethnicity, occupation, and age, as parameters and considers how strongly the parameters are correlated with one another. When they are correlated only weakly with one another—when, to take an example, the members of different ethnic groups are found throughout the occupational hierarchy—this is a condition he defines as *intersecting parameters*. When, on the other hand, they coincide strongly with one another—when, to continue the example, the members of different ethnic groups are concentrated in specific occupational strata—then this is the condition of *consolidated parameters*. Consolidated parameters hinder intergroup associations, but intersecting parameters promote them. Why?—because in a society where intersecting parameters obtain, an individual cannot easily satisfy all of his or her in-group preferences in a relation; usually, some of them must be sacrificed. This is true because in such a society, there are only a small number of others who are like the individual in all relevant ways—ethnicity, education, age, and so forth—and the chances of meeting such a person are small. This logic based on size suggests why in-group association is not problematic when the social structure is characterized by consolidated parameters.[31]

What follows quite directly from Blau's discussion of intersecting parameters is that forces such as geographical or social mobility that reduce the homogeneity of ethnic minorities will in the end promote their structural assimilation. Consider, by way of example, the situation of an unmarried, college educated Polish American. Because not all Polish Americans are college educated (this follows from the condition of intersecting parameters), there will only be a small number of Polish Americans suitable for her to marry in the sense that they are also appropriately educated, of the right age, have suitable tastes and lifestyles, and so forth. Hence to marry, she may have to sacrifice either her preference for a Polish American spouse or her preference for one who is compatible in other ways. Some individuals will choose to do the latter, but others will choose to do the former, especially since not everyone has a preference for a spouse of the same ethnicity. Thereby, the rate of intermarriage increases.

Blau's theory ultimately implies that the extent of social mobility is critical for assessing the staying power of ethnicity. Widespread opportunities for mobility open to the members of ethnic groups will lessen ethnic homogeneity and increase structural assimilation. In this respect, the theory suggests that social mobility will have a more detrimental impact on ethnic cohesiveness than pluralist writers recognize.

A final contribution to a possible assimilationist interpretation has been made by Herbert Gans, whose conception of *symbolic ethnicity* reconciles the renewed interest in ethnicity with the possibility of massive structural change to ethnicity's foundation. Briefly, Gans accepts that upward mobility has become the rule rather than the exception and suggests that ethnicity has become increasingly peripheral to the lives of many upwardly mobile members of ethnic groups. But these mobile individuals do not relinquish ethnic identity entirely; rather, they adapt it to their current circumstances, selecting from an ethnic heritage a few symbolic elements that do not interfere with the need to intermix socially with others from a variety of ethnic backgrounds. This symbolic identification with the ethnic group allows individuals to construct personal identities that contain some ethnic "spice," but it reflects an ethnicity with little social and psychological depth. Its marginal and intermittent nature makes symbolic ethnicity vastly different in character and implications from the ethnicity of earlier generations, an ethnicity of shared culture and daily experience into which individuals were irrevocably born. Hence, Gans describes symbolic ethnicity as an "ethnicity of last resort," and his thesis suggests that the much-proclaimed ethnic revival after 1960 is not so much a proof of ethnicity's continued vitality but, in the words of Stephen Steinberg, its "dying gasp."[32]

CONCLUSION

Since 1960, a debate over the significance of ethnicity for American society has arisen, and it remains to be resolved. The basic question is often hidden from clear view because the debate is often carried on as if it were between the assimilationist viewpoint of the early 20th century and a more contemporary perspective on ethnicity. But in fact the assimilationist position has been modified since the renewal of interest in ethnicity began in the early 1960s. No important analysis of ethnicity argues that ethnic groups are scheduled to disappear any time in the near future. The current debate is really about the importance of ethnicity for American society. Those who adhere to what might be called the "pluralist" position (recognizing that this position actually includes diverse viewpoints) generally see ethnicity not only as a long-lasting feature of American society, but also as a fundamental and even an essential one. On the whole, they see ethnicity as linked to salient social differences, which have resonances in important spheres, such as those of education, mobility, and politics. Of particular importance are the echoes of cultural differences. For instance, insofar as cultural differences engender mobility differences, they lead to concentrations of ethnic groups within specific strata (consolidated parameters, in Blau's lexicon) and thereby reinforce ethnic solidarities.

Those who adhere to an assimilationist position, on the other hand, see ethnicity as increasingly peripheral to American life, at least for the white ethnic groups descended from the European immigrants of the 19th and early 20th centuries. (Virtually no one would deny the salience of racial boundaries.) Generally speaking, the increasing marginality of ethnicity is viewed as a consequence of the openness of American society to mobility by the children and grandchildren of European immigrants and the resulting rise in contact across ethnic boundaries, a rise reflected in growing rates of intermarriage. This structural assimilation implies a dampening of cultural differences, a necessary precondition, and also of ethnic identity. Ethnicity, then, is entering a kind of twilight stage, but it is a twilight that may last for a very long time, perhaps forever.

The remainder of the book will assess the merits of these two perspectives by the light of the Italian-American experience. Italians provide a strategic testing ground for different theories about ethnicity, and not just because of the popular images of the group noted earlier. Arguments on behalf of ethnic pluralism have been applied with particular force to the groups of southern and eastern European origins, among whom the Italians figure prominently. The presumption has been that, by virtue of their comparatively recent arrival, they retain large parts of their ethnic cultures intact. This in turn seems verified by the ethnic stirrings occurring within these groups in recent years, as some of their members struggle for a new sense of their identity and achieve a newly found ethnic pride; the assertions of their ethnicity by Italians and others have seemed to herald a new era, as implied in the title of Michael Novak's book *The Rise of the Unmeltable Ethnics.*[33]

In the case of the Italians, the question of culture arises from another direction as well. For this group, the pluralist interpretation seems buttressed by the salient cultural feature in scholarly descriptions of the group: the same family solidarity that stands out in popular imagery. On this basis, Italian-American culture has been argued to inhibit assimilation directly through the strength of bonds to the family and indirectly by limiting mobility. Thus, the Italian-American experience raises as a central question the durability and meaning of ethnic culture. Consequently, if Italian Americans are found to be mobile and assimilating, as I will argue they are, these facts must carry great weight in our evaluation of the role of ethnicity in American life.

CODA: THE DEFINITION OF ETHNICITY

A few words need to be said about the definition of ethnicity before the book proceeds any further. The fact that nationality, racial, and religious groups can all be labeled "ethnic" groups gives rise at times to confusion; since these groups may be quite different in some respects, it is thus not always clear in what ways they can be considered to be similar.

For the purposes of this book, the most satisfactory definition of an ethnic group is that of Max Weber: a human group that entertains a "subjective belief" in its "common descent because of similarities of physical type or of customs or both, or because of memories of colonization and migration." Weber adds, "it does not matter whether or not an objective blood relationship exists."[34] To my mind, the Weberian definition puts the emphasis where it properly belongs: What matters fundamentally is the experience of the group's members, the view from inside. Thus, the members of an ethnic group recognize a boundary enclosing them; they share a "consciousness of kind," of being like others in the group, and consequently they tend to interact with them. These are the cardinal group traits for the study of ethnicity.[35]

What also matters according to the Weberian definition is that the members of an ethnic group share a common identity premised on a shared history. It is this self-definition in terms of the past that makes an ethnic group different from most other kinds of social groups and constitutes the *sine qua non* of its existence. This requirement need not be the only thing that the members of such a group share; they may also share such cultural traits as a language or dialect, kinship patterns, and cuisine. But these are merely possible accompaniments of ethnicity, not its essential ingredients. In this way, the definition is compatible with the possibility that ethnic cultures may change, even though ethnic groups live on.

By this definition, Italian Americans of course constitute an ethnic group; the "common descent" to which the definition refers is fulfilled by their ancestors' origins in Italy. So, too, do Jewish Americans, despite the fact that their group is frequently thought of as a religious group and hence different from one based on national origins. Finally, Black Americans are also an ethnic group by this definition. To bring all three of these groups, and others, together under a single definition does not assume that they are alike in all respects but, rather, suggests the importance of comparing their experiences in order to highlight those features that are decisive for group destiny.

NOTES

[1] See the definition of ethnicity on p. 17.

[2] See the reactions reported by Stephen S. Hall, "Italian-Americans: Coming into their own," *The New York Times Magazine,* May 15, 1983, pp. 28–58.

[3] For a sensitive discussion based on some life histories, see Elizabeth Stone, "It's still hard to grow up Italian," *The New York Times Magazine,* December 17, 1978, pp. 42–104.

[4] Irving M. Zeitlin, *Ideology and the Development of Sociological Theory* (Englewood Cliffs, N.J.: Prentice-Hall, 1968).

[5] See Karl Marx and Friedrich Engels, "The Communist Manifesto," in *The Marx-Engels Reader,* ed. Robert C. Tucker (New York: W. W. Norton, 1972).

[6] Max Weber, "Class, status, and party" and "Bureaucracy," in *From Max Weber: Essays in Sociology,* trans. and ed. H. H. Gerth and C. Wright Mills (New York: Oxford University Press, 1946).

[7] Stephen Steinberg, *The Ethnic Myth: Race, Ethnicity, and Class in America* (Boston: Beacon Press, 1981), p. 47.

[8] For a description of Anglo-conformity, see Milton M. Gordon, *Assimilation in American Life: The Role of Race, Religion, and National Origins* (New York: Oxford University Press, 1964), Chapter 4; and John Higham, *Strangers in the Land: Patterns of American Nativism, 1860–1925* (New York: Atheneum, 1970), Chapter 9.

[9] Quoted by Gordon, *Assimilation in American Life,* p. 116. The original is J. Hector St. John Crèvecoeur, *Letters from an American Farmer* (London, 1782).

[10] Ibid., Chapter 5.

[11] Robert Ezra Park, *Race and Culture: Essays in the Sociology of Contemporary Man* (New York: The Free Press of Glencoe, 1950), p. 150.

[12] W. Lloyd Warner and Leo Srole, *The Social Systems of American Ethnic Groups* (New Haven, Conn.: Yale University Press, 1945), pp. 283–96.

[13] Quoted by Gordon, *Assimilation in American Life,* p. 147. The original is Horace M. Kallen, *Culture and Democracy in the United States* (New York: Boni and Liveright, 1924), pp. 209–10.

[14] Marcus Lee Hansen, *The Problem of the Third Generation Immigrant* (Rock Island, Ill.: Augustana Historical Society, 1938), pp. 9–10. Hansen's Law is quoted and expounded upon by Will Herberg, *Protestant-Catholic-Jew* (New York: Anchor Books, 1960), pp. 28–31.

[15] For the primordial interpretation, see Edward Shils, "Color, the universal intellectual community, and the Afro-Asian intellectual," in John Hope Franklin (ed.), *Color and Race* (Boston: Beacon Press, 1968); and Harold R. Isaacs, "Basic group identity: The idols of the tribe," in Nathan Glazer and Daniel Patrick Moynihan (eds.), *Ethnicity: Theory and Experience* (Cambridge, Mass.: Harvard University Press, 1975). The world-wide renaissance is proclaimed by William Petersen, among others, in his introduction to William Petersen, (ed.), *The Background to Ethnic Conflict* (Leiden: E. J. Brill, 1979).

[16] Nathan Glazer and Daniel Patrick Moynihan, *Beyond the Melting Pot,* second edition (Cambridge, Mass.: MIT Press, 1970). Examples and extensions are offered by Andrew M. Greeley, *The American Catholic: A Social Portrait* (New York: Basic Books, 1977), and by William L. Yancey, Eugene P. Ericksen and Richard N. Juliani, "Emergent ethnicity: A review and a reformulation," *American Sociological Review,* 41, No. 3 (June, 1976), 391–403. Incidentally, the term *ethnogenesis* postdates Glazer and Moynihan's work; I have borrowed it from Andrew Greeley (see *The American Catholic,* Chapter 1).

[17] A good statement is by Glazer and Moynihan, *Beyond the Melting Pot,* pp. xxxi–xlii.

[18] Ibid., p. xxvi.

[19] In this connection, see Daniel Bell, "Ethnicity and social change," in Glazer and Moynihan, *Ethnicity.*

[20] Bernard C. Rosen, "Race, ethnicity, and the achievement syndrome," *American Sociological Review,* 24, No. 1 (February, 1959), 47-60. Another essay of importance bearing on the same themes is by Fred L. Strodtbeck, "Family interaction, values, and achievement," in David C. McClelland, Alfred L. Baldwin, Urie Bronfenbrenner, and Fred L. Strodtbeck (eds.), *Talent and Society* (Princeton: Van Nostrand, 1958).

[21] The phrase *cultural division of labor* belongs to Michael Hechter. He describes the so-called internal colonial model in his book *Internal Colonialism* (Los Angeles: University of California Press, 1975). It is also discussed at length by Robert Blauner, *Racial Oppression in America* (New York: Harper & Row, 1972).

[22] Greeley, *The American Catholic,* Chapter 12.

[23] Gordon, *Assimilation in American Life,* p. 77.

[24] Ibid., p. 81.

[25] Ibid., pp. 109-10.

[26] Ibid., pp. 51-54.

[27] Peter M. Blau, *Inequality and Heterogeneity: A Primitive Theory of Social Structure* (New York: Free Press, 1977). A good summary of major results is contained in Blau's article, "A macrosociological theory of social structure," *American Journal of Sociology,* 83, No. 1 (July, 1977), 26-54.

[28] Blau, *Inequality and Heterogeneity,* Chapter 1.

[29] Blau, "A macrosociological theory of social structure," p. 35.

[30] Ibid., p. 36.

[31] Ibid., pp. 44-46.

[32] Herbert M. Gans, "Symbolic ethnicity: The future of ethnic groups and cultures in America," *Ethnic and Racial Studies,* 2, No. 1 (January, 1979), 1-20; Steinberg, *The Ethnic Myth,* p. 51.

[33] Michael Novak, *The Rise of the Unmeltable Ethnics* (New York: Macmillan, 1971). On the new Italian identity and pride, see the comments in Stephen Hall's article, "Italian-Americans: Coming into their own."

[34] Max Weber, *Economy and Society* (New York: Bedminster Press, 1968), Volume I, p. 389.

[35] General reviews of ethnicity concepts are provided by Harold Abramson, "Assimilation and pluralism," and William Petersen, "Concepts of ethnicity," in *Harvard Encyclopedia of American Ethnic Groups,* ed. Stephen Thernstrom, Ann Orlov, and Oscar Handlin (Cambridge, Mass.: Harvard University Press, 1980).

CHAPTER TWO
IMMIGRATION
AND THE SOUTHERN
ITALIAN BACKGROUND

The hundred-year period from 1830 to 1930 was a century of mass immigration in the histories of the United States and the world. Many millions of people were uprooted, primarily in crowded European rural places, and flowed outward to less settled parts of the globe, especially to Latin America and the United States, but additionally to even more remote regions, such as Australia. This was the greatest migration of human beings in world history. More than 50 million left Europe, and almost 38 million entered the United States (32 million from Europe), contributing enormously to the nation's expansion and industrial dynamism (see Table 2-1). In 1830, the United States was a country of 13 million people and 24 states; a century later, it had grown to 123 million people and 48 states.

The primary cause of this massive transfer of humanity from the Old World to the New World was the social and economic strain on the creaking rural systems of Europe. The strain was due in part to the simple weight of population. Starting about 1750, European populations grew rapidly as a result of improvements in medicine and sanitation and increases in the food supply. In rural areas, the growth in population led to displacement from the soil, as there was not enough arable land to go around. Pressure was also put on rural systems by a capitalist transformation of agricultural economies. The abolition of feudalism made land into private property and ended traditional peasant privileges, such as access to the common

TABLE 2-1   Immigration to the United States by Decade, 1820-1979

	NUMBER OF IMMIGRANTS FROM:		
	ITALY	ALL OF EUROPE	OUTSIDE OF EUROPE
1820-1830	439	106,508	45,216
1031-1040	2,253	495,688	103,437
1841-1850	1,870	1.597,501	115,750
1851-1860	9,231	2,452,660	145,554
1861-1870	11,725	2,065,270	249,554
1871-1880	55,759	2,272,262	539,929
1881-1890	307,309	4,737,046	509,567
1891-1900	651,893	3,558,978	128,586
1901-1910	2,045,877	8,136,016	659,370
1911-1920	1,109,524	4,376,564	1,359,247
1921-1930	455,315	2,477,853	1,629,356
1931-1940	68,028	348,289	180,142
1941-1950	57,661	621,704	413,335
1951-1960	185,491	1,328,293	1,187,186
1961-1970	214,111	1,129,670	2,192,007
1971-1979[a]	123,900	728,200	3,234,300

[a]All figures in this interval are rounded to the nearest hundred.

SOURCE: *U.S. Bureau of the Census, Historical Statistics of the United States, Colonial Times to 1970,* Bicentennial edition, Part 1 (Washington: U.S. Government Printing Office, 1975), pp. 105-06; and *Statistical Abstract of the United States, 1981* (Washington: U.S. Government Printing Office, 1981), p. 87.

fields, thereby pushing many peasants with little land below the margin of survival. Technological advances in agriculture sharpened capitalism's effects, because only large farmers operated on a scale that made it sensible to take advantage of such improvements; as a result, small farmers could not compete effectively. The emergence of international markets accelerated the outcomes of capitalist competition, because farmers could now be ruined by events in faraway places. Everywhere in Europe, traditional systems were bursting at the seams; mass emigration was necessary to relieve some of the pressure.

Not all European countries contributed throughout the century to the human flow into the United States. What appears at a distance to be a single human tide can be seen, close up, to be composed of different waves, originating in distinct regions and nations of Europe. Early in the century, immigrants came chiefly from the countries of northern and western Europe, especially from England, Ireland, and Germany. In the parlance of immigration history, this was the "old" immigration. The reasons for this geographic concentration lie partly in the histories of the these countries—the Irish famine of the 1840s and the failure of the Revolution of

1848 produced many emigrants from Ireland and Germany, respectively—but they also lie in the technology of transportation. Before the 1860s, the journey to the New World was almost always made by sailing ship, and since it was therefore long and dangerous, ships left mostly from the western extremities of Europe.

But as the 19th century wore on, the sources of immigration began to shift to the east and south. The countries of eastern and southern Europe then began to feel intensely the demographic and economic pressures earlier felt by those of western and northern Europe, and only in the latter part of the 19th century did they remove the legal prohibitions against emigration. The shift was made possible also by the introduction of the steamship to the immigrant routes; and the competition among steamship lines led to the opening up of new ports, such as Naples and Palermo. The shift in the sources of immigration became noticeable during the 1880s, and 1896 represents the turning point. In that year, immigrants from Italy, Poland, Russia, and other countries of southern and eastern Europe—the countries of the "new" immigration—outnumbered for the first time the old immigrants from northern and western Europe. The new immigration waxed during the first years of the 20th century, when immigration grew to a frenzied pace. In these early years of the new century through 1914, more than 13 million immigrants came to the United States, mostly from the southern and eastern European countries. Their arrival in such large numbers gave strength to the anti-immigration movement. Immigration from Europe was choked off by World War I, and it did not resume with the same velocity after the war because laws to regulate the immigrant flow had begun to be put in place. By 1929, stringent immigration laws, which especially limited the new immigration, had taken effect; the prolonged spasm of immigration from Europe to the United States was essentially over.[1]

Italians were a major current in the immigrant stream. More than 5 million immigrants from Italy disembarked at American ports in the century and a half from 1820 to 1970, and more than 4½ million came during the century of mass immigration, 1830-1930. Only the number of arrivals from Germany was larger. Part of the new immigration, the immigration from Italy was tightly concentrated in time. More than 4 million Italians arrived between 1890 and 1921, and in fact 2 million arrived during a single decade, 1901-1910. (The peak year of the Italian immigration was 1907, when nearly 300,000 came.) But there was also an important return flow. Many Italians eventually returned to Italy; how many is uncertain.[2]

Italian immigration was geographically as well as temporally concentrated. Although it is difficult to be sure of the exact regional origins of Italian immigrants to the United States, it is clear that a very large proportion of Italian immigrants came from southern Italy, the *Mezzogiorno*.[3] The proportion was even larger during the peak period of Italian immigration, after 1890. Between 1899 and 1910, when more than 2,200,000 Italian immigrants came, perhaps as many as 80 percent came from the Mezzogiorno.[4] Southern Italian society has shaped profoundly the Italian-American group, as it has affected American perceptions of Italian Americans. Consequently, I begin with a description of the southern Italian social landscape.

THE MEZZOGIORNO: SOCIAL STRUCTURE
AND AGRICULTURAL CONDITIONS

Any short description of Mezzogiorno society at the time of mass immigration to America must confront the problem of generalization. Generalizations can be dangerously misleading, and no generalization can do justice to the variety of circumstances under which people lived in a region as large as southern Italy. But this diversity aside, the way of life of the southern Italian people has left a vivid impression with almost all observers, so that one feels confident that the circumstances under which most southern Italians live were, and continue to be, quite distinct. In what follows, I will review much of what is known about southern Italian society. For the most part, what is known results from anthropological studies done since the end of World War II, but this limitation does not hold completely, and what is known of the past makes clear that much of the salient outlines of Mezzogiorno society in the recent past can be extrapolated backwards to the turn of the century.[5]

Even today, the Mezzogiorno presents a classical picture of a "backward" society, in sharp contrast to the industrial and developed north. This was still more the case at the beginning of the century, when the immigrants left. The Mezzogiorno was then essentially rural, with most of its people eking out an existence in agriculture. It was also a rigidly stratified society. A hundred years ago, most of its people were born as land-poor peasants, and that is what they remained. They labored under an agricultural system that still bore the evident imprint of its feudal past—a "traditional" society, not a "modern" one.

Social Structure

Although primarily agricultural workers, the people of the Mezzogiorno lived in towns, not on the land they worked. These towns often had the appearance of fortifications, as they were set on hills to escape the malarial conditions that existed in the valleys below and also to provide defense against bandits and the invaders who came throughout southern Italian history. Adding to the fortified appearance was the physical layout; many towns were composed of tightly clustered stone or plaster houses, layered around one or a few central piazzas, each dominated by a church. The sound of the church bell, *il campanile,* was a physical fact defining the perceptible social boundary of a southern Italian's world.

Distinct social classes jostled against one another in these towns. Differences in social status were clearly marked in dress and forms of address. At the top of the social hierarchy were the *galantuomini,* a class that included substantial landowners and also professionals, such as doctors, lawyers, pharmacists, and teachers. Members of this class were addressed with the honorific titles *Don* (for men) and *Donna* (for women), and it was expected that they would not work with their hands for money. Indeed, this was perhaps the defining criterion for membership.

Much below the *galantuomo* class but probably above the mass of peasants, at least in terms of prestige, was the artisan (*artigiano*) class, composed of persons engaged in a variety of urban (i.e., nonagricultural) occupations. These ranged from skilled crafts to business and service occupations. While many in the artisan class may not have been much better off economically than most peasants, their cultural outlook was quite different, as artisans were more likely to be literate and to be attuned to a wider world than were those who worked in the fields.

Numerically, the most important group, especially for understanding immigration, was the peasant (or *contadino*) stratum: This included anyone who worked the land in order to live. In a rough way, the peasant stratum can be divided into two classes, based on land ownership; however, it is really more accurate to think in terms of a continuum, because there was such a diversity of circumstances that one class shaded into the other. At one end were the peasants who owned enough land so that, at least in good years, they need not work for others. At the other end of the spectrum was the landless agriculturalist, who obviously had to work for others in order to live. The better off among landless peasants had the exclusive use of someone else's land, perhaps on an annual basis in a sharecropping arrangement, by which the landowner provided the capital for the planting season (tools, seeds, etc.) and the sharecropper provided the labor, with the yield divided between them at the end of the season in accordance with agreed-upon proportions.

But in essence this two-class division is an oversimplification. The diversity in access to land and work was great, and the reality quite complex. Many who owned land owned so little that they were forced to work for others in addition to working their own land. Even those who owned enough land might find themselves having to work for someone else in a bad year. And among those who worked land owned by someone else, it made a difference whether they leased the land for a fixed rent or sharecropped it; the former were likely to be thought of as working for themselves, to make a profit, and hence to be placed higher in the scale of social class. It also made a difference how long a lease was for. If it were only short-term, perhaps for a year only, the position of peasant was so vulnerable that he might be forced to rent it on very unfavorable terms; very different was the situation of peasants whose families had, perhaps for several generations, a traditional relationship to the family of a landlord. Also included in the peasant stratum were those who tended flocks, usually of sheep or goats. Generally, herders did not own the flocks, and, since they were forced to live with the animals during seasonal migrations, would rank near the bottom of the scale.

At its lower end, the peasant stratum faded into another class that appears to have been growing at the time of mass emigration—that of the casual laborer, who was often called a *giornaliero*, literally a "day" laborer, or *bracciante*. The growth of this class was a product of the dislocations suffered by Mezzogiorno society, as more and more people were forced out of regular agricultural work. Casual workers worked on a short-term basis at whatever employment they could find. At times, especially during seasonal periods of peak demand for farm labor such as harvesting, the work would be agricultural; at other times, it would be non-agricultural (during the years just before mass emigration, many laborers found employment at public-works construction, road building, and the like). In general, the situation of many laborers appears to have been quite desperate, verging on chronic unemployment. Unsurprisingly, this class contributed many to the emigrant stream; those who left, however, may well have been individuals who hoped to return to an agricultural life, by earning enough money abroad to become small landowners.[6]

Agricultural Conditions

The agricultural life of southern Italy was harsh. Although Sicily was considered the granary of the Roman Empire, by the 19th century the physical conditions throughout the Mezzogiorno were no longer favorable to a prolific agriculture. Deforestation had occurred over centuries, spurred by the exploitation of the land under the many conquerers of southern Italy. One consequence was the erosion of the topsoil, leaving behind a thin, poor layer of dirt that covered the essentially mountainous terrain and through which outcroppings of rock protruded. A second consequence was a scarcity of water, since the remaining soil had little power to retain the rain.

The greatest natural obstacle to an agriculture of abundance was, and is, the semitropical climate. The temperature in winter only occasionally dips down as far as the freezing point, which might seem a blessing to agriculture, but summers are very hot. The heat is compounded by the annual cycle of rainfall. The Mezzogiorno receives an ample amount of rainfall on an annual basis, but the rains come most heavily in the fall and winter, when they are not needed. The spring and summer, when crops are maturing, are the driest seasons. The precarious agriculture is threatened further by the hot, dry winds, the *sirocco* and the *favonio*, that blow from the direction of North Africa during the arid months.[7]

Landownership was the pivotal element in the plight of southern Italian agriculture.[8] In many areas, the ownership of land was highly concentrated in the hands of a few families, and the majority of peasant families were without any land or possessed only marginal amounts. One visitor to Italy in 1900 observed that "sixty-five percent of the acreage of Italy consists of immense estates, varying in size from three thousand to fifteen thousand acres"[9]; her figures were for all of Italy, and the percentage must have been higher in the south. The largest of these estates were known as *latifundia* and seem to have been especially characteristic of some areas of the south, notably western Sicily. Generally, the land outside of the estates was broken into extremely small parcels, and this fragmentation was progressive as a result of inheritance patterns. Peasants usually divided their land among all their heirs, at least all their male heirs, with the consequence that an inheritance might consist of several very small pieces of land, of uneven quality and separated from one another by some distance. Jane and Peter Schneider report that in the area of western Sicily that they studied in the 1960s, fragmentation had proceeded so far that in some cases a single tree was owned by several people.[10]

Since so many owned land insufficient to support their families, or no land at all, the great majority of southern Italian peasants had of necessity to work on someone else's land. In some areas of the south, this meant working on the *latifundia,* but not directly under the supervision of the owners. The owners of these great estates were for the most part absentee landlords, living in cosmopolitan centers such as Palermo off the rents produced by their lands. The estates were leased to agents, who might in turn lease portions to other intermediaries. Further down this chain, peasants would lease small portions under terms that varied from one place to another. The lease might be in terms of a fixed rent to be paid in cash or kind; or a sharecropping arrangement might prevail.

A great disadvantage of the *latifundium* system was that it provided little incentive to improve the land or even to maintain it in its present state. Leases might be for a period of several years, and customary rights to plots of land extending over several generations were not unknown; but frequently, leases were for a single year only. In the Sicilian town studied by Rudolph Bell, landless peasants presented themselves in the town piazza each August to seek a contract for the next year. The agents "might grant them the same plot, a different one many kilometers away, or none at all."[11] With such insecure tenure to the land, there was little reason for peasants to improve it. But there was also little reason for the agents to do so. Since they too were just tenants, with no permanent right to the land, their principal interest was in gaining the maximum return in the present. Hence the system was conducive to exploitation of the land for maximum short-term productivity, exhausting the soil as a result.

The same point applies for a different reason to many of the plots owned by peasants. Here, the smallness of the holdings and the fact that they were frequently not contiguous meant that there was little to be gained from improvements. The scale was simply not large enough.

The conditions bred an inefficient agriculture. Just to get to the land they worked, which might be a considerable distance from town, peasants might have to walk several hours a day. Adding to the inefficiency was the primitive state of the tools used by southern Italian peasants, as well as their lack of fertilizer. The yields from southern Italian lands were considerably lower than those obtained in the northern part of the country. In the early 20th century, cereal crops grown on average lands in Lombardy, in the north, and in the northern parts of Campania, the northernmost part of the Mezzogiorno, netted 500 and 600 *lire* per hectare of land; by contrast, the best grain fields further south, on the Sicilian *latifundia,* yielded 100 *lire* per hectare.[12]

The southern Italian peasantry appears to have lived generally just above the margin of subsistence and in bad years to have lived below it. Edward Banfield's description of a *contadino* family, the Pratos, in the 1950s illustrates the poverty of many Mezzogiorno peasants and demonstrates that conditions had not improved greatly even by this late date, despite the exodus to America and elsewhere that had presumably relieved some of the pressure on the land. The Pratos were far from the worst off in their town in Basilicata, a region in the arch of the Italian boot, since they owned some land. Even so, the family survived only because the husband worked as a day laborer as often as he could; and other family members worked as well. But work was uncertain and paid very little. The family's manner of living was correspondingly impoverished. The husband ate his breakfast and lunch, both consisting of a little bread, figs, and tomatoes, while working in the fields. The only meal the family ate together was supper, which consisted of more bread, a bean soup, perhaps a little sausage or salami if meat remained from the pig the family slaughtered annually, and some fruit. The family had wine, cheese, fish, or other meat at most once a month, on feast days.

As was true for most southern Italian peasants, the Pratos lived in a one-room house. These single rooms provided shelter not only for the peasant families but also for their livestock. More affluent peasants lived in two-story houses, each story of which was a single room. Such houses had a great advantage because the animals could be kept on the first level, while the family lived on the second, able to observe their livestock through a hole in the floor. Even in the 1950s, as surely would have been true of peasant dwellings earlier in the century, the Pratos had no electricity, no running water, and hence no toilets. Since the Pratos lived on the edge of town, family members could relieve themselves at a discreet distance from their house without disturbing anyone else; other peasants might use the animal stalls.[13]

The difficulties of merely surviving under these conditions gave rise to a distinctive bleak outlook, known as *la miseria,* in many parts of the south. Rudolph Bell describes *la miseria* as it was reflected among the Calabrian peasants he came to know in the 1970s:

> Although poverty is hardly unique to the mountains of Calabria, it is here that the psychosis of *la miseria* takes its most complete form. Of course *la miseria* means being underemployed, having no suit or dress to wear for your child's wedding, suffering hunger most of the time, and welcoming death. But for Rosa and the Calabresi it means more: houses with cracked and crumbled walls, unborn children you know will be malnourished, abandoned lands, hostile lands, faces and hands burned by the sun. *La miseria* is a disease, a vapor arising from the earth, enveloping and destroying the soul of all that it touches. Its symptoms are wrinkles, distended bellies, anomic individualism, hatred of the soil, and the cursing of God.[14]

THE CULTURE OF THE MEZZOGIORNO

A landscape as harsh as this required a culture that is no longer familiar to the citizens of industrial and postindustrial societies. The word *culture* is used here in a sense made most explicit in anthropology—a "design for living," a system of precepts and beliefs that defines and justifies ways of thinking, feeling, and behaving appropriate for the circumstances under which a group lives. Culture thus provides an integrated and elaborate code of conduct that is adapted to a group's situation and supplies solutions to the problems its members face.

A circumspection born of self-awareness is a scientific, and even a moral imperative when it comes to discussing another group's culture. Outside observers tend to perceive an unfamiliar culture in terms of the deeply ingrained categories acquired from their own cultures. This *ethnocentrism* results in distortion; metaphorically, the eyeglasses of the observer's culture throw certain features of another into sharp relief, because they either parallel or oppose salient features in one's own, while making scarcely visible other features that are less directly related to the observer's culture. Other results may be an invidious evaluation of a different culture because it seems bizarre or strange from the vantage point of the observer, and an implicit glorification of one's native culture as "advanced." Such evaluations can be hidden beneath the superficially objective language of the social scientist, while still deeply coloring the description of the culture.

Likewise, one must beware of reifying a culture, presenting it in absolute and rigid terms and detaching it from the conditions in which it is embedded. All cultures contain considerable flexibility, because no society is completely static and uniform, and individuals must have sufficient latitude to cope with varying situations; for similar reasons, all cultures are malleable. Nor is there cultural uniformity from one place to another within a single society, because local circumstances vary. The possibility of variation must be borne in mind in considering the description of southern Italian culture that follows, because what we know of it appears to be the culture as it existed in the smaller towns and villages of the remoter parts of the countryside, the places that have interested anthropologists most. We know less about the larger places and cities. It must be said, however, that the culture described in the literature appears consistent with the general picture of immigrant life in the United States.

An example that brings to life the cautions concerning ethnocentrism and reification involves *fatalism*—the belief that the determination of one's fate was out of one's hands, combined with a resignation to accept what destiny brings. Southern Italian peasants are frequently described as fatalistic, but the description is misleading if it is left at that. To be sure, in accordance with the lack of control peasants had over their lives, there was an undertone of fatalism in Mezzogiorno culture, as well as pessimism—a feeling, lying just beneath the surface, that calamity could come at any time and destroy what one had worked for. The calamities that occurred might be acts of God or nature, such as sudden sickness or a *sirocco* wind that destroyed one's crops; or they might be acts of more powerful individuals. In the course of his research during the 1950s, Edward Banfield employed a psychological test to elicit characteristic themes in the peasants' world view, asking his informants to tell stories appropriate for the pictures on cards they were shown. The stories provide distressing illustrations of the sense that calamity is ever present. The following typical story was told by the wife in the Prato family described earlier, in response to a blank card—one, in other words, for which she could have told any story:

> A woman is watching a dead child with grief. There was a family—very poor—which lived by the work and sacrifice of the parents. They had only one child and consequently loved him immensely and for him made all of the sacrifices. But one day he fell ill. They believed it was nothing, but instead the illness

did not pass and in fact became worse. In order to save him, the parents spent the little they had, but the doctors were useless. After five or six months of illness he died, leaving the parents in pain and misery.[15]

The story and the pessimism behind it emphasize the futility of human action, but they should not be interpreted as implying that attempts to improve one's life were discouraged. Just as in any society, southern Italians emerge from anthropological descriptions of them as calculating human beings, elaborating plans in accordance with their self-interests. Indeed, another value in the culture was *furberia,* shrewdness, which emphasized that the wise individual was also shrewd in attempting to extract from any situation the maximum benefit for himself or herself.[16] This is hardly the stuff of fatalism if that word is taken in its absolute sense. And, of course, it is impossible to reconcile fatalism in this absolute sense with the fact that so many southern Italian peasants were willing to come to an unknown land in the hope of improving their lives. Yet fatalism did exist as one strain in the culture. What it may especially have discouraged was living one's life according to a systematic and comprehensive plan for improving it far in the future—what has become famous in sociology as the "Protestant Ethic."

Closely connected with this was a different sense of time. Americans think of time in a progressive way; each year is different than the last, and there appears to us to be a line of development or progress in the sequence of the years. This is reflected, for example, in our economic thinking: Even during periods of economic stagnation, our evaluation of the economy remains based on the expectation of continual improvements in standards of living. This way of thinking is especially oriented towards the future, but southern Italian peasants were more concerned with the past and present. Their view of time was in terms of cycles, synchronized with the rhythm of the agricultural seasons but having little sense of cumulative development. Years might differ from one another because some were good and others bad, but there was no straight line of progress to be discerned. In addition, the past weighed heavily, as evidenced by the black mourning dresses so many peasant women wore. Joseph Lopreato describes how this sense of time was reflected even in the grammatical structure of the language that peasants spoke:

> Little wonder that even today the future tense among the southern Italian peasantry is virtually unknown and the preterit (what the Italian grammarians call "remote past") is virtually their only past tense. *Si levau 'u suli* (the sun arose), a Calabrian peasant will say even today to impress upon his family the fact that it is dawn. His time outlook may be expressed with the following paradigm: "X happened; it happens today; it happens always."[17]

Probably the most significant aspect of Mezzogiorno culture for an understanding of Italian Americans lay in the ethos of personal relationships that it imposed on individuals. The southern Italian world was one of severe scarcity in the most basic resources of life: work and food. In such a world a basic problem confronts every individual: whom to trust? Because everyone needs more, everyone is a competitor threatening one's very existence. But an individual also needs to be able to count on at least a few others, to whom he or she can turn in times of extreme need. For southern Italians, the culture addressed the problem of trust, prescriptively carving the world into spheres of social intimacy, outside of which lay a great mass of "strangers."

One manifestation of the tension between trust and distrust was the parochialism known as *campanilismo*. The southern Italian perceived a strong social boundary between the world of his town or village (including its fields, of course) and those of other towns or villages. The name *campanilismo* refers to the town bell, *il campanile*, implying that the margin of this world was where the bell ceased to be heard. Except for the military service of the men, which gave them a taste of the wider world, it was not unusual for a peasant to spend his or her entire life within this boundary, with infrequent visits to neighboring towns and villages and few or none at all to larger urban places.[18]

The residents of other towns and villages were viewed as outsiders and strangers, even foreigners, and were the subject of ridicule: They are cuckolds, liars, or whatever. Since *furberia*, or shrewdness, was especially justified in dealings with someone not from the same town, such outsiders did not merit trust. One of Banfield's informants explained why it would be all right to sell something defective to someone from another town but not to a fellow townsman, a *paesano*:

> Because the *forestière* [foreigner] buys it and goes off. It is his problem after that. But if I sell it to a *paesano*, what can I do? I see him every day. It would not be good.

When asked if it is "right to steal from a *forestière*," he replied, "That is not stealing. He tries to gyp me and I try to gyp him. It is a different matter altogether. *È un imbroglio*."[19]

But *campanilismo* was not merely a defensive and hence an essentially negative sentiment; it was also something positive. Villagers took pride in their village, generally their place of birth as well as place of residence. With reverence, they could recount how the histories of their families entwined with that of the village. The village and its surroundings were something intimate, familiar, where every stone, tree, and field was connected to this personal sense of history and place. Thus, when southern Italians migrated to the United States, they tended to settle where others from the same place had settled, and their primary self-identification was in terms of their village, and not as Italians.[20]

The Family

Most revealing of the imprint of the landscape of scarcity on southern Italian life was the central place accorded the family, *la famiglia*.[21] It has been observed many times that Mezzogiorno society was a society of families, not individuals. Moreover, the family was the only truly valued social group; larger social groupings, including that of the town or village, were much more ethereal in quality.

The family was understood in a larger sense than is true for most Americans. One's family included not only the immediate family, i.e., parents, spouse, and children, but also the more extended family, including even distant cousins, and even the extended family of one's spouse. Southern Italians were acutely aware of the exact degree of a kinship connection. Anyone acquainted with southern Italians or Italian Americans of the first two generations in the United States is familiar with their almost uncanny ability to identify readily the exact family connections between themselves and any relative and to express precisely degrees of relationship that most Americans perceive only vaguely. Nevertheless, the extended family did not generally live together under the same roof; usually, households contained nuclear families, a married couple and their children, and perhaps a relative who was unable to take care of himself or herself. But a clear distinction was recognized between those who were one's kin and anyone else, and a sense of obligation was felt towards any relative, although the obligations were greater as the family connection was closer. (This meant, of course, that families were not always harmonious. The sense of obligation and the fact that relatives were often part owners of the same properties as a result of inheritance led easily to quarrels and conflict. As Chapman says in explanation of the frequency of conflict among kin, "less is expected of outsiders.")[22]

The family was a group from which individuals could expect help when they stood in need of it, and toward the welfare of which they were expected to contribute. In a much-cited passage, Robert Foerster perhaps exaggerated a bit but touched on a fundamental truth when he wrote:

> Life in the South exalts the family. It has been said of Sicily that the family sentiment is perhaps the only deeply rooted altruistic sentiment that prevails.[23]

The family was the subject of the essential moral code of the Mezzogiorno, the *family ethos,* the first principle of which was an individual's obligation to kinfolk, an obligation against which all else paled. A child whose parents died would almost certainly be taken in and raised by a near relative. (This happened in the case of my own father and aunt; when orphaned, they were taken in by their aunt and uncle, who were raising five children of their own as well.) Moreover, when a death occurred, the members of *la famiglia* were obligated to help with the funeral expenses and to render more immediate help to the survivors; family members might move in temporarily to cook, clean house, and even to do the work in the fields. Of course, the obligations to family did not become operational merely when someone died; they were continuously felt throughout life. If a southern Italian were migrating somewhere else, he might well choose to go where he had relatives because he knew he could count on them for support. Or a brother would be obligated to work in order to help his sisters achieve the dowries necessary for marriage.

By being born into a family, the individual acquired a social place that stamped him or her for life (a woman, when she married, would also be perceived in terms of her husband's family). This means, first of all, that an individual would be born into the family of a *contadino,* an *artigiano,* or a *galantuomo,* and this circumstance of birth would largely settle his or her destiny. Social station was hard to change (but not impossible). But the stamp of family was much more than this. Families represented little traditions. Thus, families acquired reputations, and this fact bound their members even more tightly, since the actions of any family member might affect the family's reputation, or honor, and thereby every family member. In her study of a Sicilian village, Chapman described a comic side of this. Many families had acquired nicknames of obscure origins and usually demeaning (e.g., "big potato" and "chicken lice"). These nicknames were publicly recognized —they could even be used in addressing mail—and were bestowed by villagers on each new generation in a family, without any thought as to their appropriateness.[24]

Because the family was truly the basic social atom in Mezzogiorno society, the interests of the family took precedence over those of the individual; the individual was expected to subordinate himself or herself to the needs of the family. There was even a clearly recognized mechanism for voicing these needs with authority, because the family code vested an absolute authority in the father. On any family matter, he might listen to the advice of other family members, particularly his grown sons, but the decision was his alone and was final. One instance of the supremacy of family interests is the economic value attached to children. Among *contadini,* children generally were expected to make an economic contribution to the family as soon as they were able to work, usually by the age of 12. The contribution of girls was often within the household itself, while boys would work in the fields as apprentices. Children were expected to turn over their entire earnings to their parents, who would use them as they saw fit. This early initiation to work brought a quick end to childhood; adulthood came at a young age in the Mezzogiorno. The early onset of work also spelled the end of formal schooling, assuming that children had attended school in the first place. (Many hadn't; it is estimated that 70 percent or more of southern Italians were illiterate in 1901.)[25] The early end to education was, in any event, in harmony with the family code; too great an educational difference between parents and their children might threaten the family's solidarity.[26]

The supreme expression of the primacy of family interests was in marriage.[27] In a society composed of families, marriage was between families more than between individuals. An individual's marriage affected the position of the whole family; an inappropriate marriage, to a social inferior, weakened the family's position, while a fortunate one, to a member of a good family with property, elevated it. The family therefore had a natural interest in whom one of its members married, and until fairly recently, marriages were more or less arranged. This does not mean necessarily that the choice of a spouse was dictated by the family, even against the wishes of the eligible family member, although this did happen. Rather, the preferences of the individual were guided by the parents, who had good knowledge of the families of the various prospects and could judge their suitability. (Guidance could be effective because romantic love was not regarded as a motive for mate selection.) At a minimum, the family exercised a veto power to bar an unsuitable marriage. Couples who did prefer each other were not without a way out in the event that one or both sets of parents were against their marriage. They could elope in order to get around their parents' wishes. All that was required was to disappear together for a short period of time. Since the culture laid great store on the chastity of women, which was tainted by any suspicion, parents would usually have to accede to the marriage, since the woman's position in the marriage market was ruined by the disappearance.

Given the stakes involved, families took an active part in the events leading up to a marriage. An individual generally did not propose to someone he hoped to marry. Rather, a member of one family inquired, in accordance with a script of indirection, of a member of the other. Involved was not only the willingness of the families to be joined through the marriage of their members but also agreement on the property that each family would contribute to the marriage; the woman's dowry was especially crucial. The engagement would be formalized at a meeting between the two families, somewhat like that depicted in *The Godfather*. With his family (and not only his immediate family), the man would appear on a Sunday at the home of his prospective bride, where her family would also be present; gifts would be exchanged to seal the betrothal. In the period between the engagement and the marriage, whenever the engaged couple met, which was not very often, the families still hovered about to make sure that sexual intimacies did not occur.

Another aspect of the family ethos was the value attached to honor (*onore*). Honor refers to the moral worth of an individual or family as evaluated by others and implies "a quick response to offense, intolerance of any encroachment upon one's person or patrimony [property] or the person and patrimony of others to whom one is loyal."[28] Honor can be understood in terms of the central place of the family. Since the family was the basic social unit and in many respects the only social unit, the individual was utterly dependent on it, even for protection from violence and harm. Thus, the honor of a family symbolized its strength and solidarity and served as a warning to outsiders not to trespass against its members.

The code of honor intertwined with sexuality in a way that bore directly on marriage as the ultimate expression of the supremacy of the family. Southern Italians attached great consequence to the chastity of their female relatives, especially those who were unmarried. After a female reached puberty, her contact with men was strictly regulated, partly on the basis of belief that sexual relations between a man and a woman were virtually unavoidable if two should find themselves alone. It was incumbent on a family's men to guard the chastity of its women. In Sicily, where the sexual code of honor reached its most rigid form, unmarried women generally did not go out alone; and if the companion were a male, he had to be a close relative (so that he was not eligible as a partner). If it should become known that an unmarried woman was not a virgin, her marriage prospects would be greatly reduced. In the past, the emphasis on virginity at marriage was so strong that, in some places, the sheet on which a newly married couple spent its first night would be hung out the window to be inspected by the families as well as by passersby. Proscriptions on the sexual behavior of married women were also very strong. To be labeled a "cuckold" was one of the strongest insults in the southern Italian vocabulary.

The sexual prescriptions of the code of *onore* make sense within the context of the supreme value attached to the family. To begin with, the requirement that individuals subordinate their personal interests to those of the family as expressed by its male head demanded that there be no competing interests, as would have been engendered by sexual relationships created at the individual's initiative. Even more important, the need for the family to have control over the choice of a marriage partner for one of its members required that contact between unmarried men and women be extremely limited, so that they would not be capable of forming strong preferences on their own. Given the division of labor between the sexes, this was most easily accomplished by keeping the young women in a kind of seclusion. Their work was primarily in the household in any event, while many of the young men had to go to the fields.

Godparentship

So far in this portrait, the family stands alone in the Mezzogiorno landscape. Given the natural competition that existed in this world of scarcity, this leaves the impression that southern Italian life was an unrelieved war among family phalanxes, which were solidary within and disconnected from one another. This in fact is the way the Mezzogiorno has been presented sometimes. Edward Banfield, for example, believed its "backwardness" had a moral or cultural basis, which lay in what he took to be its core value: "amoral familism," or conformity to the rule, "Maximize the material, short-run advantage of the nuclear family; assume that all others will do likewise."[29] But families were not so mutually disconnected, and hence life was not a war of all against all. There were definite ways in which families threw out connections to one another to strengthen their positions, as a ship might throw out mooring lines. One way, of course, was through marriage. Another was through the institution of godparentship.

Godparentship has an importance in southern Italian and some other Latin societies that is hard for most Americans to appreciate, since it has become by and large a mere formality in our own society. But in these other societies, the child and his or her godparents stand in a special relationship throughout life, a fact that is emphasized by the special forms of address between them. Moreover, the child's parents and godparents also stand in a special relationship to each other, and herein lies the key to the significance of the godparent institution. They too have special forms of address, calling each other *compare* (co-father) and *comare* (co-mother); and the significance of these relationships is suggested by the fact that a corrupted form, *goombah,* of the dialect word for *compare* has passed into the American language as a term associated with Italian Americans. The relationship between parents and godparents has the character of a friendship over which has been draped the mantle of kinship. It is like a kin relation in its permanence—it cannot be canceled by a change of heart—and its participants can turn to each other for favors they would not ask if they were unrelated. But in some of its qualities, it is superior even to kinship. In particular, quarrels of the sort that may easily occur between relatives are proscribed between co-parents; trust and esteem are their moral duties in relation to each other. Given the privileged nature of the links created by the godparent relation, it was usual for a peasant family to have at least one godparent of higher rank and thereby to strengthen a relation to an actual or potential benefactor.[30]

The social landscape of the Mezzogiorno was thus crisscrossed by particularistic relations linking families and individuals through kinship, marriage, godparentship, and also friendship. This external social fact was a manifestation of the quintessential feature of the southern Italian outlook, which was personalistic in the extreme. In an exchange between individuals, what mattered was the pre-existing relationship between the two and whether it entitled one or the other to special treatment. This stands in sharp contrast to a basic principle in the American outlook, which is suited for a society dominated by large, bureaucratically organized institutions: Namely, individuals expect to obtain equal treatment in most relationships; favoritism is condemned (even if practiced). The difference is illustrated by an exchange of Chapman with the villagers she studied. When she remarked that American storekeepers did not generally make special prices for their friends, the villagers interpreted this as meaning that Americans did not know the real meaning of friendship.[31]

THE MAFIA

No account of southern Italian society would seem complete unless it touched on the criminal societies, most notably the Mafia, that loom so large in the American perception of Italian Americans and their heritage. No account could in fact be complete unless it attempted to correct some of the fallacies that surround the Mafia. The conventional account of American organized crime, supported by federal law-enforcement agencies, is quite straightforward in its view of the ethnic derivation of this social problem. In the beginning, so it runs, there was in Sicily a secret criminal society of ancient origins. It had arisen out of good intentions, to combat Sicily's invaders, but its purposes had been corrupted over time, and its members lived by violence and extortion. When southern Italian immigrants came to the United States in large numbers, members of the Mafia were among them. Once here, they attempted to establish the kind of life they had known in Sicily by creating "Black Hand" bands that extorted money from immigrant workers. This form of crime was contained within the boundaries of the ghetto, but criminal organization was given the opportunity to flourish beyond these boundaries by Prohibition, during which enormous amounts of money could be earned by supplying Americans with alcohol. When Prohibition ended, this money capitalized new criminal ventures. Organized crime has prospered to the point that, today, it has infiltrated many legitimate businesses and threatens to become America's invisible government.[32] What makes these developments so ominous is the degree to which organized crime is "organized." According to a presidential crime commission of the 1960s,

> Today the core of organized crime in the United States consists of 24 groups operating as criminal cartels in large cities across the Nation. Their membership is exclusively men of Italian descent, they are in frequent communication with each other, and their smooth functioning is insured by a national body of overseers.[33]

This account is by no means entirely wrong—and to forestall any misunderstanding of my own position, I want to acknowledge at the outset the existence and importance of Italian-American organized crime—but it is very misleading in its emphases. It distorts the relation of ethnicity to crime in its preoccupation with events in Sicily and with the southern Italian ethos, and it falsely portrays organized crime as an alien and almost accidental growth in American soil, the seeds for which happened to be transported by a single immigrant group, the Italians, rather than as a native product that demanded the energies of numerous ethnic groups. More will be said about Italian-American organized crime in later chapters, but what is appropriate here is to indicate how the conventional account begins to go astray in the beginning, in its understanding of the Mafia in Sicily. On this matter, much has been learned from the research conducted over the last few decades in Sicily, mainly by anthropologists. These studies have subjected the historical and contemporary phenomenon of the Mafia to close scrutiny.[34]

To understand the phenomenon of *mafia*[35]—the switch to lowercase is meant both to distinguish the actual phenomenon from the romanticized version that appears in the conventional account and to accent the absence of true formal organization—one must understand something of the political history of Sicily. As was true of southern Italy generally, the island was ruled for many centuries by outsiders, falling under the hegemony of one power after another (some Sicilians might view the island as ruled from the outside, i.e., from Rome, even today). The process began with the Hellenic colonization of the eastern coast of the island, dating from the eighth century B.C., and over the ensuing centuries, the Romans, Arabs, Normans, Germans, Angevins, Aragonese, Catalans, Spaniards, French, and others struggled for control. This rule of the island from the outside, often with the intent of exploiting its resources, had disastrous consequences for its political and economic development.

One was the ineffectiveness of governmental power, even to guarantee public order. The natural antipathy of Sicilians for outside rulers undermined governmental authority; and during the long Spanish rule, at a time when modern states were emerging in much of Europe, the central authority, the viceroy, was unable to establish effective control over local barons and the countryside. By the 18th century, the transportation infrastructure had seriously deteriorated, as roads dating as far back as Roman and Arab times fell into disrepair. The police forces of the central authority showed themselves only occasionally in many parts of the hinterland. At the same time, banditry was rife, and travelers in the countryside risked their lives and property. Banditry in fact lasted well into modern times, and one of the most famous of Sicilian bandits, Salvatore Giuliano, was killed after World War II.

Conditions such as these strengthened the family ethos, since Sicilians could not count on governmental protection from harm. And they gave rise to a morality in which justice was regarded as a private matter, not a public one. This, incidentally, is the real meaning of the code of *omerta,* the so-called code of silence. But most important, in the absence of a legitimate system of effective power, a system of parasitic power emerged—*mafia.*

Mafia was not a highly structured criminal society, as it is depicted in much of the literature on organized crime. Such an organization would make no sense in Sicilian circumstances, given that the personalistic ethos of southern Italians and the fragmentation of the island were hardly conducive to the emergence of a large organization. Rather, *mafia* was a characteristic form of social organization. The classical *mafioso* was a rural power broker who, in pursuit of private ends, enlisted others to form a clique in a village. The ends were generally control over valuable resources and markets, and the means were frequently criminal. *Mafiosi* practiced extortion—demanding, for example, money from land and livestock owners to protect their properties from the harm inflicted by *mafia* henchmen—and they employed violence and intimidation to attain their ends. But also, to acquire power, they cultivated relationships involving reciprocal obligations. Unlike the bandit, who was in open opposition to legal authority, the *mafioso* generally acted in "connivance," as Anton Blok puts it, with those in authority,[36] and was often their political ally. *Mafia* cliques in the same region were not necessarily integrated on a larger scale; though cooperation might exist, frequently they remained independent of one another or even were in conflict. In sum, the secret of *mafia* power lay not in organized criminal society but in the *mafioso*'s central location within a complex web of relationships, as well as in his control over violence.

The *mafia* phenomenon, moreover, was a highly specialized one, requiring very specific circumstances to flourish. Generally unknown to Americans is that the *mafia* was not found everywhere in Sicily, but that it predominated in the western part of the island. The explanation appears to lie in the large estates found there but not in eastern Sicily. Associated with these estates were several developments that provided the specific conditions for *mafia* emergence and growth. The barons who owned them generally organized their own private police forces to maintain public order; these armed groups frequently recruited men on the wrong side of the law and entered into arrangements with local bandits. *Mafiosi* emerged partly from the ranks of the private police and partly from the ranks of the peasant entrepreneurs to whom landowners leased their land and who in turn leased it to the peasants who would actually work it. The emergence of *mafia* appears to have happened during the 19th century, after the barons had abandoned the countryside for the cities, where they could live in cosmopolitan splendor while essentially ignoring what happened on their estates.

The ultimate irony of the conventional account of the Mafia as the animating spirit of American organized crime is that it assumes the transferability into an urban, industrial society of a mode of organization that grew up on the foundations of a rural and almost feudal society. Indeed, although it needed specific local conditions to first emerge, *mafia* fit the general cultural contours of southern Italy like a hand to a glove. In a way, it represents an extension of the personalistic ethos. In the *mafia* form, this was represented especially by the cultivation of friendship (*amicizia*), which bound individuals in a privileged relationship based on reciprocal favors. As Jane and Peter Schneider emphasize in their discussion of "broker capitalism," in the scarcity of the rural Sicilian landscape, which was peripheral to world economic centers, relationships were an asset of the first order. A person was therefore wealthier the more relationships he had, and hence, the better he was able to effect some desired end by stimulating a chain of particularistic relationships into action. The *mafioso* represented the epitome of this phenomenon.[37]

THE DEPARTURE FROM THE MEZZOGIORNO

Like the other European peoples that left the countryside by the millions, southern Italians did not depart lightly from the intimate embrace of the land that had sustained them for generations, in spite of the apparent harshness of life there. But the margin of subsistence was so thin that it did not take much to shake people loose. The emigration from Italy was fed by some of the same underlying causes that led to the massive exodus from other parts of Europe. One of the most important was the population explosion that occurred in European societies after 1750. The growth in the population increased the pressure on the land, especially in areas like the Mezzogiorno, where the pattern of inheritance led to a drastic fragmentation of peasant land holdings. Many peasants were left barely clinging to the fields and hence vulnerable to any agricultural setback. In bad years, people starved.[38]

Perhaps the single most important factor was the wrenching economic transformation of Mezzogiorno agriculture associated with the gradual ending of feudalism and the penetration of capitalism, both of which occurred during the 19th century. Some of the forces bringing about this transformation were in a sense intrusions from the outside, reflecting the Mezzogiorno's disadvantaged position in the emerging international capitalist economy. For example, the edge southern Italian wheat growers had once held in export markets because of their hard, and hence durable, wheat was taken away by improvements in transportation that allowed wheat to be brought from distant places without spoilage; the result was a prolonged economic depression in the Mezzogiorno's wheat-growing areas, particularly Sicily and Apulia.[39]

The impact of these forces sharpened the struggle for economic advantages within Mezzogiorno society. Consequently, the condition of the peasantry appears to have worsened over the 1800s in tandem with the terms on which it gained access to land. A decline in customary rights and feudal privileges and a rise in short-term contracts under unfavorable conditions—to which the increasing number of land-poor peasants had to resort—are a major part of the story. A sign of the profound metamorphosis was the growing need that peasants had for money, which had been of minor consequence in the peasant economy in preceding centuries. In some places, peasants needed money to pay the rent on the land they worked, and in others, to pay the usurious interest on the loans extended by landowners and contractors at the beginning of the growing season. Everywhere, it appears that peasants became enmeshed in a web of debt, to which were added oppressive taxes such as those on land. The need for money drove some peasants to seek supplemental work to add to their incomes. Others were forced into the ranks of casual labor, hired out on a daily basis.[40]

The growth in population and the economic dislocations exerted steady pressures. In terms of migration, these were most acutely felt not so much by those at the very bottom of society, but by those who were a little better off and feared themselves to be slipping down the social ladder.[41] Often, release of the pressure by mass emigration was triggered by specific events. In the Mezzogiorno, these were not as catastrophic as they were in some other places, such as Ireland, where millions were whipped from the land by the prospect of immediate starvation in the aftermath of a potato blight; but they were still grim enough. In the 1880s, Italian wheat prices plummeted as cheap American grain entered European markets on a mass scale; as a consequence many proprietors had their land taken from them because of insolvency. In the same decade, the southern Italian citrus industry was dealt a blow by the emergence of a North American industry, in Florida and California. The competition reduced American imports of Italian fruit, driving out of business many citrus growers in Calabria, Basilicata, and Sicily, and adding to the desperation of Italian agricultural workers. Between 1888 and 1898, a Franco-Italian tariff war reduced the French importation of Italian wines, to the detriment of wine growers and their workers in Apulia, Calabria, and Sicily; and the Italian protective tariff on wheat raised bread prices, thereby eating into peasants' margin of survival. Nor were workers successful in improving their lot by direct means. In the early 1890s, peasants organized themselves in many parts of Sicily to secure lower rents and higher wages. The movement had some initial successes, but its back was broken by the imposition of martial law throughout Sicily in 1894 and the suppression of the peasant organizations. Natural calamities—major earthquakes and the eruptions of Vesuvius and Etna in the early 1900s—added to the level of human misery.[42]

The result was an enormous outpouring of Italians. It is estimated that more than 25 million Italians have emigrated, either temporarily or permanently, since the mid-19th century.[43] This is a vast siphoning from a nation whose population was around 35 million in the early 20th century, and a very substantial portion came from the ranks of the peasantry in the provinces of the south. Italians did not emigrate only to the United States. The sons and daughters of Italy have contributed to the growth of countries in Europe, north Africa, South America (notably, Argentina and Brazil), Australia, and in North America, to Canada as well as the United States.

These emigrants did not all leave to stay away forever, and this seems to have been especially true of the southern Italian peasants who left in the late 19th and early 20th centuries. Many appear to have left with the intention to work abroad and earn enough money to purchase land when they returned. One indication that this is true is the large number of young men unaccompanied by their families who were counted as part of the immigration to the United States. This feature of the Italian and some other immigrations from southern and eastern Europe was viewed with alarm by Americans, who interpreted the presence of such "birds of passage" as the harbinger of a rootless population that would not be able to assimilate successfully. Of course, many who came intending to return did not do so and eventually brought their families. But many did go back, although their number is uncertain, because the statistics on repatriation are even more inadequate than those on emigration. Uncertainty aside, the number who eventually returned to the Mezzogiorno was clearly large. One estimate is that 1.5 million Italians returned from the United States in the years between 1900 and 1914.[44]

CONCLUSION

The arrival on American shores set in motion a process that was to be fateful for the immigrants and their descendants. Within a few generations, it was to change them utterly.

Yet looking back at the landing of the southern Italian *contadini*—so many of whom, ironically, first set foot on American soil at Ellis Island, within sight of the stone forest of Manhattan's office buildings—it would be hard to be sanguine about their prospects without knowledge of the intervening years. These "greenhorns" were greener than most, their way of life remote from the demands that were to confront them in the new society. Sociologists and others tend to interpret the success or failure of a group in industrial society in terms of its own traits, the cultural "input" that it brings to the machinery of mobility; and such interpretations often make eminent common sense. They imply that the most important baggage immigrants bring with them is that in their minds, and that this is not so easily discarded as their Old World clothes. These cultural explanations focus on traits such as individualism, zeal for education, faith in the efficacy of human effort, and systematic planning for the future as being emblematic of a "modern" outlook that conforms to the requirements for integration into industrial society. By this kind of cultural scorecard, Italians rank near the bottom, epitomizing a "traditional" outlook that is presumed to mesh poorly with a dynamic, urban society. Their traditionalism is indicated by their personalistic ethos and, above all, by the solidarity of their family bonds, which brings about a closure to new experience and an adherence to the ways of ancestors.

Southern Italians had a proverb: "Chi lascia la via vecchia e piglia la via nuova, sa quello che lascia ma non sa quello che trova (He who leaves the old way for the new, knows what he leaves but knows not what he will find)."[45] Whether this is true and whether culture deserves the primacy it is often accorded are questions that are tested by the Italian-American experience.

NOTES

[1]General references on American immigration and the Italian place within it are by Maldwyn Allen Jones, *American Immigration* (Chicago: University of Chicago Press, 1960), especially Chapters 4 and 7; and Alan M. Kraut, *The Huddled Masses: The Immigrant in American Society, 1880–1921* (Arlington Heights, Ill.: Harlan Davidson, 1982), Chapters 1 and 2. Valuable for the Italian point of view is Ercole Sori, *L'emigrazione italiana dall'Unità alla seconda guerra mondiale* (Bologna: Il Mulino, 1979).

Valuable statistics are found in U.S. Bureau of the Census, *Historical Statistics of the United States, Colonial Times to 1970*, Bicentennial edition, Part 1 (Washington, D.C.: U.S. Government Printing Office, 1975), pp. 105–09; and Kingsley Davis, "The migration of human populations," *Scientific American*, 231, No. 3 (September, 1974), 53–65.

[2]Betty Boyd Caroli, *Italian Repatriation from the United States, 1900–1914* (New York: Center for Migration Studies, 1973).

[3]The Mezzogiorno is roughly designated as part of Italy south of Rome, including the regions of Abruzzi-Molise, Apulia, Basilicata, Calabria, Campania, Sardinia, and Sicily.

[4]The 80 percent figure is from statistics of American immigration authorities, who began to keep separate counts of "northern" and "southern" Italians starting in 1899. These counts are not fully trustworthy because the intent of their distinction was racial, and accordingly, a peculiar definition of a *southerner* was employed, which included anyone from central and even some from northern Italy. According to the Bureau of Immigration's definition, "southern" Italians included anyone from the "peninsula proper" (as well as the islands of Sicily and Sardinia), so that "even Genoa [the northern port city] is South Italian" (see U.S. Senate, *Reports of the Immigration Commission: Dictionary of Races or Peoples* [Washington, D.C.: U.S. Government Printing Office, 1911], p. 81).

Nonetheless, that southerners were indeed the most important part of the immigrant stream early in this century is corroborated by Italian statistics on emigration, though they are also inexact. See Sori, *L'emigrazione*, Chapter 2.

[5]The important studies include: Edward C. Banfield, *The Moral Basis of a Backward Society* (New York: Free Press, 1958); Rudolph M. Bell, *Fate and Honor, Family and Village: Demographic and Cultural Change in Rural Italy Since 1800* (Chicago: University of Chicago Press, 1979); Charlotte Gower Chapman, *Milocca: A Sicilian Village* (Cambridge, Mass.: Schenkman, 1971); Leonard Covello, *The Social Background of the Italo-American School Child* (Totowa, N.J.: Rowman & Littlefield, 1972); Joseph Lopreato, *Peasants No More: Social Class and Social Change in an Underdeveloped Society* (San Francisco: Chandler, 1967); and Jane and Peter Schneider, *Culture and Political Economy in Western Sicily* (New York: Academic Press, 1976).

Two of these studies, it should be noted, are considerably older than their publication dates and hence closer to the society known by the immigrants. Chapman's anthropological research on a Sicilian village was actually carried out in the late 1920s, at the close of the period of mass emigration; Covello's seminal study was conducted in the late 1930s and early 1940s and was based in substantial part on the recollections of immigrants.

[6]Southern Italian social structure is detailed by Covello, *Social Background*, Chapter 4; Chapman, *Milocca*, Chapter 3; and Bell, *Fate*, Chapter 6.

The category of laborers receives special attention from: Sori, *L'emigrazione*, Chapters

2 and 3; and John W. Briggs, *An Italian Passage: Immigrants to Three American Cities, 1890–1930* (New Haven, Conn.: Yale University Press, 1978), Chapter 1. On the basis of the size of this category in the immigrant stream, Briggs mistakenly challenges the common characterization of southern Italian immigrants as largely peasants, and his assertions have been accepted as accurate by others. But the immigrant laborers appear to have been mostly dislocated agriculturalists. Sori's authoritative account, which reveals the complex changes underway in Mezzogiorno society, provides the proper corrective. Unfortunately, his book is only available in Italian.

[7]On the physical environment, see Covello, *Social Background,* Chapter 3; and Schneider and Schneider, *Culture and Political Economy,* pp. 36–40.

[8]Landownership and land use are discussed by Covello, *Social Background,* pp. 45–58; Bell, *Fate,* Chapters 2 and 6; and Schneider and Schneider, *Culture and Political Economy,* Chapter 4.

[9]Elizabeth Latimer, quoted by Covello, *Social Background,* p. 45.

[10]Schneider and Schneider, *Culture and Political Economy,* pp. 63–64.

[11]Bell, *Fate,* p. 19.

[12]Covello, *Social Background,* p. 44.

[13]Banfield, *The Moral Basis,* pp. 52–54. For additional information on living conditions, see Chapman, *Milocca,* pp. 12–19; and Covello, *Social Background,* pp. 71–75.

[14]Bell, *Fate,* p. 113. Also Banfield, *The Moral Basis,* pp. 62–66; and Lopreato, *Peasants No More,* pp. 244–46.

[15]Banfield, *The Moral Basis* (copyright © 1958 The Free Press), pp. 105–106.

[16]Schneider and Schneider, *Culture and Political Economy,* pp. 82–86.

[17]Joseph Lopreato, *Italian Americans* (New York: Random House, 1970), p. 57.

[18]Chapman, *Milocca,* p. 19; Bell, *Fate,* p. 154.

[19]Banfield, *The Moral Basis* (copyright © 1958 The Free Press), p. 117.

[20]Bell, *Fate,* pp. 151–53.

[21]For general discussions, see Covello, *Social Background,* Chapters 6 and 7; Chapman, *Milocca,* Chapter 4; Bell, *Fate,* Chapter 5.

[22]Chapman, *Milocca,* p. 70.

[23]Robert Foerster, *The Italian Emigration of Our Times* (Cambridge, Mass.: Harvard University Press, 1924), p. 95.

[24]Chapman, *Milocca,* pp. 71–72, 236–38.

[25]Covello, *Social Background,* p. 246.

[26]Covello, *Social Background,* p. 257. Culture was hardly the sole explanation for low educational levels. The poor state of southern Italian schools also hindered many children from receiving an education. This is detailed by Briggs, *An Italian Passage,* Chapter 3.

[27]On marriage, see Chapman, *Milocca,* Chapter 5.

[28]Schneider and Schneider, *Culture and Political Economy,* p. 86. For general discussions, see Schneider and Schneider, pp. 86–102; Chapman, *Milocca,* pp. 38–41.

[29]Banfield, *The Moral Basis* (copyright © 1958 The Free Press), p. 83.

[30]Godparentship is taken up by Chapman, *Milocca,* Chapter 6; and by Roy A. Miller and Maria Gabriella Miller, "The golden chain: A study of the structure, function, and patterning of *comparatico* in a south Italian village," *American Ethnologist,* 5, No. 1 (February, 1978), 116–36.

[31]Chapman, *Milocca,* p. 67.

[32]Influential versions of the conventional account are The President's Commission on Law Enforcement and Administration of Justice, *Task Force Report: Organized Crime* (Washington, D.C.: U.S. Government Printing Office, 1967); and Donald R. Cressey, *Theft of the Nation: The Structure and Operations of Organized Crime in America* (New York: Harper & Row, 1969).

A very different interpretation is by Dwight C. Smith, Jr., and Richard D. Alba, "Organized crime and American life," *Society,* 16, No. 3 (March/April, 1979), 32–38.

[33]The President's Commission, *Task Force Report,* p. 6.

[34]These include Anton Blok, *The Mafia of a Sicilian Village, 1860-1960: A Study of Violent Peasant Entrepreneurs* (New York: Harper & Row, 1974); Henner Hess, *Mafia and Mafiosi: The Structure of Power* (Westmead, England: Saxon House, 1973); and Schneider and Schneider, *Culture and Political Economy.*

[35]The origins of the word *mafia* are shrouded by antiquity, although recorded uses of it go back several centuries, when it was used to signify something excellent or outstanding. It appears that the word did not acquire the meaning of a criminal association until the middle of the 19th century, and this was popularized by a dialect play of the 1860s. For further information, see Hess, *Mafia and Mafiosi,* pp. 1–3.

[36]Blok, *The Mafia of a Sicilian Village,* p. 94.

[37]Schneider and Schneider, *Culture and Political Economy,* pp. 10–14.

[38]Jones, *American Immigration,* Chapters 4 and 7; Bell, *Fate,* Chapter 8.

[39]Schneider and Schneider, *Culture and Political Economy,* pp. 114–15. I am indebted to Jane Schneider and Donna Gabaccia for impressing upon me the crucial significance of the crisis in grain prices.

[40]Sori, *L'emigrazione,* Chapter 3.

[41]Humbert S. Nelli, *From Immigrants to Ethnics: The Italian Americans* (Oxford: Oxford University Press, 1983), pp. 32–33.

[42]Jones, *American Immigration,* p. 200; Bell, *Fate,* pp. 192–93; Kraut, *The Huddled Masses,* pp. 33–34; Schneider and Schneider, *Culture and Political Economy,* pp. 120-25; Shepard B. Clough, *The Economic History of Modern Italy* (New York: Columbia University Press, 1964), pp. 114–21, 382.

[43]Guiseppe Lucrezio Monticelli, "Italian emigration: Basic characteristics and trends with special reference to the post-war years," in Silvano M. Tomasi and Madeline H. Engel (eds.), *The Italian Experience in the United States* (Staten Island: Center for Migration Studies, 1970), p. 3.

[44]Caroli, *Italian Repatriation,* p. 41.

[45]Covello, *The Social Background,* p. 257.

CHAPTER THREE
THE PERIOD
OF SETTLEMENT:
1880–1930

This and the next chapter consider what happened to the Italians and their descendants from the time of their arrival in the new land through the recent past, until 1970. Such a narrative is essential to understanding how the group arrived where it is today—which is so distant from where it began and yet still bears recognizably "Italian-American" traces. Because the focus of this book is on the integration of Italians into American society, the overarching themes of this narrative are social mobility and assimilation. These carry us into a consideration of such topics as immigrant communities in American cities, the use Italians made of American schools, the emergence and evolution of an Italian-American identity, and above all to the family ethos, which even as it underwent a drastic mutation, remained the driving gear in the group's adaptation to the new society.

THE QUESTION OF TIME

There are two ways of dividing time in the study of ethnicity and, hence, of framing the underlying stages of change. In addition to the obvious alternative of dividing chronological time into historical periods bracketed by years or decades, ethnic processes can be described in terms of generations. *Generation* here signifies distance from the point of immigration, with the immigrants counted as the first generation. Thus, their children, actually the first native-born generation, are counted as the second, and their grandchildren as the third. The generational division of time is significant because each new generation of an ethnic group potentially represents another step on the way to accommodation (which is not necessarily the same as assimilation) to the host society. Typically for American ethnic groups, each new generation is more acculturated than the last, at least for the first three or four generations. Consequently, the description of ethnic change frequently resolves into one of the differences among generations.

In the case of a group like the Italians, who came in a very compressed period of time, there is not a great deal of difference between the alternatives of generation and historical period. The Italian immigration was essentially a very short burst, with more than 3 million arrivals in the years 1900–1914—nearly 60 percent of the total Italian immigration from 1820 to 1980. As a result, each historical period is dominated numerically by a single generational grouping, whose experiences define the period's character. For the same reason, each generation has tended to come of age within a short historical span, and therefore its experiences have been framed by a common set of opportunities and constraints, determined in large part by the acceptability of Italians and Italian Americans to other Americans and by the penetration the group had made into the weave of American institutions. The relationship between these two ways of thinking about temporal change is portrayed by Figure 3-1, which presents the generational composition of the group at different points in time through 1980.

If I have elected, then, to emphasize historical period in the titles of this and the next chapter, the choice is not a fundamental one; it does not exclude a generational perspective. But it is not without meaning, either; in particular, it is intended to underline what can easily be lost in a sociological account: the significance of "large" historical events, such as both world wars, for the evolution of Italians and other immigrant groups. The choice of an opening date for this chapter is obvious—it is the onset of mass immigration from Italy. The closing date is less obvious but no less appropriate: It represents the absolute close of the period of mass immigration, brought on by restrictive immigration laws forced by growing American antagonism towards immigrants, especially those from southern and eastern Europe. Before the 1930 date, the Italian population of the United States was still unsettled, affected not only by the continuing flow of immigrants into the country (although this flow did slacken considerably after 1914 and again after 1921), but also by the departure of many repatriates, returning to Italy. Undoubtedly, among those who remained through the end of the period, there were some who intended to return eventually; but after 1930, movement in and out slowed considerably.[1] The population stabilized; and probably many of those who had come with the intention of going back, but who had remained for whatever reasons, now recognized that they were here to stay.

The period through 1930 was dominated by the first, or immigrant, generation. But the rising line of the second generation in figure 3-1 shows its rapid growth after 1910; and by 1930, substantial numbers of this first native-born

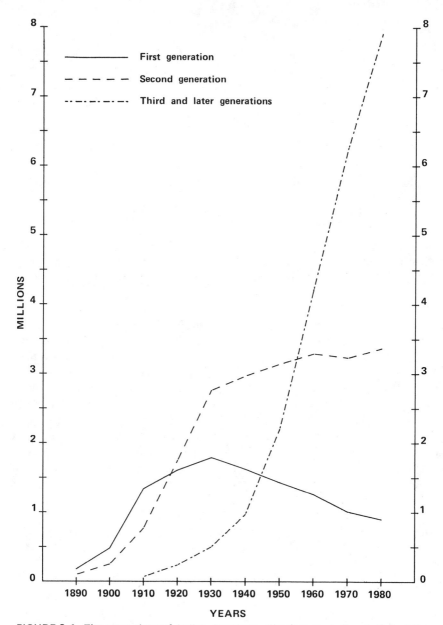

FIGURE 3-1 The generations of Italian Americans. The first generation is that of the immigrants; the second that of the American-born with at least one immigrant parent. The third and later generations include individuals with American-born parents having some Italian ancestry.

[SOURCE: Adapted from Rudolph J. Vecoli, "The coming of age of the Italian Americans: 1945–1974," *Ethnicity*, 5, No. 2 (June, 1978), p. 121; and from Massimo Livi Bacci, *L'immigrazione e l'assimilazione degli Italiani negli Stati Uniti* (Milan: Editore Giuffrè, 1961), p. 95. Data sources: U.S. Bureau of the Census, *Historical Statistics of the United States, Colonial Times to 1970,* Bicentennial edition, Part 1 (Washington, D.C.: U.S. Government Printing Office, 1975), pp. 116–117; and my computations from the November, 1979, Current Population Survey, conducted by the Bureau of the Census.]

generation were reaching maturity. During the last two decades of the period of settlement, then, the emergence of a sizable cohort of immigrant children, combined with a sharp fall-off in immigration after 1914, shifted the focus of communal concern: The immigrants' anxiety about finding a niche, however temporary, in American society was succeeded by that of passing on a way of life to the new generation, one whose members were being raised in an environment vastly different from that which lived on in their parents' memories. Thus, although the ascendancy of the second generation was not established until the 1930s, its emergence left a mark on the decades of the 10s and 20s.

THE IMMIGRANTS SETTLE IN

Patterns of Settlement

The Italians who immigrated to America came predominantly from the rural areas of Italy, and it would have seemed natural if they had gravitated toward rural areas in the United States. But they did so only to a limited extent. Northern Italians became an important force in California agriculture, a fact reflected in the frequency of Italian names on the labels of California wines; and everywhere they went, Italians excelled in vegetable gardening and truck farming.[2] But despite their rural origins, Italians settled more often than not in urban places, and frequently in the most highly urban places. Thus, in 1910, at the height of immigration, New York City had 340,000 Italians, well ahead of its nearest rivals, Boston, Chicago, and Philadelphia, none of which had more than 45,000. Other places trailed far behind these major cities.[3]

There are many reasons for this switch of locale. Many immigrants came with little money and, hence, were forced to settle where they landed. This simple fact does much to explain why New York had such a large Italian population (it is estimated that 97 percent of the immigrants disembarked there).[4] Moreover, the agriculture of the United States was very different from that familiar to Italians, especially southern Italians. The different soil, environmental conditions, and crops and the comparatively large size of American farms probably rendered the agricultural skills of many southerners irrelevant; and the large distance between farms meant loneliness for Italians used to living in towns. But most important is that Italians immigrated in the hope of a change in fortune. Many came intending to earn money as quickly as possible and then return to Italy to purchase their own land. Becoming a farmer in America didn't make sense because it would require not only a great effort before it began to produce a return, but also a long-term investment of earnings. Much more sensible, given the intention to return, was to work for others and save as much as possible. And the fact was that employment was most easily found in cities.[5]

In the cities, the Italians crowded into areas that contained other Italians. Their settlement in ethnic colonies or enclaves—"Little Italies"—was much like that of other groups, such as the Irish. Initially, the Italian areas were near business and commercial sections. These central-city areas had been areas of first settlement for previous immigrant groups, many of whose members departed, like a retreating army, at the signs of the mass arrival of the Italians. Others, however, for financial or other reasons, remained behind and provided some initial contact with outsiders for the "greenhorn" Italians. Few of the Italian neighborhoods were entirely Italian.

Physical conditions in the areas of first settlement varied considerably from place to place. Especially in the large cities, these areas tended to be true slums; in some other places, Italians occupied more comfortable, if somewhat dense, quarters. But given the group's concentration in the largest cities, it is the tenement districts of New York, Chicago, and other major cities that are often cited as typical. In some of them, to take advantage of the immigrant trade, buildings had been slapped together on every available patch of land, stacked one behind the other, with little access to sunlight and fresh air. Even stables and warehouses were made over to accommodate the immigrants, as humans were packed together within whatever space was available. Like other immigrant groups, Italians accepted this crowding during the first few years after their arrival in order to save as much money as possible and get themselves started. In their case, the desire of many to return to Italy with enough money to buy land added an extra spur to the usual motives. But to the outside observer, the dilapidated housing, the minimal sanitation, the great density of people, and the consequent ease with which diseases spread made the immigrant ghettoes horrible to behold. The photographs of Jacob Riis drew attention to the conditions in the immigrant areas of New York City, including those in one Italian slum area, Mulberry Bend in Manhattan.[6]

The Italian areas were built up by a phenomenon known as "chain migration." Knowing little of the country to which they were migrating, immigrants from all countries generally followed pathways laid down by those who preceded them; and in the case of the Italians, this universal tendency was strengthened by the general importance of family and village ties. Frequently, the men would come first and, once settled successfully, would bring over their wives and children, while encouraging other relatives and *paesani* to come as well. In her book on the Italians of Buffalo, Virginia Yans-McLaughlin gives the example of Francesco Barone from Valledolmo, Sicily. He left Sicily in 1887 and settled in Buffalo, eventually succeeding as a saloonkeeper. As a result of his encouragement, fourteen of his relatives and their families had moved there by 1905. By 1947, the migration to Buffalo from Valledolmo, not an especially large place, reached the astounding total of 8,000 persons, equal to the town's population in the late 19th century.[7] Obviously, a movement like this, linking two distant points as if by magic carpet, was a matter of chains within chains, as members of the initial chain started new ones, whose members then initiated others, and so on.

The result was to give the Italian enclave a speckled appearance in terms of the regional origins of its residents. Immigrants from the same towns and provinces settled near one another, on the same block or in the same tenement. Thomas

Kessner describes New York's Little Italy, for example, according to the following Old World geography:

> Mott Street between East Houston and Prince held the Napolitani; the opposite side of the street was reserved for Basilicati. Around the corner the Siciliani settled Prince Street, while two blocks away the Calabresi lived on Mott between Broome and Grand. Mulberry Street was strictly Neapolitan, and Hester Street, running perpendicular to Mulberry, carried the local color of Apulia.[8]

These "Little Sicilies" or "Little Calabrias" were generally not made up exclusively of individuals from these areas—immigrants from other places were interspersed among them—but they permitted immigrants to live in a world as familiar as possible under the vastly different circumstances of the new world. Hence, the *campanilismo* of the old world carried over into the new one, and town and provincial identifications remained important. At least during the early period of settlement, parents often expected their children to marry someone from the same area of Italy, and the evidence suggests that in fact this happened with some frequency.[9]

The pattern of settlement within the colony points up its larger function: to provide a buffer against the shock of the new surroundings and thereby to permit the gradual adjustment of the immigrants. Even in a physical setting that seemed superficially so different, the immigrants managed to recreate many of the sights, sounds, and smells of the Old World. One such recreation was the *festa* in celebration of a patron saint's day. In Italian East Harlem, for instance, the most popular *festa* was that of the Madonna of Mount Carmel, on July 16. Every year on that date, the neighborhood would be festooned with Italian and American flags, its stores and pushcarts crammed with watermelon, *dolci* (sweets), and other good things to eat, and its streets crowded with the 30,000 or 40,000 people who would come, many from other parts of New York, to be in attendance. A high point of the *festa* was a procession centered around a large statue of the Madonna, carried on the shoulders of four men, and followed by a banner bearing the dollar bills pinned to it by the faithful. In the evening, there would be music and fireworks. In the words of an East Harlem native, it was "the biggest day of the year."[10]

The residents of Italian colonies also created institutions to support them in the new place—although it must be said that the organizational life of Italian enclaves was not as rich as that found among some other nationalities, because the family-centeredness of the immigrants tended to preclude deep involvement in extra-familial groups. The chief organizational form that emerged was that of the mutual-benefit society. As befits the early *campanilismo* of the enclave, many of these societies were formed around a provincial or regional identity, such as Chicago's *Unione Siciliana*; but eventually societies open to all Italians came into being. The most important of these was the Order of the Sons of Italy in America, which was founded in 1905 and by 1923 had almost 300,000 members in over

1,000 lodges. The mutual-benefit societies provided not only a format for socializing, but as their name implies, they rendered help in times of need. They provided benefits to members suffering from sickness or injury, and they offered death benefits and help with funeral expenses to members' families. These contributions were essential for an ethnic group whose members did much of the most dangerous work in a society.[11]

The enclave provided the population concentration for other specialized institutions to survive, if not thrive. Thus, businesses with an ethnic clientele knew where their customers were; in fact, Italian colonies appear to have offered fertile ground for the enterprising immigrant. As an example, one six-block area of Pittsburgh in 1910 supported six Italian grocers as well as a number of other merchants.[12] Also, Italian-language newspapers knew where to find their readers. Such newspapers flourished during the era of mass immigration, the high-water mark being attained in 1918, when 110 of them were published in the United States. Most were specific to a single city, but one paper, *Il Progresso Italo-Americano* of New York City, did succeed in being somewhat national in scope. Its daily circulation in 1921 exceeded 100,000, and it is still in existence today.[13]

Population concentration had, moreover, important implications for the political advancement of the group, given the machine politics that dominated most American cities. Even though not very many Italians registered to vote in the early period of settlement, because their gaze was still focused on the Italian homeland, enough did so to draw the attention of political leaders. And since the Italian vote was so concentrated geographically, politicians had to make concessions to the Italian group in order to hold on to the districts it occupied. To be sure, Italians did not advance rapidly in politics. Like other minorities, they had difficulty competing for higher-level offices, which demanded that Italian candidates appeal to non-Italian voters; and, in many cities, the Italian advance was partially blocked by Irish-American politicians, who clung tenaciously to the controls of the Democratic machine, even in areas where Irish-American voters had been replaced by Italian ones. Some of the early Italian political leaders were, in fact, intermediaries between Italian voters and Irish machine bosses. This was true of "Big Jim" Colosimo of Chicago and Paul Kelly (originally named Paolo Antonio Vaccarelli) of New York, neither of whom ever held elective office. (They shared the additional trait of involvement in organized crime.) The family ethos may also have played a role in the slow political advance of the group, by hindering the emergence of ethnic political leaders who had the solid support of the community. But the crucial point is that Italians did get ahead in politics, especially after 1920.[14]

The importance of the enclave as a "decompression chamber"—shielding its inhabitants from the uncomfortable pressures of a strange environment and allowing them to adjust gradually to its demands—bears on the nature of segregation, at least as far as immigrant groups are concerned. The enclave is often portrayed as a ghetto, created by discrimination against its residents. Italians did, in fact, suffer from the discrimination envisioned in this picture and were prevented by it from moving into many better neighborhoods. But discrimination does not explain the *existence* of the enclave; this is explained by the need of immigrants to huddle together in a strange land, to re-create something familiar. An additional impetus in the case of Italians was the desire of many immigrants to return eventually to Italy. Those intending to return felt no need to adjust to America but, rather, wanted to maintain themselves in an existence as nearly as possible like that to which they would return. What discrimination does explain is the *location* of the enclave. Discrimination tended to compel the immigrants to accept during the early period of settlement the worst housing and neighborhoods.

Even so, the boundaries of Italian colonies did not remain fixed in place. One study of Chicago documents the movement of its Italian residents over the period of early settlement. Initially confined to a central-city district, Italians gradually migrated outward to new areas, especially as they became more prosperous. This outward trek did not mean abandonment of the central-city colony by the group, because newly arrived immigrants moved in to replace those moving out.[15] Another study demonstrates statistically that this pattern was a fairly general one, found in a number of American cities and for many ethnic groups. Nevertheless, the fluidity of the boundaries of the areas of Italian settlement did not, at least up to 1930, mean a decline in their segregation from others. The latter study shows that the segregation of Italians from third- and fourth-generation Americans remained high at the end of this period.[16] Thus, in the sense of an area enclosing the familiar social world of a group, and indicating its lack of integration into the larger society, the enclave remained, even though its boundaries had expanded and now included better housing than before.

Work

As a body, the Italian immigrants who poured into American cities after 1880 possessed few skills of value in an industrial economy. The much smaller northern Italian immigration that preceded this date had been more varied and contained substantial numbers of craftsmen and professionals, including a note-worthy component of musicians and others who worked in the arts. One such person, admittedly not typical, was Lorenzo da Ponte, who had been Mozart's librettist for *Don Giovanni* and became Columbia University's first professor of Italian. The mass immigration was more homogeneous. During its early years, it was composed predominantly of men of prime working ages coming from the agricultural villages of the south; later, they were joined by their wives and children. The bulk of the men were unskilled laborers. For example, of the 1,768,281 Italian immigrants with previous occupational experience who entered the United States in the years 1899-1910, 563,200 were counted as farm laborers and 767,811 as other laborers, the two categories comprising three-quarters of the total.[17] To be sure, the mass immigration was not devoid of highly skilled individuals. Frequently, however, these were not individuals with skills of use in the expanding and dynamic indus-trial sector, but men who were stonemasons, shoemakers, and barbers, possessing skills that could not be applied in a factory setting, but in the out of doors, small shops, and in personal service.

Italians therefore entered the American labor force *en masse* in the ranks of manual labor. In this respect, they were not different from other groups that had been drawn to America from rural backgrounds, notably the Irish. Many immigrants fresh from peasantry discovered upon their arrival that only "peek and shuvil" work was open to them; they were expected to contribute only their muscle power to the industrial behemoth. In 1905 in New York City, at the height of immigration in the city with the largest concentration of Italians in the United States, nearly 60 percent of Italians did unskilled or semiskilled manual labor, working on construction gangs or as ragpickers and longshoremen. Another 18 percent did work that could be classified in the "lower white-collar" category, which included many small shopkeepers, but also a fair number of street peddlers. Only a tiny percentage were in the upper white-collar category, which included professionals, and the remainder, over 20 percent of the total, were skilled blue-collar workers, including an increasing number who worked in the skilled trades of New York's garment industry.[18]

In New York, then, four out of five Italians had manual occupations, and most of these were concentrated in the lowest ranks of the blue-collar class. This concentration appears to have been quite typical, and other factors besides the rural European backgrounds of the Italians contributed to it. One was the *padrone* system, which existed during the early years of the Italian immigration (a similar system existed also among some other southern and eastern European groups). The *padrone* was a labor contractor, who arranged seasonal work for immigrants, usually on construction gangs such as those that built the railroads. The *padrone*, who was usually Italian, found his men in the cities with large Italian populations; New York and Chicago were both major centers of *padrone* activity. He would meet ships and trains carrying immigrants and would offer work to the debarking men. Some would accept immediately, and others who initially refused would eventually turn to him after discovering the difficulties of finding work in a strange society.

Americans frowned on the *padrone* system, which to them smacked of a submissive group unsuited for the demands of a democratic society, and which had a number of built-in possibilities for abuse. Immigrants paid the *padrone* a fee (called the *bossatura*) for finding them work, and the most unscrupulous *padroni* would quickly discharge immigrant workers and take on new ones, thereby collecting new fees. The basic conditions of work also bred exploitation. The *padrone* would organize the immigrants into work gangs, sending these out into the countryside to construction sites. He arranged for their transportation, for which he charged them. And while the men were working, they lived in camps for which the *padrone* supplied the provisions, again for a charge. In both cases, the charges were often well above regular prices, and the *padrone*'s ability to enforce unfair charges was strengthened by the fact that he generally transmitted the men's wages to them.

The high-water mark for this labor contracting system occurred before 1900, and it had receded considerably by the time of the heaviest southern Italian immigration, 1900-1914. The efforts of American social workers and others opposed to the system are partly responsible for its decline. But more importantly, immigrants no longer needed it. The *padrone* system was a feature of the earliest stage of immigration, when there were not yet a large number of Italians having sufficient experience with American working conditions and knowledge of English to assist their newly arriving relatives and *paesani* in finding jobs. After 1900, this was no longer true, and the *padrone* system largely disappeared.[19]

Another major factor contributing to the early concentration of Italians in the lowest ranks of manual labor was the intention of many immigrants to stay only temporarily in America and to return to Italy as soon as they had earned enough money to purchase land. Because of this sojourner mentality, Italians sought out jobs that required no investment of money or self and paid ready cash. The expectation of transience discouraged the establishment of small businesses, which would tie up immigrant money and might take a considerable period of effort to pay off. (Nonetheless, there were many Italian shopkeepers.) This expectation also made the prospect of mobility of little or no concern in choosing a job. Hence, the intention to return added to the acceptability of unskilled manual labor.

Culturally engendered expectations about the nature of work, carried from the Mezzogiorno, further constrained occupational possibilities. That many immigrants took jobs in construction or on the docks was in part a result of preference, because the men looked for outdoor work, seeking to reproduce the familiar work cycles and conditions of rural Italy. Outdoor work was seasonal, thus reproducing an annual rhythm found in agricultural work, but of course this fact meant winters of unemployment for many immigrant workers. Italians also preferred outdoor labor to factory work because they shunned the relentless discipline, the machine-imposed rhythm, of the factory. This culturally produced preference tended to consign Italian men to irregular work outside the regular channels of blue-collar mobility, which were found in the factories. With respect to this important disadvantage, Italians were different from most other immigrant groups, including those from peasant backgrounds, whose members more readily took to industrial work.[20]

The culture brought from the Mezzogiorno also limited the work horizons of immigrant women. One of the culture's strongest prohibitions was directed against contact between women and male strangers, and this powerful norm went far toward defining what was an acceptable work situation for Italian women. Work in the home was strongly preferred, both on the grounds of the prohibition and because it allowed women to earn money without neglecting their families. Many wives were able to contribute to the family income by taking in boarders, who were usually relatives or *paesani* in order not to compromise the family honor. Women also took in work that could be done in the home, such as laundering or the manufacture of clothes or artificial flowers. Some women did find jobs outside the home, but this probably happened with less frequency among the Italians than among some other groups; and when it did, it was generally under circumstances compatible with cultural roles. This was the case when the family worked together as a group and also when women worked in factories, such as those in the garment industry, where they were surrounded by other immigrant women. But because of the cultural prohibition, Italians did not do what many other immigrant women had done before them, become domestics in other people's homes.[21]

By the end of the period of settlement, the concentration of Italians in the lowest ranks of manual labor had been diluted somewhat, although it remained strong. One study of New York City shows that many of those Italians who remained in America were mobile and improved their occupational situation over the decades. In particular, a rise out of the depths of unskilled labor into the grades of skilled and semiskilled blue-collar work took place for many immigrants, or their children.[22] Also, in some industries, Italians were so numerous that they gained a nearly dominant position, and this helped to produce great success for some of their countrymen. In New York City, this happened in the construction industry, where highly successful Italian builders and contractors emerged. The four Paterno brothers (Charles, Michael, Anthony, and Joseph), for instance, constructed the apartment buildings at some of the city's fancier addresses, including Fifth Avenue, Sutton Place, and West End Avenue.[23]

Moreover, by the 1920s, many of those who intended to come only temporarily had returned to Italy, and others had mentally transferred their futures from the Mezzogiorno to America. One measure of this shift in orientation is the increasing proportion of the Italian-born who had become American citizens. An analysis of ten American cities shows a steady rise in this proportion from 1910 to 1930. In 1910, at the height of immigration, generally a third or fewer of adult Italian immigrants had become naturalized citizens. By 1920, this had climbed to about half or more in most of the cities. At the end of the period, in 1930, it generally had reached two-thirds or more. Still, among these ten cities there were three (Boston, St. Louis, and Columbus, Ohio) in which more than 40 percent of the Italian-born were noncitizens; and in the majority of the ten, Italians had the highest proportion of noncitizens among immigrant groups and also the highest percentage who did not speak English.[24]

Another index of the shift in orientation to America and away from Italy is the frequency of home ownership by immigrant families at the end of the period—also, of course, an index of increasing prosperity. Owning a home was of great symbolic importance to families of peasant origins, since it partook of the near-sacred value attached to land and provided a way to attain a cherished and familiar status in an alien setting. But owning a home in America also represented a commitment to the new country, literally a sinking of savings into its earth. Once they decided to buy a home, Italian families appear to have been willing to make great sacrifices to realize their ambition, for example, removing their children from school and sending them to work as early as the law allowed.[25] The just-cited study of ten cities shows that in most of them around half of the immigrant families owned homes by 1930. Despite the stereotype of Italians as working-class home-owners, however, the Italians appear to have been no different from the members of other immigrant groups in this respect.[26]

THE SECOND GENERATION EMERGES

Despite the seeming insulation of many Italians from the influences of the American environment—an insulation stemming from their intention to return to their homeland and strengthened by the protective embrace of the enclave—the immigrants could not escape altogether the impact of their stay in America. The effect, of course, was all the more profound when they transferred their aspirations from Italy to the United States. Nonetheless, the extent to which an immigrant generation can undergo a cultural transformation and become acculturated is limited. Granting the existence of numerous exceptions, most immigrants from whatever country remain distinguishable from other Americans even after prolonged residence. This could hardly be otherwise. Most come as adults, having been raised and having spent their early lives in another society; hence, their personalities are largely formed when they arrive and cannot be expected to change radically under the impact of a new environment. Typically, immigrants of long residence remain identifiable by such external features as accent, clothing, and mannerism; and if they remain different in these external ways, then how much more so they must be in internal ways, in cultural values.

Matters are quite different with their children, who form what is called the "second" generation in discussions of ethnicity. Theirs is the first native-born generation, and with the exception of perhaps a few individuals who are brought temporarily back to the Old World by their parents, they are raised wholly on American soil and attend American schools. But they are also influenced deeply by the culture of their parents. Thus, although the second generation typically represents a giant step in the direction of accommodation to the host society, it is in important respects a transitional generation, caught in between the demands of the immigrant culture and the exigencies of a new way of life. Strain is built into its situation; and in the nature of that strain and the adjustments that are made to relieve it, much is revealed about the overall direction the group's adjustment will take.

Strain and Adjustment in the Family System

To observe that immigrants generally seek to recreate a world that conforms to the familiar outlines of the culture of their homelands is not the same as saying that immigrant cultures are carbon copies of the originals. The period of immigration and early settlement is a time of "sorting out" for a group's culture. The culture brought by Italian immigrants was adapted to a rigidly stratified, underdeveloped rural environment, but its appropriateness for the industrial and urban places into which immigrants came was problematic. As was true for the cultures of other groups as well, the impact of immigration produced a reshuffling of cultural elements. Some faded in importance because they were incompatible with the group's new needs; others either ascended—their importance enhanced by the requirements of the very different situation—or they were transformed. The important point is that cultures were malleable; they were not eternal givens, directing group destiny like the fingers of a puppeteer.

The impact of immigration was deeply felt in the family system. The impact here has been misconstrued in the past. Some of the most famous sociological and historical interpretations of immigration have portrayed the process as a disastrous transition from a rural folk society to a complex industrial society, disorganizing the family, leading to high rates of family abandonment and breakup. But this did not happen to the Italian family. One change in fact was of a very different kind: the strengthening of the extended family.[27] Although the family ethos of the Mezzogiorno idealized the solidarity of the extended family, the socioeconomic realities of southern Italy prevented it from becoming fully realized. Households were composed of nuclear families, i.e., parents and their children, with perhaps an additional relative or two. Nuclear families were also the basic economic units, since the landholdings of peasants were generally too small to support large numbers of individuals. But extended family ties were activated by immigration; they were crucial links in the migration chains. Immigrants often went to specific American cities because relatives (or *paesani*) had preceded them and could help the newcomers to establish themselves. During the very early period of settlement, when immigrants were attempting to save as much money as possible, groups of immigrants lived together in the same cramped quarters or immigrant families took in boarders; in both cases, extended family ties were frequently involved.

But if one immediate impact of immigration was a strengthening of the family system, strain was not far behind. It became evident with the emergence of the second generation, and then the strains seemed to come from many directions. To begin with the obvious, the second generation was educated in American schools and exposed to American culture in many other ways, such as movies and popular music. The awareness of a very different set of cultural standards in the surrounding society, of which it was more a part than its parents, weakened its loyalty to Mezzogiorno culture. Especially seductive was the greater tolerance, the individualism, in family and sexual matters.

Changes in relative position within the constellation of the family acted as a catalyst for greater acculturation. One such shift occurred between parents and children. In the Mezzogiorno, the absolute authority of parents over children derived legitimacy from the parents' greater knowledge of the society and its ways. But in America, it was children who possessed the greater knowledge, because they were more acculturated—they were able to speak English while many of their parents were not, for example. Hence they were better positioned than their parents to take advantage of American opportunities. With this important prop of parental authority removed, the generations were placed in conflict. One expression of the conflict lay in tension over parental control of their children's earnings, tensions bred by the individualism implicit in the American labor market. In southern Italy, the family itself often constituted the work unit. Husband, wife, and children would go into the fields at times of peak work, such as the harvest, and all would contribute to the same goal, even if their individual tasks might be different. Under these circumstances, it made sense to pool the earnings of individuals into a single family wage, which the parents received. But in America, children past school age generally had their own jobs, and first put into their own pockets the money they had earned. Accordingly, it became difficult for them to automatically turn all their earnings over to their parents, especially given that the acculturated second generation might earn more than its parents.[28]

Significant changes in the position of women were also wrought by the American environment. It was no longer possible to maintain the kind of family surveillance over young women that had been attainable in the Italian south. Daughters could not attend school nor go to work in the company of family members acting as chaperones. (However, the prohibition on contact between unmarried women and unrelated men did channel the employment possibilities for second-generation women in the direction of jobs held primarily by women, like those in the needle trades.) Second-generation Italian women thus had a taste of personal freedom, one that was accentuated, moreover, by their growing consciousness of the standards by which young American women were judged.

The shift in the position of women and the structural forces producing it are most visible in relation to courtship and marriage. The control exercised in southern Italy by parents, and the family generally, over the marriages of their children hinged on greater knowledge of the field of eligibles. But this was a knowledge acquired over many years in a fairly static village, with a stable complement of families, and it largely disappeared in the new setting. Parents who attempted to maintain the same control in an American city placed their daughters in a difficult position, as this plaintive description by one second-generation Italian-American woman reveals: "Our parents think you can just sit home and wait for a man to come asking for your hand—like a small town in Italy." She added a remedy that made sense only in the American environment, "They don't realize that here a girl has got to get out and do something about it."[29] Many apparently did do something about it, slipping away without their parents' knowledge to go to dances or meet men. But still there was a lot of confusion over the proper limits on the behavior of young women. Some were allowed great freedom, others were kept at home as they would have been in southern Italy, and the situations of the majority were in between these two extremes. There were even variations within the same family, as the struggle between the generations was most intense for the oldest daughters, and parental resistance often abated for the younger sisters.[30]

A survey conducted by Caroline Ware in Greenwich Village in the early 1930s offers a snapshot of family norms in motion. She divided the sample into

TABLE 3–1   Changes in the Family Ethos between the Generations:
Percentages Disagreeing with Mezzogiorno Family Norms

	OVER 35 YEARS	UNDER 35 YEARS
Does *not* believe that:		
Marriages should be arranged by parents.	70%	99%
Large families are a blessing.	48%	86%
Girls should not associate with men unless engaged.	45%	83%
Husband's authority should be supreme.	34%	64%
A child should sacrifice his personal ambition to welfare of family group.	31%	54%
Divorce is never permissible.	12%	61%
Children owe absolute obedience to parents.	2%	15%

SOURCE: *Greenwich Village, 1920–1930* by Caroline Ware. Copyright 1935 by Caroline F. Ware. Copyright renewed © 1963 by Caroline F. Ware (Boston: Houghton Mifflin, 1935), p. 193.

respondents over 35 and those 35 or under, a division that no doubt correlates with generation, since a large part of the older group must have been Italian-born, and probably most of the younger group were American-born. For the two age groups, the contrast in the percentages disagreeing with Mezzogiorno family norms, presented in Table 3–1, reveals the discord between the generations. In every case, the younger group departed further from the family ethos, and in several instances, the differences between the two groups were very large. The younger group was much more willing not only to allow young women to associate with men to whom they were not engaged but also to accept divorce. This group was also more likely to deny that the husband's authority should be supreme, that children must sacrifice for the good of the family, and that large families are a blessing. Virtually no one in the younger group believed that marriages should be arranged by parents, but a third of the older group continued to believe this.[31]

The changes in the family system demonstrate that the influence of the American environment penetrated deep beneath the cultural crust, subtly but powerfully transforming and rearranging fundamental elements. The shift in family norms was necessitated by the incompatibility between the Mezzogiorno culture, if faithfully adhered to, and American situations. Yet the changes did not mean a complete acceptance of American culture, either. The second generation represented an important step in the direction of acculturation, but its members still felt strongly the influence and indeed the desirability of the Mezzogiorno family ethos. As we will see in the next chapter, a kind of metamorphosis was occurring: The ethos took on forms that meshed with the situation of the Italian group in America.

The Mezzogiorno Ethos and American Schools

One area in which the Mezzogiorno ethos left an indelible imprint on the second generation was education. Formal schooling was of little significance in southern Italian society, even though legislation enacted shortly after Italian unification required three years of school attendance for every child. But in the south, schools were inaccessible for much of the population, and where they were accessible, they were underfinanced and in poor condition; and in many places, schooling for peasant children was actively opposed by the propertied classes. Consequently, few peasant children attended schools for more than a brief period, if at all, and at the time of mass immigration, the great majority of peasants were illiterate. Most of what peasant children had to know to function as full-fledged members of their society was taught within the bosom of the family.

Contributing to the low levels of education was a tension between the schools and peasant society, recorded in the culture. Southern Italians distinguished between being *buon educato,* well versed in the mores of the society, and being *ben istruito,* well instructed in the knowledge obtainable from books; the former was unquestionably good, the latter of doubtful value. The tension arose in part because the schools were frequently agencies of upper-class and northern Italian interests; but it also derived from a fundamental incompatibility between the intellectual values embodied in the educational system and the material, pragmatic values that were not taught in school but were essential to the proper raising of peasant children.[32]

The conflict between the school and peasant society in southern Italy was intensified by the needs of the family system. From the perspective of the family, the school appeared to pose a threat because of its potential to inject new values into a traditional society, disrupting the accepted hierarchy of authority within the family and interfering with the transmission of its values and mores from one generation to the next. The ultimate danger was of fission within the basic social atom, if the younger generation became alienated from its elders. The danger inherent in the school was highlighted by implication in southern Italian proverbs, such as "Chi lascia la via vecchia e piglia la via nuova, sa quello che lascia ma non sa quello che trova (He who leaves the old way for the new, knows what he leaves but knows not what he will find)" and "Fesso chi fa i figli meglio di lui (Stupid and contemptible is he who makes his children better than himself)."[33]

The emphasis on knowledge that was practical (and hence preparation for an adult trade) as well as moral (compatible with the strict family ethos) did not disappear in America. For this reason, the use that Italian families made of American schools was very different from that made by Jews, a group with whom the Italians are often compared, since both entered many of the same American cities in large numbers about the same time. As many observers reported, eastern European Jews swarmed to take advantage of every educational opportunity, flooding libraries and night schools, and it was not long before they were knocking on the doors of the most prestigious colleges and universities.[34] The contrast with the

Italians could not be greater. Italian children had high rates of truancy and frequently left school as early as the law allowed, with the obvious consequence that their ultimate educational attainment was quite low. Even as late as 1930, only 11 percent of Italian Americans who entered New York City high schools graduated from them, at a time when over 40 percent of all the city's high school students stayed through to receive their diplomas.[35] Moreover, there were Italian-American students who did not even reach high school.

Of course, a comparison with the educational achievements of eastern European Jews was bound to be unfavorable to the Italians. Jewish immigrants were not really rural dwellers in Europe; and their occupations had been chiefly industrial and commercial. In fact, in their possession of industrial skills, they ranked at the top of American immigrant groups.[36] Moreover, both their religious and secular cultures endowed learning with a special sanctity. A comparison with other immigrant groups from rural backgrounds would not have been so unfavorable. Nonetheless, the point remains that the educational differences among groups in their early periods of settlement were rooted to a significant degree in their cultures, even if these were explicable in terms of the European background.

The conflict between the school and the Italian family system was renewed in America. Laws mandating school attendance up to a certain age were regarded as a particularly obnoxious intrusion on the prerogatives of the family. Only a few years of schooling were viewed as necessary to impart to children what they would need to survive. Additional years were destructive of their moral fiber, instilling in them ideas that were alien to their parents and the family ethos. This was especially true in light of the acculturating influence of the American school. No matter how well ensconced a family believed itself to be in an Italian cultural enclave, the siren song of American culture was unavoidable once its children began to attend American schools. They then began to come home with new ideas, which they didn't always embrace, of course; but whether these concerned the proper food to eat, the unscientific nature of folk superstitions such as the *malocchio* (evil eye), or American standards of physical attractiveness (implicit in school readers portraying blond, blue-eyed children), they portended a loss of cultural innocence, of the certainty of folkways, that could never be repaired.

It is impossible to convey all the points of contact and friction when such different cultural worlds collide, but two examples suggest their pervasiveness and their subtlety. The Italian-American educator Leonard Covello reports in his autobiography the experience of taking oatmeal home from school:

> This food was supposed to make you big and strong. You ate it for breakfast. My father examined the stuff, tested it with his fingers. To him it was the kind of bran that was fed to pigs in Avigliano.
>
> "What kind of a school is this?" he shouted. "They give us the food of animals to eat and send it home to us with our children! What are we coming to next?"[37]

Italian parents also found the recreational activities of American schools in-imical to the family ethos. The concept of play in American society as the antith-esis of work was uncomfortable for Italians, for whom work and play were to be combined in socializing children. Moreover, in southern Italy the period of child-hood, a period of relative freedom from responsibility, was of brief duration, and the transition to adulthood was abrupt. Hence, the fact that schools provided rec-reation for their students, even those of high-school age, was astounding to immi-grants and was perceived as dangerous, because it risked injury and endorsed what was seen as idleness. Representative of their views is the complaint of one Italian mother, "I always thought of the school as a place where one has to study. But play? *Questo giuoco è la rovina della famiglia* [This play business is the ruination of the family] ."[38]

Undoubtedly, one of the most important conflicts between the school and the family system centered on the economic contribution expected of children. In the Mezzogiorno, children had been expected to make an economic contribu-tion at a very early age, but in America this was postponed by compulsory atten-dance laws, which generally required attendance to the mid-teen years. Depriving the family of the income that could be earned by its children angered Italian parents, especially since schools permitted students the frivolity of play. In the years immediately after immigration, some Italian parents ignored compulsory attendance laws on the grounds that they intended to return with their children to Italy, where the education acquired in American schools would be no help. (Some estimates have it that as many as 10 percent of Italian immigrant children in New York City managed to avoid school altogether.)[39] Later on, some parents abetted the truancy of their children; and many, perhaps most, withdrew them from school and sent them to work as soon as the law allowed.[40]

The children were often willing to leave school as soon as they could. Italian students as a rule did not do well in American schools. Around the turn of the century, educational statisticians were fond of measuring group differences in terms of so-called retardation rates, the percentages of students who were a grade or more behind for their age. Retardation was often simply a function of lack of familiarity with English, but whatever the explanation, one study of New York City elemen-tary schools in 1908 found that more than a third of the Italian pupils were re-tarded academically, the highest proportion among ethnic groups.[41] A decade later, the intellectual inferiority of the Italians seemed confirmed for them and others by their poor scores on IQ tests (although they shared low scores with many other immigrant groups, including Jews).[42] Italian pupils were frequently dis-cipline problems. Perhaps they perceived the rebuff of their group and its culture in the classroom, and certainly the contradictory influences of school and family converged on them, putting them in a psychologically untenable position.

The Italian resistance to education and indifference to the opportunities it opened up profoundly restricted the occupational mobility of the second genera-tion, at least that part of it that grew up in the shadow of mass immigration. The

low educational achievement of American-born Italians reared in immigrant ghettoes channeled them toward jobs where educational credentials were not important.
By 1910, for example, only 14 children of southern Italian immigrants had become
schoolteachers (and only a tiny number were attending college).[43] No doubt, the
conflict between the school and family cultures hampered educational achievement
even when children liked school and wanted to continue their schooling. Those
parents who were willing to allow them to go on were generally not willing to sub-
sidize education beyond the minimum necessary to get a job, and this lack of
support placed many second-generation Italian students under greater strain than
that endured by students from other backgrounds. In addition, the practical emphasis in the Italian view of education pushed students in the direction of studies
that were explicitly vocational in nature. Italians would have to wait for a while
before producing their share of scholars.

ORGANIZED CRIME

Ever since the fascination with the "Mafia" and "Cosa Nostra" took hold of
the American consciousness in the mid-1960s, Italian-American organized crime
has been perceived in increasingly mythological terms. Mythology has especially
shrouded its presumed Sicilian origins and early development in America—a consequence of the widely accepted but erroneous belief that Italian-American organized crime is essentially synonymous with American organized crime. Because
of this belief, the explanation for organized crime in general has been sought
almost exclusively in events among the Italians. For the same reason, there has been
a strong tendency to see a single line of development, starting in Sicily and leading
up to crime organized on a national level in the United States, as if this form of
crime were unique and separate from wider ethnic evolutions.

But no such single line of development exists. The exclusive focus on Italian-
American organized crime, which lends itself to an explanation cast entirely in
terms of ethnic culture, masks crime's crucial features: in particular, the forces in
American society that engender organized crime; and the participation in it by
many ethnic groups during various stages of their assimilation. Also obscured is
the important point that among the Italians, as among other ethnic groups, the
forms of crime were constrained by the level of the overall group's integration into
American society. Crime is not *sui generis*.

The organized crime that was present in Italian communities during the
earliest stages of settlement did not foreshadow the developments that took place
in the 1920s and 30s, but reflected the many-faceted insulation of immigrant
enclaves from American life.[44] In the first two decades of the century, the prevalent form of Italian organized crime was the Black Hand (*Mano Nera*) gang.
Numerous Black Hand gangs, which do not appear to have been organized at a
higher level, operated within the boundaries of immigrant enclaves, extorting
money from their more prosperous inhabitants. Their characteristic mode of

operation began with a letter threatening harm to the victim unless he paid a sum of money. If he did not comply at once, "friends," often part of the gang, would offer help in negotiations with the extortionists. Negotiations would follow, leading to agreement upon a sum, which would then be paid.

Black Hand crime was successful because threats of violence, including bombings and murder, were frequently carried out if the intended victim proved recalcitrant. In fact, the success and publicity received by this form of extortion produced an epidemic of imitators. Some non-Italians tried to use the Black Hand tactics, and within the enclave, amateurs imitated the practices of professional gangs. But despite its success, the Black Hand phenomenon had essentially died out by 1920. One factor contributing to its demise was stricter federal enforcement of laws against the use of the mails to defraud. A second was the emergence of a new field for criminal endeavor—bootlegging.

Prohibition was a turning point for American organized crime in general. Organized crime already existed in many American cities, where gambling and prostitution were organized to a greater or lesser extent and flourished in vice districts under arrangements made among criminals, police, and politicians. Italians participated in this form of illicit enterprise in the pre-Prohibition era; however, they were not a very important force in it, with the exception of Chicago, where the organization headed by James Colosimo and John Torrio was one among a few major prostitution operations. Italians were also significant in New York City, but only because the number of Italian residents of the city was so great that large-scale gangs operating wholly within the boundaries of ethnic enclaves were possible.

Prohibition added the possibility of enormous profits, and gangs sprang up to take advantage of the new opportunity. These gangs recruited from most of the new immigrant groups and also from the Irish, Germans, and even WASPs; but Jews and Italians stood out from the rest in many cities, because the recency of their arrival and their sheer numbers meant that many criminals had names indicating Jewish or Italian ancestry. Generally, each major city had several major bootlegging gangs. Some of these were ethnically homogeneous, such as the notorious (Jewish) Purple Gang of Detroit and the (Italian) Mayfield Road Mob of Cleveland, but surprisingly many contained ethnically diverse memberships. For example, the Capone group in Chicago, which had previously been headed by Colosimo and Torrio, was run by Frank Nitti, Jack Guzik, and Ralph Capone while Al Capone was in prison, and it contained a number of non-Italian members besides Guzik, including his brother Harry, Murray Humphreys, Dennis Cooney, and Hymie Levin.

Although Italians were important contributors to the Prohibition underworld, it would be incorrect to say they were its dominant force—no ethnic group was. The Italian gangsters were drawn to some extent from the ranks of former Black Handers as well as from those who had gained criminal experience in pre-Prohibition vice crime. Other petty crooks also saw a golden opportunity in bootlegging; and finally, young men were recruited from the street gangs that flourished in all ethnic neighborhoods. The Prohibition era powerfully transformed Italian and other ethnic organized crime, which spilled out of the confines of the enclave and into American society. Moreover, by its very nature, which required some contacts between ethnic gangsters and other Americans, Prohibition-era crime shifted the competitive edge from Old-World-style gangsters (called "Moustache Petes" among the Italians) to more Americanized ones. In this respect, changes in crime clearly paralleled wider ethnic dynamics, particularly the growing acculturation of recently arrived ethnic groups and the emergence of their second generation. During the 1920s, a cohort of Americanized Italian gangsters, such as Lucky Luciano and Frank Costello, rose to prominence. They were destined to take over Italian-American organized crime in the next decade.

The flowering of organized crime during Prohibition had important consequences for the Italian-American community, as it did for those of other ethnic groups. The enormous liquid profits generated by the business in booze entered the Italian community as a reservoir of capital, which financed legitimate, ethnically owned businesses; and in turn, these businesses provided employment for members of the community. The connection between licit and illicit ventures was sometimes direct, when mobsters would use the profits from illicit business to start to buy legitimate ones, and sometimes indirect, when the illegally earned money would be lent to legitimate businessmen to start a business or keep one running. The banking aspect of organized crime may have been particularly important for Italians, because their access to credit from established banks was undoubtedly limited. There is nothing surprising in this spillover from underground to above-ground businesses. The connection between the two is an intrinsic feature of organized crime, in general, since this phenomenon in a sense covers the illicit part of the spectrum of high-risk entrepreneurial activity.[45] The connection is visible today in discussions of the narcotics trade in South Florida, where it is alleged, some banks have become conduits for millions of illegally earned dollars.

AMERICAN REACTION TO ITALIAN IMMIGRATION

Two episodes bracketing the period of settlement illuminate the American response to the Italians. The first occurred in the aftermath of the 1890 murder of the New Orleans police chief David Hennessy. The shooting occurred under mysterious circumstances, and although Hennessy denied while dying that he knew the identities of the men who shot him, he was heard to mutter that "dagos" did it. The suspicion immediately arose that the "Mafia" had murdered him, and a number of Italians were arrested and charged—largely on the basis, it seems, of an enmity that was presumed to exist between the police chief and an Italian group on the docks. The murder and subsequent arrests raised fears about the criminality of many of the Italian immigrants who had recently flooded into the Louisiana port city. These fears grew more acute when nine of the accused Italians were put on trial and, owing to a lack of evidence, the jury acquitted most of them and was unable to agree on a verdict concerning the others. Since the guilt of the men on trial was widely assumed, the verdicts stunned many New Orleans citizens. Having concluded that the jury had been bought, they took justice into their own hands the next day. A mob headed by some of the city's leading citizens, who incited it to action with inflammatory speeches, stormed the jail where the men were still held and lynched eleven Italians.

The lynching in New Orleans—which was not, incidentally, the only lynching of Italians in the United States—was the product of a climate of xenophobia, fear of aliens, that thickened visibly as the sources of immigration shifted to southern and eastern Europe. Symptomatic of the atmosphere is the lightninglike appearance of dark suspicions. Reportedly, one immediate stimulus to the lynch-mob's action was the raising of an Italian flag on the waterfront to celebrate the Italian king's birthday, an event misunderstood by some Americans as a celebration of the Mafia's victory at the trial. And the lynching itself was rather indiscriminate; four Italians who had no connection with the case were among its victims.

The affair was resolved only at the international level. Because some of the lynched men were Italian citizens, the Italian government protested the mob action, and tensions between the two countries increased rapidly. With the threat of war moving into the foreground, the American government eventually agreed to pay an indemnity. But no member of the lynch mob was punished for his actions.[46]

Thirty years later, in 1920, the killing of a guard and the paymaster during a robbery in South Braintree, Massachusetts, unleashed the forces of xenophobia again. Two Italian anarchists, Nicola Sacco and Bartolomeo Vanzetti, were arrested and tried for the crime. Their 1921 trial took place in the immediate aftermath of a tidal wave of antiforeign and antiradical hysteria, which had reached its zenith in the anti-Red raids ordered by U.S. Attorney General A. Mitchell Palmer to round up thousands of aliens for deportation on the suspicion of radicalism. The evidence in the Sacco and Vanzetti case was contradictory, but the prosecution made much of the facts that the defendants were anarchists and Italians. By the evidence of their private remarks, later made public, the judge and the jury's foreman appear to have been hostile to the defendants, and Sacco and Vanzetti were found guilty.

Their trial became a *cause célèbre*, caught up in the political passions of the times. Because of the contradictory evidence, subsequently supplemented by new evidence favorable to the defendants, and because of the apparent unfairness of the trials, the verdicts were appealed several times. The trial judge, Webster Thayer, also heard the appeals, rejecting each in turn. Soon after one rejection, he boasted to a former Dartmouth classmate, "Did you see what I did with those anarchistic bastards the other day?" Made public, the comment became one of several famous epitaphs for the defendants.[47]

In 1927, their appeals exhausted and their guilt affirmed by a specially appointed review panel headed by the president of Harvard University, Sacco and Vanzetti were executed. The final review seemed to many to symbolize the forces that were pushing the two men unjustly to their deaths—namely, the contempt in which respectable New England society held immigrants and radicals. But unlike the lynching in New Orleans, this contempt was nearly matched by the strong support shown by many sympathetic Americans for Sacco and Vanzetti. Thousands demonstrated on their behalf before their execution and marched in their funeral procession after it. The passions evoked by the case have not quieted even today, and books continue to be written about the case, which has been called, with justice, "the case that will not die."[48]

The issue in both the Hennessy affair and the Sacco and Vanzetti case is not guilt or innocence. We have no way of knowing who killed the New Orleans police chief, the trail having long since grown cold; it is certainly possible that some of the Italians charged with the crime actually committed it. The guilt or innocence of Sacco and Vanzetti is still hotly debated; and one contemporary writer argues with plausibility, though not absolute proof, that Sacco was guilty and Vanzetti innocent.[49] But the issue of guilt or innocence aside, both cases suggest the depth of antipathy to Italians, although they provide no key to its interpretation.

The key lies in the American reaction to immigration generally, which has almost always had a touch of ambivalence, even when the country was a vast continent waiting to be filled by Europeans. The ambivalence is not all that surprising, because a common human reaction to ethnic strangers is ethnocentrism: viewing them through the special lenses of one's own culture. As far back as colonial times, Benjamin Franklin had worried about the impact on Pennsylvania society of the influx of Germans, fearing that interpreters would be necessary in the colony's legislature.[50] But for the most part in the 18th century, the immigration to America had been reassuringly homogeneous, dominated by Protestants from the British Isles. Concerns about the effects of immigration on American society took a sharp upward swing when large numbers of famine-stricken Irish Catholics began to arrive in the 1840s. Fear of a Catholic menace to American institutions, and also of economic competition with the newcomers, set in motion a political movement—epitomized by the Know-Nothing Party—to restrict immigration and naturalization and limit the power of foreign-born Americans. By taking the form of a political agenda, ethnocentrism had become nativism.[51]

The Know-Nothing Party did not survive the 1850s, but nativism did. When the sources of immigration shifted from northern and western Europe to its southern and eastern regions, beginning in the 1880s, nativism received renewed vigor; on the west coast of the United States, the Chinese immigration, and later the Japanese immigration, had the same effect. Americans grew anxious about what appeared to them as a torrent of foreigners very different in character from those Europeans who had peopled the nation. The anxiety was fed by doubts that these strangers could be assimilated and by fears of the social evils they might introduce; moreover, continued immigration posed an economic threat, which played a predominant role in the intense anti-Asian sentiment in California and other parts of the West. Anxiety was further magnified by the visibility of the foreigners, who congregated in the most congested parts of American cities. The revived agitation to curtail immigration achieved an early success in the Chinese Exclusion Act of

1882, which essentially ended Chinese immigration, but success was far more elusive as far as European immigration was concerned.

The concern over the new European immigrants did not focus on only one or two nationalities but, in its sweep, took in a panorama of Europe—Italians, Jews, Slavs, and others were all included in its field of vision. All of these groups were viewed more or less in terms of the undesirable characteristics of the new immigrants, but Americans also perceived differences among them according to specific ethnic stereotypes. In this respect, two groups, Jews and Italians, stood out from the rest because of the frightful stereotypes associated with them. The imagery in which the Italians were cloaked was probably the more dire. The unfavorable associations were partly physical: Italians were "swarthy," to use one of the favorite words for characterizing them, and to the eyes of Americans they bore other physical signs of degradation, such as low foreheads. Italians were also stigmatized by the view of them as having dangerous social tendencies, especially criminal:.y. The belief that the Mafia and other criminal societies came to America in the midst of other Italian immigrants originated almost as early as the southern Italian immigration, in the 19th century. Italians were believed additionally to be prone to crimes of passion and vengeance, a tendency symbolized for Americans by the stiletto. The drift of the criminal stereotype is rendered with marvelous visual clarity in an 1890 article by a penologist that appeared in *Popular Science Monthly* under the title, "What shall we do with the 'Dago'?" The author writes, "The knife with which he cuts his bread he also uses to lop off another 'dago's' finger or ear. . . . He is quite as familiar with the sight of human blood as with the sight of the food he eats."[52]

Two forces worked to whip the xenophobic reaction to the new immigrants into a hysteria lit up by a vision of national apocalypse. One stemmed from World War I. Associated with the large-scale immigration that populated America had long been a fear of subversion from within. During the 19th century, Catholics were a special focus of the fear, because of the belief that they were subject to the control of a foreign power, Rome. The war gave the fear a special twist: During it, anxiety mounted about the loyalty of recent immigrants and their potential to form fifth columns, acting at the orders of foreign powers. In many American states the wartime fever led to actions against immigrants from the Central Powers, America's enemies—such as prohibitions against the teaching or even the speaking of German. The temperature did not subside at the end of the war but broke out in a new manifestation: panic over political radicals in the midst of the immigrants, a panic stimulated in part by the Russian Revolution. The Red Scare came to a climax in the already mentioned Palmer Raids of 1919-20 and caught up Sacco and Vanzetti in its aftermath.

The fever of the war and postwar periods added to the pressures generated by a newly born campaign for the rapid Americanization of the immigrants, who were viewed as "hyphenated" Americans with divided loyalties. The campaign demanded "100 percent Americanization," the complete making over of the immigrants into ordinary Americans, an endeavor symbolized by a pageant enacted by the worker-students at Henry Ford's English School. Immigrant workers wearing the national costumes of many different nations would march into a giant pot on stage, labeled as the melting pot, and emerge wearing identical suits of American clothes and carrying American flags.

The fever just described stemmed from a deep fear for American social institutions, given the presence of so many culturally different strangers. The second force intensifying the xenophobic reaction added a different sort of fear, the submergence of the American people under a flood of racially inferior humans. It was born of the racist thinking that developed to a high level in the late 19th and early 20th centuries. This racism drew distinctions among European peoples that strike a peculiar note today but seemed plausible then; specifically, it elevated Nordics, the peoples of northern and western Europe, above all others. European thinkers contributed most significantly to the development of racist philosophy, but it contained a special meaning for the American experiment, implying that the immigration policy of free entry from Europe risked the biological degradation of the superior peoples who had originally colonized America. Racist thinking had very wide acceptance among old-stock Americans in the early 20th century, including many who belonged to the social and intellectual elite. Racist theories, for example, gave impetus to the development of IQ tests by social scientists; and, in turn, the evidence derived from these tests—which showed Italians and other immigrant groups to have much lower scores on average than native-born Americans—appeared to bear the theories out.

The racism of the earlier part of this century cast a shadow over all of the groups immigrating from southern and eastern Europe; again, however, two groups stood out in the dark, if only for their large numbers. Jews figured in the racist vision as a degenerate and hence dangerous race. They formed the special object of opprobrium for one of the most famous of American racist tracts, *The Passing of the Great Race,* by Madison Grant, patrician founder of the New York Zoological Society. Italians, too, stood out by virtue of their dark complexions, along with their social characteristics. Astonishing as this may seem in the light of contemporary racial perceptions, many Americans doubted that Italians were "whites." Illustrative is the reply of one man when asked during his appearance before a Congressional Committee if he considered the Italian a white man: "No, sir, an Italian is a Dago." [53] It would go too far to say that Italians were believed to be nonwhites, but their problematic racial position is suggested by a common epithet for them, *guinea,* which is probably derived from a name attached to slaves from part of the western African coast. [54]

The nativist objective, the limitation of immigration and particularly that from southern and eastern Europe, was finally accomplished in the 1920s, after decades of attempts. The 1911 Report of the Dillingham Commission, established by Congress to investigate immigration questions, purported to demonstrate with 41 volumes of statistics the inferiority of the new immigration, strengthening the restrictionist movement. At long last, in 1921, Congress passed a law that set quotas on the numbers of immigrants who could enter each year from the European nations. The quotas were based on the proportions of the countries' immigrants among the foreign-born in the United States as reported in the latest available census, that of 1910; and they implicitly established an upper bound, about 350,000, on annual immigration from countries outside the western hemisphere. The 1921 law was not entirely satisfactory to nativist sentiment, however, since it still allowed too many new immigrants in. (Because the 1910 census was taken in the middle of the most intense period of immigration from southern and eastern Europe, new immigrants were plentiful among the foreign-born.) And so another law was passed in 1924. It further reduced the total number of immigrants allowed to enter annually, to 150,000; and it barred the entry of Japanese, thereby completing the exclusion of Asian immigrants, begun by the earlier Chinese Exclusion Act. But its primary significance was to erect a new system of national quotas based on the presumed national origins of the entire American population, not just the foreign-born. Under the new system, which took effect in 1929 and was to stand until 1965, the quotas allotted to the countries of southern and eastern Europe plummeted, and so did the immigration from them. The immigration from Italy, which had stood at over 200,000 in many of the years between 1900 and 1914, received an annual quota under 4,000. An era of mass immigration was over.[55] Americans had erected an immigration system to preserve what they took to be the ethnic character of the American people. For Italians and members of other new groups already on American shores, the shutting of the gates meant a turning away from connections to European homelands and toward America as the land where the remainder of their lives would be spent.

CONCLUSION

At the end of the period of settlement, Italians occupied a low position in American society. Immigrant workers were concentrated in the humbler ranks of manual labor; and the limited educational achievement of their American-born children, a result of the still powerful ethos of the Mezzogiorno, did not bode well for great occupational advancement in the generation just growing into adulthood. Italians were the objects of intense prejudice on the part of native Americans, and in the prevailing climate of racist ideologies, their place among so-called whites was not even secure.

A comparison with Jews, who arrived in America about the same time and were also greeted by prejudice and discrimination from native-born Americans, illuminates the considerable disadvantages borne by the Italians. The occupational background of eastern European Jews was very different. Unlike the Italians, Jews had not been agriculturalists but had pursued industrial and commercial occupations; and they had more urban experience. Consequently, they were far better prepared than the Italians for the urban and industrial environment of America. And to add to their relative advantages, their culture sanctified learning, thus preparing them to take full advantage of educational opportunities. The great early differences between the two groups in American success are reflected in the prejudice that attached to them. The stereotypes associated with the Italians were those of an unruly lower-class group. In contrast, those associated with Jews were images of avaricious social climbers who pushed themselves where they were not wanted.

Another important difference also helps to account for the gap between these two groups in early success. Although they both arrived on American shores at about the same time, they did not arrive simultaneously in American society. Jews were fleeing European persecution, and they did not look back. Because they did not want to return to the European societies from which they came, Jews immediately set about adapting to American society, learning English, and acquiring American citizenship. In these respects, Italians lagged nearly a generation behind. Many Italians entered the United States intending to work for a time and return to Italy after earning enough money to purchase land. Those who nonetheless remained often realized only slowly that they were to be permanent inhabitants, not sojourners. Because the view of the Italian colony as a way station for travelers lingered, adaptation to the surrounding society was delayed. The delay only ended completely with the closing of the gates on mass immigration in 1929, which brought to a halt the constant renewal of the immigrant society by fresh recruits and settled once and for all the question of orientation to the new society.

Finally, at the heart of any discussion of Italians' adaptation to the New World must be their family-centered culture. This colored their perceptions of American opportunities and curtailed the use they made of them. Broadly put, the culture discouraged any interest competing with the family, and this tended to limit the educational and occupational horizons of the immigrants and their children. The stamp of the family ethos was visible in many other ways, from the kinds of work Italian women sought to the energy with which immigrant families pursued the purchase of a home. The sacrifices Italian families were willing to make to achieve the goal of home ownership, such as sending their children to work at the earliest opportunity, suggests the basis of the frequent observation that Italians and other groups from rural Europe preferred to become property owners than to invest in occupational mobility.

Thus, the culture of the Mezzogiorno carried over into the new land, shaping the niche the immigrants were able to carve out for themselves and their families. Merely by coming to a different place, the immigrants were not reborn as new men and women. They perceived unfamiliar situations in terms of what they had valued in the homeland. Nonetheless, the culture did not survive the journey unchanged. The exigencies of American circumstances provoked a transformation and reshuffling of cultural elements, setting in motion a process of cultural change evident in the family system. These changes represented a form of acculturation; nevertheless, they were not a wholesale acceptance of American culture, but rather a gravitating toward it within an overall framework that retained an Italian character. Yet on balance, the malleability of culture was as significant as its continuity.

The groundwork had been laid for a remarkable transformation of the Italian group in America.

NOTES

[1] See Table 2-1.

[2] The Italian experience in American agriculture is discussed by Luciano J. Iorizzo and Salvatore Mondello, *The Italian-Americans* (Boston: Twayne Publishers, 1971), Chapter 7. On the success of northern Italians in California, see Humbert S. Nelli, *From Immigrants to Ethnics: The Italian Americans* (Oxford: Oxford University Press, 1983), Chapter 5.

[3] Nelli, *From Immigrants to Ethnics*, p. 62.

[4] Ibid.

[5] Humbert S. Nelli, "Italians," in *Harvard Encyclopedia of American Ethnic Groups,* ed. Stephen Thernstrom, Ann Orlov, and Oscar Handlin (Cambridge, Mass.: Harvard University Press, 1980), pp. 549–50.

[6] Nelli, *From Immigrants to Ethnics,* Chapter 4; Virginia Yans-McLaughlin, *Family and Community: Italian Immigrants in Buffalo, 1880–1930* (Ithaca, N.Y.: Cornell University Press, 1977), pp. 117–118; Thomas Kessner. *The Golden Door: Italian and Jewish Immigrant Mobility in New York City, 1880–1915* (New York: Oxford University Press, 1977), pp. 20–21.

[7] Yans-McLaughlin, *Family and Community,* p. 17.

[8] Kessner, *The Golden Door,* p. 16.

[9] Josef J. Barton, *Peasants and Strangers: Italians, Rumanians and Slovaks in an American City, 1890–1950* (Cambridge, Mass.: Harvard University Press, 1975), pp. 53–61; Caroline F. Ware, *Greenwich Village, 1920–1930* (Boston: Houghton Mifflin, 1935), pp. 155–59. The evidence presented by John W. Briggs, *An Italian Passage: Immigrants to Three American Cities, 1890–1930* (New Haven, Conn.: Yale University Press, 1978), pp. 81–94, suggests that the marriage pattern was quite complex because many provincial groups were too small in individual American cities to support a pattern of exclusive marriage.

[10] Marie J. Concistrè, "Italian East Harlem," in Francesco Cordasco and Eugene Bucchioni (eds.), *The Italians: Social Backgrounds of an American Group* (Clifton, N.J.: Augustus M. Kelley, 1974), pp. 223–25,

[11] Nelli, *From Immigrants to Ethnics,* pp. 115–18. There is some dispute as to whether the mutual-benefit societies were a form acquired in the New World and hence an incipient acculturation, or whether they were brought from the Old World. Nelli (see "Italians," p. 552) favors the former and Briggs (*An Italian Passage,* Chapter 2) the latter.

[12] John Bodnar, Roger Simon, and Michael P. Weber, *Lives of Their Own: Blacks, Italians, and Poles in Pittsburgh, 1900–1960* (Urbana: University of Illinois Press, 1982), p. 81.

[13] Nelli, *From Immigrants to Ethnics,* pp. 124–25.

[14] Ibid., Chapter 6; Ware, *Greenwich Village,* Chapter 9.

[15] Humbert S. Nelli, *Italians in Chicago: 1880–1930: A Study in Ethnic Mobility* (New York: Oxford University Press, 1970), Chapter 2.

[16] Stanley Lieberson, *Ethnic Patterns in American Cities* (New York: Free Press, 1963), pp. 101–20, 209–18.

[17] Kessner, *The Golden Door,* pp. 33–34.

[18] Ibid., pp. 51–59.

[19] Nelli, *From Immigrants to Ethnics,* pp. 77–81.

[20] Yans-McLaughlin, *Family and Community,* pp. 35–44.

[21] Ibid., pp. 50–54, 200–17; the importance of culture in defining the work possibilities for Italian (and other) immigrant women is disputed by Stephen Steinberg, *The Ethnic Myth: Race, Ethnicity, and Class in America* (Boston: Beacon Press, 1981), Chapter 6.

[22] Kessner, *The Golden Door*, Chapter 5.

[23] Nelli, *From Immigrants to Ethnics*, p. 83.

[24] Lieberson, *Ethnic Patterns*, pp. 209-18.

[25] Yans-McLaughlin, *Family and Community*, pp. 174-79.

[26] Lieberson, *Ethnic Patterns*, pp. 209-18.

[27] This insight is developed at length by Yans-McLaughlin, *Family and Community*, especially Chapter 2. Her argument is partly directed against the famous interpretation of Oscar Handlin's *The Uprooted* (Boston: Grosset & Dunlap, 1951).

[28] Paul J. Campisi, "Ethnic family patterns: The Italian family in the United States," *American Journal of Sociology*, 53, No. 6 (May, 1948), 443-49. Joseph Lopreato, *Italian Americans* (New York: Random House, 1970), pp. 57-74. The point about earnings is revealed by Irvin L. Child, *Italian or American? The Second Generation in Conflict* (New Haven, Conn.: Yale University Press, 1943), pp. 106-08.

[29] Ware, *Greenwich Village*, p. 182.

[30] Ibid., pp. 180-88.

[31] Ibid., pp. 192-94.

[32] Education in southern Italy is discussed at length by Leonard Covello, *The Social Background of the Italo-American School Child* (Totowa, N.J.: Rowman & Littlefield, 1972). Chapter 8; and by Briggs, *An Italian Passage*, Chapter 3.

[33] Covello, *The Social Background*, p. 257.

[34] Some of these schools established quotas to limit the numbers of Jewish students; see Stephen Steinberg, *The Academic Melting Pot: Catholics and Jews in American Higher Education* (New York: McGraw-Hill, 1974), Chapter 1.

[35] Covello, *The Social Background*, p. 285.

[36] Steinberg, *The Academic Melting Pot*, Chapter 4; Kessner, *The Golden Door*, Chapter 2.

[37] Leonard Covello, "Autobiography," in Cordasco and Bucchioni, *The Italians*, p. 265.

[38] Covello, *The Social Background*, pp. 325-26.

[39] Kessner, *The Golden Door*, p. 96.

[40] Covello, *The Social Background*, pp. 288-311.

[41] Diane Ravitch, *The Great School Wars: New York City, 1805-1973* (New York: Basic Books, 1974), p. 178.

[42] Stephen Jay Gould, *The Mismeasure of Man* (New York: W. W. Norton & Company, 1981), Chapter 5.

[43] Richard Gambino, *Blood of My Blood: The Dilemma of the Italian-Americans* (Garden City, N.Y.: Anchor, 1975), p. 256.

[44] The supporting evidence that follows in the rest of this section is drawn largely from Humbert S. Nelli, *The Business of Crime: Italians and Syndicate Crime in the United States* (New York: Oxford University Press, 1976).

[45] A good description of the relationship between licit and illicit business within the same family is by Francis A. J. Ianni with Elizabeth Reuss-Ianni, *A Family Business: Kinship and Social Control in Organized Crime* (New York: Russell Sage, 1972).

[46] The case is analyzed fully by Nelli, *The Business of Crime*, Chapter 3.

[47] Francis Russell, *Tragedy in Dedham: The Story of the Sacco-Vanzetti Case* (New York: McGraw-Hill, 1971), p. 265.
The most beautiful epitaph is provided by the famous words of Vanzetti, spoken offhandedly to a reporter visiting the condemned men: "If it had not been for this thing, I might have live out my life talking at street corners to scorning men. I might have die, unmarked, unknown, a failure. Now we are not a failure. This is our career and our triumph. Never in our full life can we hope to do such work for tolerance, for joostice, for man's onderstanding of man, as now we do by an accident"(Ibid., p. 387).

[48] Some recent books include Roberta Strauss Feuerlicht, *Justice Crucified: The Story of Sacco and Vanzetti* (New York: McGraw-Hill, 1977); Herbert B. Ehrmann, *The Case That Will Not Die: Commonwealth vs. Sacco and Vanzetti* (Boston: Little, Brown, 1969); and the already cited book by Francis Russell. The books by Feuerlicht and Erhmann argue that the men were innocent; Russell delivers a split verdict—Vanzetti was innocent but Sacco was guilty.

[49] Francis Russell makes the argument in *Tragedy in Dedham.*

[50] Milton Gordon, *Assimilation in American Life: The Role of Race, Religion, and National Origins* (New York: Oxford University Press, 1964), p. 89.

[51] The classic book on nativism is by John Higham, *Strangers in the Land: Patterns of American Nativism, 1860-1925* (New York: Atheneum, 1970), which has supplied many of the details for this section.

[52] The quote is taken from Higham, *Strangers in the Land,* p. 66. Also relevant are pp. 87-96.

[53] Ibid., p. 66. Racist ideologies are discussed in Chapter 6 of Higham's book.

[54] This derivation is suggested by H. L. Mencken, *The American Language,* abridged edition (New York: Knopf, 1963), p. 373. Also, *guinea* is indicated as a shortened form for *guinea negro* by *A Dictionary of American English on Historical Principles,* ed. Sir William A. Craigie and James R. Hulbert (Chicago: University of Chicago Press, 1940), Volume II, pp. 1192-93.

[55] Higham, *Strangers in the Land,* Chapter 11; Maldwyn Allen Jones, *American Immigration* (Chicago: University of Chicago Press, 1960), Chapter 9.

CHAPTER FOUR
THE EMERGENCE OF
THE ITALIAN AMERICANS:
1930–1970

The closing of the gates on mass immigration and the realization by Italians that their future now lay in the United States did not mean that they now regarded themselves as purely and simply Americans. Still, these events were part of a process by which a foreign group, dependent for its identity on a live connection to its homeland, became an American ethnic group, recognizing an identity based on ancestry and shared American experience rather than an immediate tie to Italy.

Another important shift was part of the same process. At the height of immigration, the *campanilismo* of southern Italy had been re-created in the checkered settlement of the ghetto, whereby immigrants settled near others from the same village and province. In this period, immigrants regarded themselves not as Italians but as residents of a particular *paese*. These parochial identifications were reflected, among other places, in immigrant mutual-aid societies, which were formed and named on the basis of village and provincial ties. But as the period of settlement wore on, the focus of identity enlarged to take in the rest of the Italian peninsula. "Italian," or "Italian American," as a self-identification, increasingly replaced such labels as Neapolitan or Catanian. This identification with the entire group may not have affected so much the immigrant generation, whose self-identification was well-developed and stable, as it did the second. Identification with a village they had never seen was obviously not easy for the American-born; and in any event, other

Americans did not recognize these place distinctions but treated, or more usually mistreated, all those of Italian background as "Italians."

Common treatment at the hands of Americans cemented solidarity among the Italian Americans, but so too did events in the homeland. The Mussolini regime and the rising Italian power in Europe and Africa created among the immigrants and their children a pride in Italy and an admiration for its leaders that their ancestors in the Mezzogiorno had not felt and that they themselves probably would not have felt had they still been in the Italian south. Thus, the Italians conform to the much-noted irony that European nationalisms frequently required American soil to flower.[1] The emergence of an Italian-American identity was indicated in a number of ways, such as the emergence and growth of organizations not tied to a particular region of Italy (e.g., the Order of the Sons of Italy) and an increasing frequency of personal relations across provincial lines.[2]

THE DILEMMA OF THE SECOND GENERATION

The birth of the new ethnic group was very much tied to the ascendancy of the second generation. With immigration reduced to a trickle, the Italian Americans entering maturity in the 1930s were predominantly the children of immigrants, and the problems they faced were very different from those of their parents. Caught between two cultural worlds, raised in an immigrant home but socialized on the streets and in the school according to American ways, their fundamental dilemma was to define their identity—to choose between "Italian" and "Italian American" on the one side and "American" on the other. The very possibility of identifying themselves as Americans was a giant step beyond where their parents could go; even when immigrants recognized that their lives were to be spent in America, they continued to think of themselves in terms of Old World identifications.[3] In the dilemma of the second generation the dynamic of assimilation revealed itself.

The dilemma is captured in detail by two portraits of second-generation Italian Americans during the 1930s. Irvin Child depicts its psychological aspects in his study of New Haven Italian Americans, *Italian or American?*[4] In Child's view, the second generation was snagged in an uncomfortable conflict between two alternatives, each of which was hedged in with risks. One was to identify with the Italian group. This afforded the satisfaction of membership in a group of ethnic peers, but it risked complete exclusion by other Americans and the loss of any chance for social mobility. The other was to identify with the American group. This was attractive because it lay on the pathway to mobility, but it was riskier than the first. There was no assurance that others would accept an individual of Italian ancestry; prejudice against Italians was prevalent, as indicated by the widespread use in ordinary conversation of such epithets as *wop* and *guinea*. Moreover, the individual who identified as an American risked a double rejection; he or she might also be rejected by other Italians, angered by the apparent desertion of the group.

There were three possible strategies for coping with this psychological dilemma. One, labeled by Child as the "in-group" response, was to emphasize identification with the Italian group. The in-grouper chose an identity as an "Italian" or an "Italian American" and intended to maintain an Italian way of life as much as was possible in a very different society. The opposite response was labeled by Child as the "rebel" reaction. The rebel identified as an "American" and rejected Italian culture and customs as unsuited for American society. The rebel's rationale was that one should behave as other Americans do and, indeed, that the prejudice directed against Italian Americans was a result of their failure to embrace an American way of life. A third strategy represented an attempt to avoid the dilemma. Labeled the "apathetic" reaction, it entailed a denial of the conflict. The person responding in this way tried to deny that nationality distinctions were meaningful and even to deny the existence of prejudice and discrimination directed against those of Italian background. Like the others, this strategy could not be a complete success; the persons employing it usually betrayed in a variety of ways that they recognized the significance of the very things they were attempting to deny.

Child's study suggests that those breaking away from the Italian group were still a definite minority in the 1930s. The apathetic reaction seems to have been most prevalent among the individuals Child interviewed. Generally, the individuals displaying this reaction remained, through inertia rather than intention, within the Italian group. For those born into Italian-American communities, and hence naturally embedded in a matrix of Italian-American social life, deliberate action was required for any move into non-Italian social circles and ways of life. Only the rebels, who were a minority among the respondents, displayed such intentions.

That assimilation and mobility were regarded as a risky possibility, pursued actively by only a minority, is demonstrated also by the classic study from the 1930s, William F. Whyte's *Street Corner Society,* a description of Boston's North End Italian-American community.[5] Whyte observed an important distinction among its second-generation residents, between "corner boys" and "college boys." The college boys had set their sights on mobility that would carry them upward in the social scale of American society and out of the North End. At the time when Whyte knew them, they were still in the midst of their educations, attending colleges in the Boston area; and, ultimately, most did leave the ghetto. But educational credentials *per se* were not the sole secret of their mobility; contact with non-Italian Americans helped to strengthen their orientation to the larger society outside the ghetto. Relationships with the social workers who ran a settlement house in the area were an early form of this contact. Later, some of them formed other important relationships through political activities. In addition, since few Italians attended college in the 1930s, the fact that these men did necessarily brought them into contact with non-Italians.

The orientation of the corner boys remained within the ghetto. The label that Whyte applied to them and through them to the society of the North End (in the book's title) derived from the overriding fact of their lives: membership in a tight-knit group of young men who hung out on a street corner. The attachment to their corner group was sufficiently important to most of these young men that they continued to return to the corner even after they were married or, in some cases, after they had moved out of the area. For the corner boys, loyalty to the group took the place of the mobility aspirations of the college boys. And while loyalty is not the sole explanation for their lack of occupational mobility—Whyte's study was done at the tail end of the Depression, and many of the men had difficulty finding any sort of steady work—the fact remains that the corner boys were not mobile, and there appeared to be little prospect that they would be.

The loyalty that tied the men to the corner reflects the persisting influence of the personalistic ethos Italians brought from the Mezzogiorno and illustrates how the apathetic response was compatible with continued membership in the Italian group. Whyte does not describe the corner boys in ways that suggest they were "in-groupers," in Child's terminology. That is, he does not describe them as explicitly loyal to an Italian-American way of life. Rather, they felt loyalty to a particular group of young men, who happened to be Italians because they all grew up and resided in the North End. This loyalty, then, proved to be a kind of inertia that kept them within the Italian-American orbit without a specific intention on their part to remain so.

THE IMPACT OF WORLD WAR II

Both the Child and Whyte studies were carried out under the looming shadow of war in Europe. The shadow subtly colored the responses of second-generation Italian Americans to their group. On the one hand, the bellicose nationalism of the Mussolini government added to the prestige of Italy and caused many Italian Americans to feel a pride of identification with a renascent *Italia*. On the other hand, the antipathy of Americans to the fascist Italian state was evident, and many Italian Americans perceived by the late 1930s the possibility that America would enter a European war against Italy. This possibility added a new thorn to the dilemma of the second generation: It provided another reason why too strong a partisan Italian identification might provoke the antagonism of other Americans, while at the same time it added to the perceived probability that they would reject an Italian American, whatever his or her attitude. The sting this added is revealed in this comment by one of Child's informants:

> Then a lot of times in the show you see Mussolini on the screen and they all start to razz him. Then I feel, "How the hell do I stand?"[6]

The crux of the international situation in the late 1930s and early 1940s is that ethnic identity was turned into a matter of national loyalty. Consequently, the impact of the war on immigrant groups was profound. Despite the added burden that the war imposed on Italian and German Americans (and, in a very different way, on Japanese Americans), in the end it hastened assimilation, making it more necessary and attractive and perhaps making it more possible.

War is frequently underestimated as a social force, because it is easy to over-look the fact that it can transform even those societies that it leaves physically unravaged. To understand the impact of World War II, it is important to appreciate the theme of national loyalty in American history. The American nationality is comparatively new on the world stage and vulnerable by its youth, at least until recently. Its hardiness has been tested in one way by the absorption of millions of immigrants. It has been tested with equal thoroughness by the wars Americans have fought, beginning as far back as the War of Independence against the country from which much of the American heritage was derived. As a consequence, the theme of national loyalty has held an unusual place of celebration in American culture, as the historian Richard Hofstadter has expressed insightfully:

> What other country finds it so necessary to create institutional rituals for the sole purpose of guaranteeing to its people the genuineness of their national-ity? Does the Frenchman or the Englishman or the Italian find it necessary to speak of himself as "one hundred percent" English, French, or Italian? Do they find it necessary to have their equivalents of "I Am An American Day"? When they disagree with one another over national policies, do they find it necessary to call one another un-English, un-French, or un-Italian? No doubt they too are troubled by subversive activities and espionage, but are their countermeasures taken under the name of committees on un-English, un-French, or un-Italian activities?[7]

The experience in this century of going to war against several nations that had sent millions of immigrants to American shores is unique. To be sure, the bound-aries of European nations, such as Czechoslovakia and Poland, have included siz-able populations with national affinities to neighboring states; indeed, this was one of the important factors in the pre-World War II tensions. But in Europe these populations were regionally concentrated, whereas in America they were dispersed. The presence of millions of people in America with ancestry derived from its war-time enemies fed anxieties about loyalty to the American nation.

During World War I, there was a national anxiety crisis about subversion from within. Anxieties were also provoked by World War II; their ugliest manifestation was the internment of Japanese Americans from the West Coast. But by the 1940s, the flood tide of immigration had receded; the groups with the potential for loyalty to enemy nations were no longer composed predominantly of immigrants but of the native-born, and foreign mannerisms no longer dominated American percep-tions of the European ones. Consequently, xenophobia gave way to the desire to bring about national unity to fight the war. The theme of unity in the war effort was emphasized by "town meetings for war" sponsored by the Office of Civilian Defense, by civil defense preparations that enlisted millions of volunteers and in-cluded mock air raids staged on cities such as Chicago, by campaigns on behalf of war bonds, and by drives for scrap materials, such as rubber, metals, and even kitchen fat.[8]

The solidarity ignited by the Japanese attack on Pearl Harbor expanded to include most Americans of recent vintage. The unification of Americans of different nationalities was symbolically promoted by festivals to celebrate the contributions of immigrant groups to America, which according to the historian Richard Polenberg became a ritual during the war.[9] Wartime reporting and films about the war made for domestic consumption also self-consciously highlighted the spirit of unity among American fighting men from different backgrounds. Ernie Pyle's popular books, *Here Is Your War* and *Brave Men,* portrayed American fighting forces as a national cross-section. In films, fighting groups were presented deliberately as the melting pot in miniature; the men were given names and accents to indicate ethnic variety.[10]

This cultivated unity was a necessary national response to the strain of the war, and Italians particularly benefited from it. At the outset of hostilities, a cloud of suspicion gathered over Germans, Japanese, and Italians. Many first-generation members of these groups were not American citizens at the outbreak of the war— nearly 600,000 Italians were not—and these noncitizens immediately came under the force of restrictions applied to "aliens of enemy nationality." They were required to register with the government and to apply for permission to travel outside their hometowns, and they were forbidden from traveling in airplanes and from possessing cameras, shortwave radios, and other paraphernalia that might be used in spying. But throughout the war, Italians, both in America and in Europe, were not viewed in terms of stereotypes as harsh as those applied to the Germans and Japanese, and the restrictions on so-called enemy aliens were quickly lifted from Italian noncitizens, on Columbus Day in 1942.[11]

The significance of the wartime embrace of first- and second-generation Americans is that it was, in its way, an invitation to them to move away from close attachment to their ethnic groups, and the invitation was given additional weight by the stigma attached to extreme ethnic loyalty under wartime conditions. Many accepted, at least to a degree. Ethnics had high rates of enlistment in the armed forces, where they served in integrated groups with others from a variety of backgrounds. (This, however, was not true of Japanese and Black Americans, who for the most part were placed in segregated units, which frequently had limited or specialized duties.) Movement toward acculturation is visible in the waning of the foreign-language press that occurred during the war. The number of radio stations broadcasting in immigrant languages, for example, dropped by 40 percent between 1942 and 1948. The war also produced a surge in the adoption of American citizenship by the foreign-born. Over 1,750,000 took the pledge of allegiance.[12]

The wartime unity was a precursor of the war's ultimate fruit as far as ethnicity was concerned: namely, a different vision of America, which included ethnic Americans, or more precisely those who were white, in the magic circle of full citizenship. This vision did not take shape immediately, but it is clearly reflected, among other places, in the novels about the war that were published during it and afterwards. Norman Mailer's *The Naked and the Dead,* James Jones's *From Here to Eternity,* Harry Brown's *A Walk in the Sun,* and John Hersey's *A Bell for Adano,* all of which were made into successful films, presented a vision of an American society that was at least integrated on a moral plane, if in no other way. These novels portrayed fighting groups that contained the ethnic diversity of America in microcosm. Illustrative are the names and origins of the men in the platoon on which Mailer's bitter novel focuses, such as Croft, a WASP from Texas; Martinez, a Mexican American, also from Texas; Valsen, a Swedish American from Montana; Gallagher, an Irish American from Boston; Goldstein, a Jewish American from Brooklyn; and Minetta, an Italian American from New York City. The war novels openly acknowledged the prejudice present in American society. Indeed, that was one of their major themes, as they showed ethnic Americans in the lower ranks subordinated to prejudiced and often incompetent WASP officers. But where their vision was triumphant was in the portrayal of ethnic Americans, who were presented free of stereotypes as fully developed human beings, men who were, moreover, contributing to American victory with an everyday heroism, exerting themselves to their limits.[13]

It is not important whether these novels provided an accurate description of the American armed forces during the war. What is important is their view of the moral worth of ethnic Americans, which previously had been hidden behind a curtain of stereotypes. This view hinted at the human power that would be released if America truly were a melting pot. These were, in addition, highly popular books (as were several of the films made from them) that served to interpret the war experience to other Americans. This does not mean that the novels and films convinced other Americans of the truth of their interpretation, but rather that they gave credible and coherent expression to fragmentary perceptions that many other Americans had. And the popularity of the novels proclaimed the popularity of the vision they contained, demonstrating that they gave voice to the *Zeitgeist.* The stage was set for some opening up of American society to the ethnics in its midst.

A truism has it that wars provide groups with the opportunity to earn with their blood a place in American society. Clearly, this is part of the explanation for the vision inspired by the war, but it is far from the whole of it. The war stirred consciousness of the fragility of an American nationality that was parceled out among many insular ethnic communities, and thus it made integration and assimilation matters of some urgency. Undoubtedly, this was felt not only by "core Americans," whose families had been Americans for many generations, but also by second- and third-generation Americans. Ethnic Americans may have felt encouraged by the vision of an America opening up to take steps toward assimilation, but in addition, because of the uncomfortable spotlight the war placed on an emotional connection to another nation, many felt constrained to weaken their ethnic links, to become "more American." For ethnic change to happen on a massive level, however, another element was required, and it too was in a way a product of the war.

SOCIAL MOBILITY

The war had a profound economic impact in addition to its cultural and moral one. The industrial gearing-up for the war effort touched off an economic boom that dragged America out of the economic depression through which it had staggered throughout the 1930s and prompted a prolonged period of economic growth after the war ended. During the war, the total production of the nation expanded rapidly—the gross national product rose by over 80 percent between 1939 and 1945 —and the civilian standard of living improved significantly, despite the diversion of much of the country's goods and services to the war needs.[14] After the war, the economy did not fall back into a depression, as some economists had expected it would, but real income (i.e., income adjusted for inflation) remained stable for a time and then began a steady increase in the early 1950s. Between 1947 and 1968, the real income of American families and individuals increased by over 50 percent.[15]

At the same time, the shape of the occupational structure continued to change. Throughout this century and a good part of the last, a rumbling subterranean transformation has brought America from a largely agricultural society to, first, an essentially industrial one and, then, to one in which white-collar occupations are approaching predominance. Between 1930 and 1970, for example, the percentage of the labor force in agricultural pursuits declined precipitously from 21.2 to 2.9. (In 1900, the percentage stood at 37.5.) The proportion in blue-collar and service occupations hardly changed in the period, decreasing slightly from 49.4 percent to 45.8 percent. But within the broad blue-collar category, a significant realignment was taking place. Unskilled laborers, a category that included many Italian Americans in the earlier part of the century, declined sharply from 11.0 percent of the labor force to 4.4 percent, while other blue-collar and service categories increased to take up the slack. Lastly, white-collar occupations expanded dramatically in the forty-year period, from 29.4 percent to 44.8 percent of the labor force. Moreover, nearly half this change was concentrated in the high-ranking category of professional and technical workers, whose share of the labor force increased from 6.8 percent to 13.7 percent.[16]

Sociologists describe one consequence of such a transformation of the occupational structure as "structural mobility," because some individuals or, more likely, their children are forced to change places, to move up or down, to accommodate changing labor needs. And in this respect, the important fact about the transformation between 1930 and 1970 is that, in terms of the status of occupational slots, it entailed a sharp contraction at the lower end of the scale, in agricultural categories and unskilled labor, and a corresponding expansion at the upper end, in white-collar work generally.

Structural mobility of this large magnitude holds a special significance for the advancement of disadvantaged groups, because it does not have a "zero-sum" character. The advancement of one individual or group does not require the downward fall of another, since the essential nature of large-scale structural mobility is that it creates room in the occupational structure that cannot be filled by those already there or their children. Hence, advancement can occur without the already advantaged perceiving a threat to their interests and without, therefore, a sudden raising of group boundaries to keep the disadvantaged in their place, Steady, large-scale structural mobility allows for a gradual increase in the number of members of disadvantaged groups who work alongside members of advantaged ones; the equal-status contact between the two makes group boundaries appear less and less meaningful.

The significance of the general process of structural mobility was accentuated by parallel changes in the educational system: namely, the expansion of higher education and its transformation from a selective system, granting access chiefly to those of privileged social origins, to a mass system, open to the majority of those completing high school. World War II had a specific impact here, too, because the revolution in college-going was fueled initially by the GI Bill, which provided the financial support for many returning GIs to attend college. The resulting expansion of enrollments ignited a period of sustained, permanent growth in the *rate* of college enrollment. In 1940, only 15 percent of the college-age group actually attended college, but by 1954, the rate of college attendance had climbed to 30 percent, and by 1960, it was almost 38 percent. The expansion of higher education went hand in hand, of course, with the expansion in the upper range of the occupational structure, the great increase in the number of jobs requiring professional and technical training.[17] In its immediate impact on opportunities for socially disadvantaged groups, the transformation of higher education worked much like that of the occupational structure. It created non-zero-sum opportunities, from which the members of disadvantaged groups could profit without a concomitant decline in the privileges of others. Thus, it allowed Italian Americans and other ethnics to enter what had previously been an elite sphere, and to do so on a basis of formal equality with old-stock Protestants.

Changes in the occupational distribution and in higher education are alterations in the structural foundations of society, and it does not follow that they necessarily had effects on any specific group. One reason for thinking that they might have had effects on Italians is that these changes were not spread uniformly through the country, but were most sharply felt in those places where Italians and other European ethnics were most concentrated: in and around large cities, particularly in the Northeast and Midwest. This is made clear by an examination of where new jobs were coming into being and where old ones were going out of existence, since it is through this process of replacement that structural mobility in fact occurs. One study shows that in the period 1940–60, metropolitan, or large urban, areas were the places of greatest job growth; according to the economists Stanback and Knight, "approximately three-quarters of the jobs that opened up [between 1940 and 1960] were in metropolitan areas whereas most of the jobs that closed down were in nonmetropolitan areas." In the older metropolises of the Northeast and Midwest, this growth was primarily in white-collar rather than blue-collar jobs.[18]

But to see the precise effects of these structural processes on Italian Americans, one has to examine the experiences of different birth cohorts, groups of people born in the same period. Historically specific changes, such as the expansion of higher education after World War II, do not have the same effect on people of varying ages, because older people have life commitments that usually do not allow them to respond to changing opportunities; they cannot easily choose to go back to school or change careers. Hence, a comparison of all Italian Americans in 1940 with all Italian Americans in 1950 or 1960 muffles the changes that have taken place in the interval, because so many in the group will have been stable in their position. The litmus test for change is a comparison of groups of individuals who reach maturity at different points in an interval, because it is those not yet adults who are most able to respond to shifts in opportunity.

The needed analyses will be fully presented in the next chapter, in the context of a thorough examination of the group's contemporary situation. What is appropriate here is to point to enough evidence to indicate the relevance of structural mobility processes for Italian Americans. Such evidence emerges from the analyses of Andrew Greeley, who has examined the socioeconomic progress of Catholic ethnic groups, comparing their cohorts to those of Protestant groups. The evidence presented by Greeley is sharpest in relation to education. In essence, Greeley finds that the oldest cohorts of Italians and of other Catholic groups from southern and eastern Europe were educationally far behind Protestant core groups, but that each new cohort took a step toward closing the gap. The Italians and the other new groups began to reach parity in the cohorts born after 1930, whose members completed their educations after the war under the influence of postwar opportunities.[19]

Additional evidence is presented by Stanley Lieberson in his book, *A Piece of the Pie.* Liberson's evidence is particularly critical because he focuses on cohorts among the second generation, and hence his analyses avoid confounding birth cohort changes with expected generational improvements. Lieberson compares different cohorts among second-generation southern and eastern European groups to their equivalents among all third- and later-generation Americans. His analyses reveal important changes among all the new groups for the cohort born in 1925-35, which came to maturity during and after the war. In the case of the Italians, the educational gap, which had been fairly constant in the cohorts born before 1915, declined somewhat in the cohort born in 1915-25 and virtually disappeared in the next cohort. A pattern of rising attainment is also evident in the proportion of Italian-American men employed as professionals. In this case, the change is less gradual, and the big leap occurs between the cohort of 1915-25 and that of 1925-35, which began to enter the labor market in the 1940s.[20]

Structural mobility provided the driving force for ethnic change in the postwar period. Without it, the fluidity in ethnic perceptions created by the wartime experience and expressed in novels about the war might have remained a mere blueprint for ethnic equality, unrealizable because of the socioeconomic gulf that acted to preserve ethnic boundaries among groups. For this fluidity to crystallize in a realignment among ethnic groups, fundamental changes in the social structure were required, to allow Italian Americans and other ethnics to move upward in the socioeconomic scale and thereby to associate more freely with other Americans. Given that these changes did occur in the postwar period, it is now appropriate to examine their further consequences for the position of the Italian-American group.

POLITICS

The great strides made by Italian Americans after 1945 did not take long to be registered in the domain of politics. The suddenness of the political arrival of Italian Americans is surprising in a way, because the political advancement of a group usually lags behind its general social mobility. Political power stands atop a steep pyramid. It requires not only raw numbers at the base (i.e., masses of voters who turn out regularly) but also, at the intermediate levels, cadres of individuals with the credentials—generally a law degree—for a career in politics. In this respect, the political success of Italians had been brewing for a while. In Rhode Island, for example, a state with proportionally one of the largest Italian-American populations, an average of only one Italian American a year passed the bar examinations in the years between 1906 and 1924. But in the period from 1925 to 1946, four or five entered the bar each year; and between 1947 and 1951, the average increased to eight.[21] The attainment of political power by a group also requires a sufficient number of individuals with the wealth to bankroll campaigns. In this way, too, the social mobility of Italians propelled them to the brink of political mobility.[22]

A measure of just how far and fast the Italians came is derived from the fact that Fiorello La Guardia, who was first elected to the House of Representatives in 1916, was only the third Italian American to serve in Congress and the second to represent any area of New York, despite the large concentration of Italians there.[23] Yet, in 1948, eight Italian Americans were elected to the House, double the number in any previous year; and by the late 1960s, the number had doubled again—sixteen then served.[24]

Other political milestones were passed in the aftermath of the war. The first Italian American elected as governor of a state was John Pastore, who became governor of Rhode Island in 1946. Pastore subsequently went on to become the first person of Italian ancestry to be elected to the U.S. Senate, in 1950. Since Pastore opened these cracks in the wall, other Italian Americans have squeezed through into important positions in the American political system. John Volpe, to take a prominent example, was elected governor of Massachusetts three times, in 1960, 1964, and 1966. Success in reaching these top positions had been preceded by a much more massive success at lower levels. By the early 1950s, more than twice as many Italian Americans served in the state legislatures of states with large Italian populations (Connecticut, Massachusetts, New Jersey, New York, Pennsylvania, and Rhode Island) as had done so in the mid-1930s.[25] Italians were also successful in many municipal and other local elections. La Guardia had been mayor of New York City before the war; and in 1950, Vincent Impellitteri became the second Italian to serve in this office. Throughout the northeastern region, Italians won many other mayoralties, in both large and small places, in the postwar period.

Entry into Cabinet-level positions in the federal government took a little more time. President Kennedy was the first to appoint an Italian American, Anthony Celebrezze, to head a Cabinet department, that of Health, Education, and Welfare, in 1962. Later in the same decade, Jack Valenti was a special assistant to President Johnson; and John Volpe became Secretary of Transportation in the Nixon Administration.

By 1970, the end of the period under discussion in this chapter, the Italian advance had moved the group very far politically, but still left it short of the share of power to which its proportion of the population should have entitled it. The gap was particularly noticeable at the highest levels, in those offices that depended on a broad constituency and hence where success among non-Italians was as important for a politician as success with his, or much more rarely her, own group. Considering the number of states in which the Italian-American population is substantial, there have been few Italian-American governors, and until the 1970s John Pastore was the only person with an Italian name to serve in the U.S. Senate. Moreover, even though more than a few Italian Americans were members of the House in the late 1960s, their number there was still smaller than should have been expected on the basis of population proportions. The same underrepresentation is found in positions whose holders are appointed, rather than elected. Few Italians have been appointed to the Cabinet, and none has served on the Supreme Court. One study of the ethnic composition of the national elite in 1971-72 undoubtedly serves to summarize the situation in the late 1960s as well. The study, based on more than 500 interviews with individuals in top positions in a variety of institutional sectors, found that Catholic groups aside from the Irish were distinctly underrepresented in the elite, constituting under 9 percent of it as opposed to 17 percent of the general population.[26]

The failure of Italian Americans to achieve a proportionate share of political power has led to speculation about the explanation for their lack of full political success, speculation centering on their political style. One cultural element that has figured in this speculation originates with the alienation of southern Italians from the succession of foreign governments in the Mezzogiorno, leading to a characteristic attitude toward government in general, summarized by the phrase *ladro governo,* "government is a thief." That this attitude survived in America is demonstrated by Herbert Gans's study of the residents of an Italian-American ghetto in Boston's West End, who were unable to mobilize on behalf of their neighborhood when it was under threat.[27] Undoubtedly, such an implicitly apolitical attitude did retard Italian-American participation in politics. A second cultural element is the lower-middle-class style that, in the view of Nathan Glazer and Daniel Moynihan, typifies many Italian-American politicians. Glazer and Moynihan trace this style to the recency of the arrival of Italian Americans in the middle class and their consequent insecurity. The lower-middle-class style is a drawback to politicians seeking higher office, because it is tinged with an unattractive parochialism and conservatism. Indeed, in its emphasis on "no frills" in government, it is related to the attitude of *ladro governo.*[28]

Both of these cultural elements may have played a part, but in my own view they are less important than other facts. The most fundamental is the recency in historical terms of the acquisition by Italians of the social resources, chiefly wealth and education, needed to reach the threshold of power. Political success is not attainable overnight. Even after the general social mobility of a group, there is still a period in which its members must toil in large numbers at the humbler levels of politics—working in campaigns, for example—before it will be ready for significant success. Moreover, as Italians reached the threshold of power, they found other groups blocking the doorway. Unlike educational and occupational mobility, the political kind involves a zero-sum game; there is only one mayor in a city and one governor in a state. Hence, the advance of one group must mean a loss for another. In most of the cities where they settled, Italians found the Irish ahead of them, in control of the political machines and doling out small political favors in return for Italian votes. Italians therefore had to struggle to wrest a fair share of offices from Irish-American politicans; and when they could not get by Irish Democrats, they sometimes tried to go around them, by joining the Republican party. As a result, Italian voting strength has been divided in many places, weakening the group's claim on the nominations of either party as well as the chances of its politicians to be elected, since the willingness of Italian-American voters to support them may be undercut by partisan loyalties.[29]

One last factor limiting the political success of Italian Americans deserves to be mentioned: the rise in popularity during the 1960s of the equation of organized crime with "Mafia" and "Cosa Nostra." This equation was placed under a spotlight by the testimony of Joseph Valachi in 1963, and it was then extended and glamorized by the mass media, which elevated the Mafia to a central myth in American life. The attention given to it placed many Italian Americans in public life under a shadow of suspicion, and it became all too easy to believe that they might be connected in some fashion to gangsters. The suspicion of underworld ties that easily attached itself to anyone with an Italian name has slowed the group's political advance. As an example, the Watergate tapes reveal Richard Nixon considering the possibility of appointing an Italian American to a top federal position, only to ask, "but where would we find an honest Italian American?"[30]

RESIDENTIAL INTEGRATION AND SUBURBANIZATION

The image of transplanted peasants has had an enduring association with Italian Americans. This is particularly exemplified by the reputation the group has acquired for residential immobility. Italian Americans are popularly characterized as steadfast small-property owners, who, bound by ties to family and friends and perhaps by a touch of Old World *campanilismo,* remain rooted in one place for generations, creating viable urban neighborhoods and resisting incursions by outsiders.[31] The characterization would be important if true, because it would imply that even extensive social mobility might not erode the ethnic solidarity fostered by homogeneous neighborhoods, where the forces of physical proximity come to the rescue of weakening preferences for in-group primary ties. Like the "apathetic" individuals described by Child, those who are unconcerned about ethnicity but grow up surrounded by ethnic peers might remain in the bosom of the group.

Systematic data lend some credence to this image. According to the 1970 census, second-generation Italian Americans in the 25–44 age bracket, the prime age range for residential mobility, were less likely to move than were other Americans. Fifty-eight percent of the Italians were living in the same house they had lived in five years before, compared to only 40 percent of white Americans in the same ages.[32]

Of course, these same data demonstrate that over 40 percent of this Italian group did move within a five-year period. By any absolute standard, this is a substantial figure and suggests that even though Italian Americans may be less likely to move than other groups are, their immobility may not be sufficient to maintain ethnically homogeneous neighborhoods over very long periods. Other evidence, though flawed, buttresses this conclusion.

One kind comes from studies of the residential segregation of Italians and other new ethnic groups. These show that their segregation, which was very high in 1930, had declined noticeably by 1970. Still, the implications are not unambiguous, as segregation indices remained moderately high at the end of the period.[33] The ambiguity stems in part from two limitations that afflict all studies of residential segregation. One is due to the census data on which they are based, which until 1980 did not identify nationality beyond the second generation. Consequently, these studies are unable to speak to the segregation of the third generation, even though by the late 1960s, this generation had become a major presence among Italian Americans. A second failure concerns age. These studies fail to consider the possibility that segregation is detectable largely because older Italian Americans remain in enclaves from which their children have moved. Put another way, the studies of residential segregation hold an unreasonable standard against which to measure the residential concentrations of the group: namely, the complete disappearance of any differences between the residential distributions of Italians and others. Given the existence of such differences at the outset, their complete disappearance is virtually impossible in a forty-year period, even if younger Italian Americans were to intermix freely with non-Italians. The reason is that many of their parents and grandparents would remain in place, thereby creating concentrations detectable to the statistician's measurements. Thus, conventional indices of residential segregation probably exaggerate the significance of Italian-American segregation at the end of the period.

Fortunately, another kind of evidence is available, although it too is limited. It concerns the increasing suburbanization of America after 1950. The post–World

War II period was one of tremendous change in the residential patterns of Americans. Their increasing affluence, together with government programs to allow Americans to obtain home mortgages, stirred a tidal wave of home building and home buying. In the single decade from 1950 to 1960, the population in the suburbs increased by nearly 50 percent, from 41 million to 60 million. The suburban exodus was full of portent for ethnic groups, because it disrupted urban ethnic communities. Also, life in many suburbs demanded a certain level of assimilation, since suburban dwellers frequently were held by their neighbors to a strict standard of outward appearance, symbolized by the universal concern over lawns. Although critics of the suburbs exaggerated their middle-class homogeneity, many of them were fairly homogeneous. This was epitomized by the Levittowns, which, because they were built according to an ingenious plan for mass production, contained standardized, nearly identical houses.[34]

Given the socioeconomic advances of the Italians, it was only natural that they should participate in the suburban pilgrimage. Joan Fee, in a study of religious groups, found that of those white Catholics who lived in metropolitan regions, the proportion who lived in suburbs rather than central city areas increased very dramatically from 42 percent to 68 percent, between the mid-1950s and the late 1960s.[35] Since Italian Americans form a substantial fraction of the Catholics in metropolitan areas, this increase would not have been possible without their participation in the suburban movement. This is exemplified by the residential changes evident in the sprawling metropolitan region centered around New York City and Newark, where ethnicity could be expected to linger longer than it does elsewhere by virtue of the area's large ethnic populations. But by 1970, second-generation Italian Americans in the region had significantly dispersed to the suburbs. According to census figures, 47 percent of this generation were living in the area's smaller places, those with fewer than 100,000 residents; and 41 percent were living in places with fewer than 50,000. These figures are only slightly lower than those for whites generally (50 percent and 45 percent, respectively). However, first-generation Italians remained distinctly more concentrated in the region's larger cities. Only 35 percent were in places smaller than 100,000 in population, and 29 percent in places smaller than 50,000.[36]

What is hard to be sure about is whether movement to the suburbs by Italian Americans was accompanied, as either a prerequisite or a consequence, by further assimilation. To be sure, some suburbs became ethnic enclaves, but in general suburbanization was almost certainly associated with further acculturation and intermingling across nationality lines. Herbert Gans, in his study of a Levittown in New Jersey, noted that most of the suburb's ethnic residents appeared to have come from acculturated homes.[37] Other than this isolated remark, the evidence is indirect but still pertinent. It consists of one feature of suburban life that stands out in the accounts of it during the 1950s and 1960s: the salience of religion, rather than nationality, as a social boundary. These descriptions highlight the emergence of separate but parallel institutions (such as schools and country clubs) to serve the major religious groups, as well as the segregation between these groups in primary relationships. Andrew Greeley, for example, describes the social life of Catholics and Protestants in "Westwood" (a pseudonym) as nearly completely contained within religiously homogeneous social circles; even the golf foursomes at the community's country club, which in this case did serve both groups, were largely homogeneous.[38] The accounts of suburbia imply that nationality differences tended to diminish under the homogenizing influences of suburban life, leaving religion as the primary form of ethnicity.

In sum, the evidence on residential mobility, although far from definitive, points to a significant leakage out of Italian-American neighborhoods in the period 1930-70. Residential segregation declined throughout the period, and Italians, particularly of the second generation, took part in the movement to the suburbs. But there was still substantial segregation at the end of the period, at least by the measure of segregation indices.

OTHER CHANGES IN THE DIRECTION OF ASSIMILATION: INTERMARRIAGE, LANGUAGE, RELIGION

The key issue in the study of residential segregation is whether concentrations remained sufficient to prevent massive social assimilation, the entry of Italians into primary relations with non-Italians on a large scale. There is another angle of attack on the same issue, through intermarriage rates, and here there is no ambiguity. If the data about residential segregation leave one uncertain about whether the ecological basis for separation in primary relationships remained, the data about intermarriage demonstrate that social assimilation had begun to occur on a mass scale by the late 1950s.

The best intermarriage data for the period are available from a 1963 survey of American Catholics. According to the results of this survey, the overall intermarriage rate for Italian Americans, including those of all generations and ages, was about 40 percent. This figure was modest compared with the intermarriage rates of some other Catholic groups, such as the Irish, but by any absolute measure it was far from trivial. Moreover, this overall rate mixed together the intermarriage rate of first-generation Italians, who as newcomers are unlikely to intermarry, with that of the third generation; it also mixed together the rate for older persons, who married a half century before, with that holding for the youngest members of the group. Distinguishing among the marriage rates for different generational and age groupings reveals an upsurge in intermarriage: marriage to non-Italians but still largely to Catholics. Sixty percent of third-generation Italian Americans had intermarried, and among those who were 30 years of age or younger in 1963, a group whose members had mostly married within the preceding decade, the intermarriage rate reached almost to 70 percent. From an examination of the ethnic backgrounds of their spouses, it appears that intermarrying Italians married freely with other Catholic groups, choosing spouses of Irish, German, Polish, and other eastern

European backgrounds in rough proportion to their numbers within the Catholic population.[39]

Growing acculturation helped to make the surge of intermarriage possible. One important change was the decline of Italian as a language of everyday use. The decline was inevitable because the Italian the immigrants brought with them was too restricted to endure. The immigrants mostly spoke dialect, and the dialects from different areas were sometimes even mutually unintelligible. Moreover, the Italian of the immigrants was a language highly adapted to the circumstances of a static, rural society and hence capable of expressing only a limited range of experience. To expand its domain, immigrants borrowed many words from English, such as *shoppa* for "shop," *giobba* for "job," and *gellafrienda* for "girlfriend." But the intrinsic limitations of peasant dialects made the Italian of the immigrants ultimately inappropriate for grasping the complexities of American experience.[40] As a result, even though Italians as a group took a long time to acquire English because the intention of many immigrants to return to Italy made knowledge of English seem superfluous, once they did learn English it rapidly replaced Italian. Exact figures documenting the decline of Italian through the period 1930-70 are impossible to find, but data collected by the U.S. Bureau of the Census in the late 1970s are suggestive. The Census Bureau asked a large sample of individuals about the language spoken in their childhood homes, i.e., their mother tongue, and also about the language currently spoken in their homes. From the responses, the Census Bureau estimated that over 4 million claimed Italian as a mother tongue. The large figure, making Italian one of the most frequently named mother tongues, was due to the size of the second generation. But fewer than 1.4 million spoke the language in their current homes. Since according to the same study, the number of first-generation Italians, who would have been very likely to speak Italian at home, was 800,000, it is clear that only a small proportion of the second and third generations used Italian on a daily basis.[41]

Another notable aspect of acculturation concerned religious beliefs and practices. Although southern Italian immigrants were Catholics, their Catholicism was of a very different kind from that which dominated the American Church. For one thing, the relation of the Church to the people of southern Italy was made difficult by the temporal power of the Church, often used on behalf of the landholding class. Church-going was largely an affair of women and the very young and very old. Adult men typically expressed strongly anticlerical sentiments and attended Mass only on major holidays and for family events, such as weddings and funerals.

Mezzogiorno Catholicism, moreover, represented a fusion of diverse elements, frequently derived from the religions of the region's conquerors, and included a substratum of magical practices. Perhaps reflecting the polytheism of ancient Greeks and Romans, southern Italian Catholics experienced relationships to the supernatural in terms of relations to saints and the Madonna rather than to God directly. Prayers were directed to these intermediate figures, who were expected to act as intercessors with God, and with whom relations took on a very human tone, including punitiveness when expected benefits failed to materialize. Southern

Italians also perceived in the world various pre-Christian powers that could work for good or evil. They believed, for example, in the "evil eye" (*il malocchio*) and used various charms to ward it off. One was the horn (*cornuto*); horns could be hung over a doorway to keep malevolent spirits out of the home; or the symbol for a horn could be worn around the neck as an amulet. Such necklaces are still popular among Italian Americans as good-luck charms.[42]

Their different brands of Catholicism formed a pivotal element in the conflict between the Irish and the Italians, the two largest Catholic groups in many American cities. The Irish dominated and set the basic tone for the American Catholic Church. They were far more fervent Catholics, and far stricter in their observance of norms for religious behavior, such as that mandating weekly Mass attendance. The Church hierarchy was largely Irish, and during the early period of Italian settlement, there were few Italian priests. The Irish possession of the American Church generated considerable antipathy among the immigrants and led to what has been called the "Italian problem" by Church historians. A considerable number of Italian immigrants fell away from the Church, and some even converted to Protestantism. Few of the great majority of immigrants who remained nominally Catholic sent their children to parochial school.[43]

But in its worst manifestations, the Italian problem was of short duration. One reason was the early establishment by the American Church of "national parishes" to serve the distinct needs of different immigrant groups. Thus, Italian parishes were staffed by Italian priests, sometimes imported expressly for the purpose, or at least by sympathetic Italian-speaking priests of other backgrounds. The national parishes allowed the Italians and other immigrants to move their masses out of the basement, to which they had been literally consigned in some Irish-American churches, and to worship according to their own traditions (for example, through the festas in honor of saints, which the Irish disdained as practically a form of paganism).[44]

Additionally, the adjustment of the second generation carried it in the direction of religious acculturation, and for the most part, this meant a reconciliation with the Church. This is not to say that adjustment took the same form for all members of the second generation. As Francis Femminella has noted, there were three possibilities.[45] The response of a small minority, conversion to Protestantism, has already been mentioned. This represented an obvious kind of acculturation, namely, acceptance of the religion of the majority of Americans.

A second response continued some of the spirit of Mezzogiorno Catholicism but with revised external forms. As did others in the second generation, those who responded in this way dropped the external religious forms of their parents. Southern Italian superstitions were rejected as a part of the old country that had no place in America and were replaced with a secularism that was quite appropriate for urban America. Those responding in this way remained nominal Catholics and may well have had an important influence on the American Church, because their skepticism about the authority of its hierarchy allowed them to challenge the Church's prohibitions against birth control. Hence, they may have been critical to the disaffection from Church teaching on sexual matters that has characterized American Catholicism in recent years.

The third response has been one of acculturaticn to Irish-American norms for Catholicism, a response sometimes described as the "Hibernization" of Italian Americans. One study of New York City parishes has documented that second- and third-generation Italian Americans were very similar to Irish Americans on such matters as weekly Mass attendance, use of the sacraments, and prayer to God rather than to saints. A significant indicator of Hibernization is the increasing frequency with which Italian-American parents sent their children to parochial schools.[46] The acculturation of many Italian Americans to Irish-American Catholicism contributed significantly to the perception, widespread during the 1950s, that Catholics formed a separate melting pot within which ethnic differences were diminishing rapidly. And, in fact, since Italian and Irish Catholics were both large groups settled in many of the same American cities, intermarriages between them became a frequent occurrence.

Still, a subtle form of the Italian problem remains. Italian Americans have been slow to gain a proportionate share of the American Church's hierarchy. In part, this seems due to a reluctance to enter the priesthood, a likely reflection of continuing aloofness from American Catholicism; but it also is attributable to a pattern of ethnic exclusion maintained by the Church's leadership. In the early 1970s, about 15 percent of Catholics were Italian Americans, but only 12 percent of priests had Italian ancestry. Far worse, only one of thirty-four archbishops was Italian American and only five of 253 bishops. There was no Italian-American cardinal. Ten years later, this last had been remedied, but otherwise the situation remained essentially the same.[47]

CHANGE AND CONTINUITY IN THE FAMILY SYSTEM

The occupational and educational mobility of Italian Americans after World War II should imply changes in the family system because of the jigsaw fit between family ethos and socioeconomic position. Broadly put, one would expect at least a partial acculturation to American family patterns to occur with social mobility, both be-cause of the requirements of mobility and because mobility leads to greater inter-action with non-Italians. In the last chapter, moreover, we caught glimpses of the beginnings of acculturation in the adjustments made by young members of the second generation.

But acculturation was only partial, and the essential flavor of the Italian family ethos remained. The changes that took place tended to be ones that brought the outward form of Italian-American family life into conformity with American culture, while leaving its animating spirit, its core values, largely intact. Making the case for this description involves a bit of speculation, because we know far more about the family life of working-class Italian Americans than we do about that of the socially mobile members of the group. The key study is Herbert Gans's *The*

Urban Villagers, a study of the Italian-American residents of a Boston neighborhood, the West End, in the 1950s.[48] This is a study of working-class members of the second generation, and there exists no comparable study of its middle class. But a lot of recent personal testimony suggests that there has been something different about Italian-American family life in general: something its articulate participants perceive as rich and sating while simultaneously limited and confining.[49]

One prominent change was the blossoming of the tight-knit and controlling Italian extended family into a social circle, within which second-generation Italian Americans chose to spend much of their social life apart from work. Gans describes this phenomenon as the "peer group society," defining the peer group as composed of relatives and family friends who enjoy the same sex, age, and life-cycle status. The peer group was a group of sociability, and the compatibility it required generally excluded those of a different generation and those whose acculturation was either more or less than that of its members. The peer group came together without formal invitation one or more times a week in the homes of its members. What happened was more or less conversation, but conversation covering a limited range of topics, on which the opinions that would be offered were known in advance. What mattered was really the presence of others, one's kin and friends. The fundamental value that the peer-group society retained was that of loyalty to kin, at the same time that it concealed this within the American form of leisure-time conviviality.[50]

That the family-based social circle is a quite general pattern among Italian Americans is indicated by the visiting relations discovered in national surveys. Andrew Greeley has noted that Italian Americans are more likely than other ethnic groups to live near relatives, especially parents and siblings, and to visit with them frequently. He found these patterns to exist for both working-class and middle-class Italians. Greeley has also found that Italian Americans simply spend more time with their immediate families. Among the white ethnic groups he studied, Italians ranked third highest in time spent with children, and Italian men ranked highest in time spent with wives.[51]

Relations within the nuclear family retained even more of a characteristic Mezzogiorno flavor than those within the extended kinship circle. Divorce on the part of Italian Americans appears to have been unusual, at least until recently (see Chapter 6). Analyzing extensive data from the 1960s, Andrew Greeley found that only 2 percent of Italian-American Catholics reported their current marital status as divorced, the second-lowest rate among American ethnic groups.[52] In his study of the West End, Gans noted that marital relations were compartmentalized according to what he termed a "segregated conjugal pattern." Husbands and wives had distinct, nonoverlapping roles, and there seemed to be little communication between them. Even their friendships were largely separate, in contrast to the joint friendships of middle-class American couples; meetings of the peer group generally broke up into a male gathering in one room and a female gathering in another. The division of labor was fairly conventional. Women were responsible for home and family matters, including the raising of children; men were breadwinners. What was unconventional was the rigidity of the boundary between their roles. For example, in discussing their children with their wives, men would frequently refer to them as "your" children. Indeed, the chief role of fathers seemed to be that of occasional disciplinarian.[53]

Also strongly reminiscent of the Mezzogiorno and the immigrant generation was the attitude toward children. In contrast to the child-centeredness of American middle-class families, the Italian-American families of the West End were adult-centered. Children were expected to behave in accordance with adult wishes, to stay out of the way of adults and to behave like miniature adults when in their presence. These expectations seem descended from the foreshortened childhood of the Mezzogiorno, the early transition to adulthood there. Childrearing, moreover, was "impulsive," to use Gans's word. Parents were not concerned with being consistent toward their children or with guiding them toward some predetermined future goal, as contemporary American middle-class parents would be. Rather, they heeded their momentary reactions to their children's behavior, with the result that they might punish an act at one moment and let a similar act go unnoticed at another time. They were also concerned predominantly with keeping children's outward behavior under control, and consequently parental discipline seemed ever present:

> to a middle-class observer, the parents' treatment seems extremely strict and sometimes brutal. There is a continuous barrage of prohibitions and threats, intertwined with words and deeds of reward and affection. But the torrents of threat and cajolery neither impinge on the feelings of parental affection, nor are meant as signs of rejection. As one mother explained to her child, "We hit you because we love you." People believe that discipline is needed constantly to keep the child in line with and respectful of adult rules, and without it he would run amok.[54]

In addition to these prominent features of family life, there were numerous other nuances and shadings of the Italian-American family in which the outlines of *contadino* life in the Mezzogiorno could be recognized—such as the characteristic reserve of Italian-American men, carried over from the ideal of masculinity described by Richard Gambino as *l'uomo di panza,* "literally a man of belly, meaning a man who knew how to keep things to himself—in his guts, as it were."[55] But there was at least one decisive break with southern Italian traditions. Between the first and second generations, the average number of children born to Italian-American families declined dramatically. The immigrant family was much like the peasant family of the Old World. There was little or no attempt to limit family size, and families with five or six children were the rule. Matters were entirely reversed in the second generation. The Church's rulings on birth control apparently were widely ignored by Italian Americans, and in the second generation, family size was much lower, with two to four children the rule. This is essentially no different from urban Americans in general.[56]

Overall, the second-generation Italian-American family presents a picture of adjustment to American culture contained within a framework still set in southern Italy. This is not to deny the many outward changes. Italian-American parents of the second generation did not demand that their children leave school at the earliest possible age to help support the family, but they did instill in their children loyalty to family as a basic value. Nonetheless, it deserves to be emphasized again that what we know of the Italian-American family we know mostly of its working-class variety, and we cannot be sure just how much Italian-American distinctiveness may have been muted by social mobility and also by intermarriage. Gans, in fact, speculatively interprets the culture of the West Enders as working-class rather than ethnic in its origins, implying that middle-class Italian Americans might well be like other middle-class Americans. The possibility remains, then, that in the immediate aftermath of World War II, mobility and increasing intermarriage may have eroded the distinctive Italian-American family culture more widely than we know.

ORGANIZED CRIME

The theme of mobility is visible in the field of crime, too. Organized crime can be usefully thought of as an American institution, a sector of the economy providing illicit goods and services and serving as a channel for ethnic mobility.[57] It is, to be sure, a stigmatized institution, whose participants are branded with the mark of unrespectability and whose proferred opportunities for power and money entail great risk, including the possible loss of one's life. For these reasons, it attracts chiefly the members of low-standing ethnic groups. Their ethnic backgrounds are a disadvantage added to the usual difficulty of achieving more than modest mobility through legitimate routes; and in the event they lack the appetite to take the hard road to conventional success or are unwilling to settle for a pedestrian existence, they may perceive that the opportunities of illicit enterprise outweigh its risks. Members of established ethnic groups, having more routine access to opportunities for decent jobs, are rarely tempted into organized crime careers.

It follows as a corollary that the forms that crime takes are constrained by a group's position in the larger society; and as this position changes, so does the character of its members' participation in crime. Hence, the large-scale mobility and acculturation of Italian Americans in the period 1930–70 was accompanied by parallel changes in Italian-American organized crime. The crucial ones were a completion of the breakout from the ethnic enclave into the wider society, and a consolidation of Italian criminal groups into crime "families," loosely linked in a national network.

One important step was the "Americanization of the mobs," the replacement of Old World–style leaders by younger men who had grown up in America and were familiar with American ways.[58] Americanization did not happen everywhere at once; its timing and sequence varied from one city to another. In Chicago, Americanization occurred before 1930, under the leadership of John Torrio and then Al Capone. In New York, the same process occurred in the early 1930s, when Lucky

Luciano choreographed the elimination of two Old World-style capos. Among the younger men, mostly born in Italy but reared in the United States, who rose in the aftermath of these killings were Luciano, Frank Costello, Albert Anastasia, and Vito Genovese. Their names were to dominate the public's perception of Italian-American organized crime in the ensuing decades.[59]

The Americanization of the mobs was important for several reasons. One concerned the linkage among criminals, police, and politicians necessary for illicit enterprise to prosper. When crime is dominated by unacculturated men, their unease in an American environment makes the linkage fragile. Acculturated criminals move easily in the world outside the ghetto. The presence is more invisible and hence they are able to associate more freely with politicians and other men wielding legitimate power. Among Italian-American gangsters, Frank Costello, a gambling kingpin of the 1930s, 40s, and 50s, is perhaps the supreme example of this ease of movement in the legitimate world. His biographer, interviewing his many legitimate friends, who of course knew of his criminal career, found that they nonetheless viewed him as a "prince of a fellow."[60]

In addition, Americanized Italian gangsters were able to cooperate with criminals of other ethnic backgrounds. As a result, starting in the 1930s, the Wild West atmosphere of Prohibition was brought to an end. Violence continued, to be sure, but principally as a means of working out succession in leadership positions and of eliminating individuals who had trespassed against powerful figures, and not as a feature of a war of all against all. The most notable examples of cooperation occurred with Jewish gangsters in Northern big cities, New York, Chicago, Cleveland, and Detroit, and with national repercussions. Eastern European Jews had immigrated to the United States at the same time as southern Italians and also found many legitimate avenues of mobility closed off. Jewish gangsters therefore formed an important component of the "rackets" in many cities with large Jewish populations. In these, located in the industrial heartland of the East and Midwest, Jewish and Italian gangsters—including Meyer Lansky, Bugsy Siegel, Lepke Buchalter, Lucky Luciano, Frank Costello, and Albert Anastasia—linked up in the 1930s to form a powerful syndicate known to its insiders as "the combination" and later to the public as "Murder, Inc." The combination eliminated many of the independents and smaller groups that had survived Prohibition mayhem, and it rationalized control over the rackets, allowing crime bosses to work in their territories without constant competition from others. It was regionally based, and hence it did not truly control American organized crime. Independent criminal groups continued to exist outside the region it dominated. Nonetheless, the combination could project itself on a national and even an international scale, as is shown by its activities in Las Vegas, which it helped to establish, and in Havana.[61]

Ethnically based Italian-American criminal organizations also appear to have become consolidated during the 1930s, entering a long period of stability in which the organizational forms and even the personnel occupying them remained relatively constant. Italian-American organizations existed alongside the multiethnic framework of the combination (their collective name, "Cosa Nostra," literally

"Our Thing," perhaps signified their need to have something separate). The basic organizational unit, the crime "family," is of unclear origins. It does not coincide with Mezzogiorno prototypes, and it is not discernible in the crime of the early period of settlement. It represents an adaptation to American circumstances that appears to have become crystallized during Luciano's ascendancy. By the 1930s, the organizational form could be described in a way that more or less applied to Italian crime families throughout the country (though it should be noted, details varied from place to place). A family was headed by a *capo* or boss, aided by one or more underbosses. Underneath the level of leadership, "soldiers" were organized in small units called "regimes" or "decine" (which translates as "groups of ten"); each such unit had a head, a *caporegime* or *capodecina*. The men at the very bottom were criminal entrepreneurs, responsible for developing their own enterprises and providing those above them with a cut of the action.

Not only did the form crystallize, but so did the actual crime families. The five New York crime families that exist today existed in the early 1930s, and the same continuity occurs in other American cities. Moreover, since that time, the twenty-four Italian-American crime families in the country have been loosely linked through the mechanism of "the Commission," a small group of leaders who meet to discuss general problems and resolve jurisdictional disputes. Popular literature on the Mafia to the contrary, however, the Commission does not appear to direct Italian organized crime; crime families are essentially independent units.[62]

One other consequence of the Americanization of the mobs was essential. The acculturation of Italian-American crime bosses and their cooperation with non-Italian gangsters eased the transition from Prohibition. Prohibition officially came to an end in 1933, with the ratification of the Twenty-First Amendment; and as America became legally "wet" again, an important source of profits for organized crime dried up and a search for new sources began. Interest in gambling was renewed. In New York, Italians followed Dutch Schultz into the numbers racket in Harlem, taking over after his murder in 1935 the operations he had grabbed from Black numbers bankers. Italians and others created bookmaking enterprises, allowing bettors to gamble on horse and dog racing, and established illegal casinos to cater further to the gambling trade. The profits from gambling in turn fed loan-sharking operations, for which gamblers served as important customers. Also, perhaps following the model of Lepke Buchalter, who used the conflict between businessmen and labor unions as an entree into the garment industry and other trades, Italians burrowed into labor racketeering. To a large extent, the industries in which they established themselves were ones where Italian Americans formed a critical part of the labor force, such as New York's Fulton Fish Market and the East Coast docks. But this was not always the case. For a time in the 1930s, Italian and Jewish gangsters succeeded in controlling a motion picture and theater union, using it as a base to extort money from movie studios and theater owners.[63]

In the decades following the 1930s, Italian Americans continued their rise to power and prominence in organized crime, and by the 1950s, they were gaining ascendancy over Jewish gangsters, whose influence was ebbing. Jewish participation in crime was essentially a one-generation phenomenon, and Jewish strength was not renewed by a continuing flow of young Jewish men into careers of crime. Hence, as Jewish gangsters departed from the underworld by death or retirement, they were not replaced. Buchalter died in the electric chair in 1944; Bugsy Siegel was murdered in 1947, apparently because he was blamed for what at the time seemed to be the failure of Las Vegas. The Jewish figures who remained, such as Meyer Lansky, moved away from the front lines of crime. As individuals, some remained very powerful, but their numbers became fewer and fewer. By the 1960s, Italian-American crime families had achieved a monopoly position over a number of spheres in many American cities.

It was in the same decade that Italians came, as well, to dominate public attention to organized crime. Racketeers had received intermittent attention in the 1940s and 50s, but a new phase of public concern about organized crime was inaugurated by the spectacular revelations of Joseph Valachi, a soldier in a New York City crime family. Valachi testified about a secret society he called "Cosa Nostra" and focused the public eye squarely on Italian-American organized crime. His testimony helped give birth to a new perception of organized crime, namely, that it was the same as the "Mafia" and "Cosa Nostra."

This perception spurred a reinterpretation of American organized crime, in which a historically specific ethnic form was taken as the key to all organized crime in America. Accordingly, American crime history was revised to focus almost entirely on events among the Italians; only Prohibition remained a significant exception. Thereby, the revision, which purported to trace step by step the development of American organized crime from its antecedents in Sicily and southern Italy, suggested implicitly that organized crime in America was the product of an alien cultural ethos brought by southern Italian immigrants.

It took a while for the basic character of this new perspective on crime to become clear, but subsequent research has uncovered the extent to which it distorts basic facts about crime in America.[64] In the revised history, inconvenient events faded into the background, while others that had previously seemed unimportant were elevated to prominence and given new twists of interpretation. A revealing example concerns the so-called Purge of the Greasers, alleged to be the pivotal event in the Americanization of the Mafia. According to the revised history, Americanization was accomplished in a wave of violence in a 24-hour period (September 11, 1931), when scores of old-time Mafiosi were murdered throughout the country at the direction of Lucky Luciano. The story of "Purge Day," as it came to be called, was based in substantial part on Valachi's account, and it bolstered the image of a unified, nationwide conspiracy, capable of acting on a national scale according to a single plan. However attractive it was from the new perspective, the story is almost certainly not true. Two investigators acting independently of each other, Humbert Nelli and Alan Block, have searched newspapers and records in many American cities in an attempt to verify the murderous score. Their researches have uncovered only a very few murders that might be connected with one another, almost all in the New York–New Jersey area. The notable one, known about long before the account of "Purge Day" came to public attention, was that of Salvatore Maranzano, an important crime figure, and insofar as there is any truth to the notion of a "purge of the greasers," it appears to have been an event connected to realignments in New York City's gangland.[65]

Nonetheless, the public attention devoted to Italians in crime during the 1960s appeared to cast a shadow of ambiguity over the gains made by Italian Americans after World War II. Many Americans with Italian names felt stung by the new interpretation, which implied that the Italian-American cultural heritage was tainted with criminality, and by the vulgar popularizations of the purported story of the Mafia, which magnified the phenomenon, attributing to it a mythological aura. Some Italian Americans attempted to defend their group by denying altogether the existence of Italian-American organized crime, managing to damage their own credibility and subject Italians to ridicule, without denting the mythology. The ambiguity enveloping the status of Italian Americans seemed cemented in place by the events of Italian-American Unity Day, June 26, 1971, when thousands gathered in New York City to celebrate Italian pride. During the ceremonies, Joseph Colombo, founder of the Italian-American Civil Rights League and alleged to be a crime figure, was shot; according to the police, his shooting resulted from gangland disagreements.

CONCLUSION: A RESURGENCE
OF ITALIAN-AMERICAN ETHNICITY?

In the period 1930-70, during which the second generation formed the bulk of the Italian-American population, the group advanced along a lengthy front into American society. The period began with the emergence of one ethnic group out of the ranks of Sicilians, Calabrians, Neapolitans, and others and, hence, the weakening of the *campanilismo* of the immigrant generation. But the emergence of this group did not remove the strain of ambivalence from the identity of individual Italian Americans, many of whom found themselves torn between two identities, Italian and American, each with its pluses and minuses. The American identity in particular was a risky choice, because many Americans viewed Italian Americans as their inferiors.

The position of Italians in American society shifted very rapidly during and after World War II. The war had the effect of expanding the magic circle of citizenship to include Italian Americans and other white ethnics, and it drew a distinction between the previously despised European ethnic groups and people of color that had not been so visible before. Consequently, in the aftermath of the war, it was the white ethnics who made tremendous socioeconomic strides. In fact, the social position of Italian Americans continued to improve throughout the period under discussion, and the group's social mobility was accompanied by demonstrable cultural and social assimilation. The most significant indicator of the assimilation trend was the intermarriage rate, which rose sharply in the 1950s and 60s.

The figure of Joe DiMaggio, the New York Yankee outfielder, exemplifies the rapid shift in the position of Italian Americans. DiMaggio entered baseball's major leagues in the late 1930s and drew immediate attention through his feats. Yet at the beginning of his career, perceptions of DiMaggio were colored by the images attached to Italians. A revealing instance is a 1939 feature article that appeared in the popular magazine, *Life.* Although the intention of the author, Noel F. Busch, was clearly to praise DiMaggio, the ballplayer is viewed through the prism of stereotypes about Italians. In arguing that his Italian background was an advantage for DiMaggio, the author wrote the "Italians, bad at war, are well suited for milder competitions." Comparing DiMaggio and Joe Louis, Busch noted that "like Heavyweight Champion Louis, DiMaggio is lazy, shy and inarticulate." And to demonstrate that DiMaggio was "well adapted to most U.S. mores," the author pointed out that "instead of olive oil or smelly bear grease he keeps his hair slick with water" and "he never reeks of garlic."[66] But by his career's end, DiMaggio had become an all-American hero, a status solidified by his marriage to Marilyn Monroe, which brought together the most famous baseball player of the 1940s with the woman who represented the consummation of movie screen beauty of her time. With justice, DiMaggio's biographer could describe him as "America's last hero."[67]

Nevertheless, at the end of the period, Italians remained still a distinct ethnic group, their assimilation not yet complete. Many northeastern cities retained large Italian-American sections, and a substantial part of the group's massive second generation was to be found in the urban working class, even at its lower edges in such occupations as sanitation worker and longshoreman. Above all else, the family ethos survived in a transmuted form. The value placed on family solidarity imbued Italian-American life with its own special flavor, detectable in tight-knit families, well-kept neighborhoods, and in what Gans described as the "peer-group society."

The ultimate assimilation of the group was thrown into question by what appeared to be a resurgence of ethnic identity in the late 1960s. The seeming surge of ethnic feelings among Italians was matched by apparently similar trends among many white ethnic groups, especially those whose ancestors had entered the United States in the late 19th and early 20th centuries from the countries of eastern and southern Europe. The renewal of ethnicity even seemed to occur on a worldwide scale, and ethnic conflicts grew intense in such diverse societies as Northern Ireland, Belgium, Pakistan, Nigeria, and of course in the Middle East. Social scientists perceived a tidal wave of ethnicity, leading them to question their previous views of ethnicity on the grounds that these contained an assimilationist bias, and to seek novel explanations for ethnicity's durability. In the United States, the spirit of the reexamination was reflected in the title of a popular book, Michael Novak's *The Rise of the Unmeltable Ethnics.* Notable contributions to social-science reflection on the matter were made by Daniel Bell, Nathan Glazer, Andrew Greeley, Daniel Patrick Moynihan, and others.

In American society, it was held, the resurgence of ethnicity was stimulated in part by a lack of full acceptance of white ethnics, especially in elite sectors. Italian and Polish names, for example, seemed almost entirely absent from the boards of major corporations, the partnerships of prestigious law firms, and the faculty of elite universities. The problem was complicated by the images attached to white ethnic groups. An extreme case in point was the Mafia image applied to Italians, but in general the white ethnic groups were widely perceived to be concentrated in the lower ranks of the blue-collar labor force—a perception that carried the subtle implication that these groups didn't have the cultural wherewithal to really make it in American society.

The sense of being only half accepted became linked up with some of the political currents generated by the Civil Rights movement, which reached a high-water mark during the 1960s. On the one hand, the apparent success of the movement seemed to show there was another route to the American cornucopia. A group didn't have to accept assimilation on terms laid down by powerful groups in order to achieve its fair share, or at least so things appeared in the heady days of the 1960s protests. On the other hand, one consequence of the Civil Rights movement, affirmative action, seemed to pose a new barrier for white ethnics, just as they seemed on the verge of full acceptance. Writers taking their point of view described affirmative action as changing unfairly the "rules of the game," after ethnics had committed themselves to playing by the old rules of individual achievement. In a gloomy vision, some even went so far as to suggest that affirmative action paved the way to a society in which rights would be vested in groups rather than individuals, as if every significant domain would have to have so many Blacks, so many Jews, so many Italians, and so on.[68]

Finally implicated in the apparent resurgence of ethnic consciousness was the ascendancy of the third generation, which among the new ethnic groups began to reach adulthood in large numbers during the 1950s and swelled considerably during the 1960s. The third generation, it was suggested, no longer needed to be defensive about its ancestral origins. Hence it was capable of asserting its ethnic identity with confidence and vigor, in contrast to its parents, who had been anxious to shuck off foreign traces. Strengthening the third generation's voice were the sizable gains that had been made in educational and occupational achievement. Ethnic Americans no longer needed to hide who they were.

What, then, was to happen to the Italian Americans? Would they assimilate, as the optimistic predictions of a melting pot that prevailed after World War II had assumed? Or would they continue as one group among many on the American scene, preserving their own unique cultural heritage with its distinctive family ethos? To examine the thesis of resurgent ethnicity, it is necessary to take a close look at the most recent evidence concerning Italian Americans. Such an examination forms the subject of the next two chapters.

NOTES

[1] Nathan Glazer, "Ethnic groups in America: From national culture to ideology," in Morroe Berger, Theodore Abel, and Charles H. Page (eds.), *Freedom and Control in Modern Society* (New York: D. Van Nostrand, 1954).

[2] Caroline F. Ware, *Greenwich Village, 1920-1930* (Boston: Houghton Mifflin, 1935), pp. 157-71; Josef J. Barton, *Peasants and Strangers* (Cambridge, Mass.: Harvard University Press, 1975), pp. 82-85.

[3] A poignant memoir of this feeling in immigrant homes is Jerre Mangione's *Mount Allegro: A Memoir of Italian American Life,* recently reissued by Columbia University Press (New York, 1981).

[4] Irvin L. Child, *Italian or American? The Second Generation in Conflict* (New Haven: Yale University Press, 1943).

[5] William F. Whyte, *Street Corner Society: The Social Structure of an Italian Slum* (Chicago: University of Chicago Press, 1943).

[6] Child, *Italian or American?,* p. 88.

[7] Richard Hofstadter, "The pseudo-conservative revolt," in Daniel Bell (ed.), *The Radical Right* (Garden City, N.Y.: Anchor, 1964), p. 90.

[8] Richard Polenberg, *One Nation Divisible: Class, Race, and Ethnicity in the United States since 1938* (New York: Viking, 1980), pp. 46-54.

[9] Ibid., p. 54.

[10] John Morton Blum, *V Was for Victory: Politics and American Culture During World War II* (New York: Harcourt Brace Jovanovich, 1976), p. 63.

[11] Polenberg, *One Nation Divisible,* p. 59.

[12] Ibid., pp. 55-57.

[13] The war literature is surveyed by Blum, *V Was for Victory,* pp. 79-89.

[14] Ibid., p. 91.

[15] Herman P. Miller, *Rich Man, Poor Man* (New York: Thomas Y. Crowell, 1971), pp. 36-41.

[16] The statistics are from the U.S. Bureau of the Census, *Historical Statistics of the United States, Colonial Times to 1970,* Bicentennial edition, Part 1 (Washington, D.C.: U.S. Government Printing Office, 1975), p. 139. Their significance is discussed by Dennis Gilbert and Joseph A. Kahl, *The American Class Structure: A New Synthesis* (Homewood, Ill.: Dorsey Press, 1981), pp. 72-78.

[17] Martin Trow, "The second transformation of American secondary education," *International Journal of Comparative Sociology,* 2 (1961), 144-66.

[18] Thomas M. Stanback, Jr., and Richard V. Knight, *The Metropolitan Economy: The Process of Employment Expansion* (New York: Columbia University Press, 1970), p. 1; Brian Berry and John Kasarda, *Contemporary Urban Ecology* (New York: Macmillan, 1977), Chapter 12.

[19] Andrew Greeley, *Ethnicity in the United States: A Preliminary Reconnaissance* (New York: John Wiley, 1974), Chapter 3; *The American Catholic: A Social Portrait* (New York: Basic Books, 1977), Chapter 2.

[20] Stanley Lieberson, *A Piece of the Pie: Blacks and White Immigrants since 1880* (Berkeley: University of California Press, 1980), pp. 200-06, 328-32.

[21] Samuel Lubell, *The Future of American Politics,* third edition, revised (New York: Harper & Row, 1965), pp. 79-80.

[22] Two general discussions of the prerequisites of political achievement, with specific references to Italians, are by Lubell, *The Future of American Politics,* pp. 76-83; and by Lieberson, *A Piece of the Pie,* pp. 77-85.

[23] La Guardia, moreover, was hardly a typical Italian American. He was half Jewish in ancestry, a Protestant in his own religion, and a Republican in politics. See Humbert S. Nelli, *From Immigrants to Ethnics: The Italian Americans* (Oxford: Oxford University Press, 1983), pp. 109-13; and Salvatore J. LaGumina, "Case studies of ethnicity and Italo-American politicians," in Silvano M. Tomasi and Madeline H. Engel (eds.), *The Italian Experience in the United States* (Staten Island: Center for Migration Studies, 1970).

[24] Lubell, *The Future of American Politics,* p. 76; Lieberson, *A Piece of the Pie,* p. 80.

[25] Lubell, *The Future of American Politics,* p. 77.

[26] Richard D. Alba and Gwen Moore, "Ethnicity in the American elite," *American Sociological Review*, 47, No. 3 (June, 1982), 373-83.

[27] Rudolph J. Vecoli, "The coming of age of the Italian Americans: 1945-1974," *Ethnicity*, 5, No. 2 (June, 1978), 141. Herbert J. Gans, *The Urban Villagers: Group and Class in the Life of Italian Americans*, updated and expanded edition (New York: Free Press, 1982), Chapter 8.

[28] Nathan Glazer and Daniel Patrick Moynihan, *Beyond the Melting Pot*, second edition (Cambridge, Mass.: MIT Press, 1970), pp. 214-16.

[29] This is a conclusion that stands out from the election results reported by Mark R. Levy and Michael S. Kramer, *The Ethnic Factor: How America's Minorities Decide Elections* (New York: Simon & Schuster, 1972), pp. 178-83.

[30] Quoted by Jerre Mangione, *Mount Allegro*, p. 307.

[31] For statements of this view, see Vecoli, "The coming of age," pp. 124-26; and Glazer and Moynihan, *Beyond the Melting Pot*, pp. 186-90.

[32] U.S. Bureau of the Census, *National origin and language*, 1970 Census of Population: Subject Reports, Report PC(2)-1A (Washington, D.C.: U.S. Government Printing Office, 1973), pp. 6, 89.

[33] Avery M. Guest and James A. Weed, "Ethnic residential segregation: Patterns of change," *American Journal of Sociology*, 81, No. 5 (March, 1976), 1088-111. For an interpretation emphasizing the durability of segregation, see Nathan M. Kantrowitz, *Ethnic and Racial Segregation in the New York Metropolis: Residential Patterns among White Ethnic Groups, Blacks, and Puerto Ricans* (New York: Praeger, 1973).

[34] Polenberg, *One Nation Divisible*, pp. 127-39, provides a compact discussion of suburbanization.

[35] Joan Fee, "Political continuity and change," in Andrew M. Greeley, William C. McCready, and Kathleen McCourt, *Catholic Schools in a Declining Church* (Kansas City: Sheed & Ward, 1976), pp. 88-89.

[36] These figures are for what the Census Bureau calls the "New York, N.Y.-Northeastern New Jersey Standard Consolidated Area," which includes a number of large cities, most importantly New York City and Newark, and their suburbs, stretching from Long Island to nearly the Pennsylvania border. In 1970, the total population of this area was over 16 million, and it contained 1.4 million first- and second-generation Italian Americans, nearly a third of those counted by the Census.

The figures in the text are my calculations from data presented in Tables 17, 23, and 81 of the *1970 Census of Population, Volume I, Characteristics of the Population*, Parts 32 and 34 (Washington, D.C.: U.S. Government Printing Office, 1973).

[37] Herbert J. Gans, *The Levittowners: Ways of Life and Politics in a New Suburban Community* (New York: Pantheon, 1967), p. 24.

[38] Andrew M. Greeley, *Why Can't They Be Like Us?* (New York: Dutton, 1971), Chapter 9. Polenberg, *One Nation Divisible*, pp. 144-50, also advances the argument I am making.

[39] Richard D. Alba, "Social assimilation among American Catholic national-origin groups," *American Sociological Review*, 41, No. 6 (December, 1976), 1030-46; Richard D. Alba and Ronald C. Kessler, "Patterns of interethnic marriage among American Catholics," *Social Forces*, 57, No. 4 (June, 1979), 1124-40. Intermarriage is also discussed with use of these data by Harold J. Abramson, *Ethnic Diversity in Catholic America* (New York: John Wiley, 1973).

[40] Joseph Lopreato, *Italian Americans* (New York: Random House, 1970), pp. 56-57; Vecoli, "The coming of age," p. 135.

[41] U.S. Bureau of the Census, *Ancestry and language in the United States: November 1979*, Current Population Reports, Special Studies, Series P-23, No. 116 (Washington, D.C.: U.S. Government Printing Office, 1982), p. 14. Valuable as a general reference on languages other than English in the United States is a book by Joshua Fishman and others, *Language Loyalty in the United States* (The Hague: Mouton, 1966).

[42] Leonard Covello, *The Social Background of the Italo-American School Child* (Totowa,

N.J.: Rowman & Littlefield, 1972), Chapter 5; Richard Gambino, *Blood of My Blood* (Garden City, N.Y.: Anchor, 1975), pp. 212-44.

[43] Andrew M. Greeley and Peter H. Rossi, *The Education of Catholic Americans* (Chicago: Aldine, 1966), pp. 36-37; for a comprehensive account of ethnic differences in Catholic religious behavior, see Abramson, *Ethnic Diversity*, Chapters 5 and 6.

[44] Nelli, *From Immigrant to Ethnic*, pp. 127-29; Silvano M. Tomasi, "The ethnic church and the integration of Italian immigrants in the United States," in Tomasi and Engel, *The Italian Experience.*

[45] Francis X. Femminella, "The impact of Italian migration and American Catholicism," *American Catholic Sociological Review*, 22, No. 3 (Fall, 1961), 233-41.

[46] Nicholas John Russo, "Three generations of Italians in New York City: Their religious acculturation," in Tomasi and Engel, *The Italian Experience*; Greeley and Rossi, *The Education of Catholic Americans*, pp. 38-40.

[47] Gambino, *Blood of My Blood*, pp. 232, 239; Stephen S. Hall, "Italian-Americans: Coming into their own," *The New York Times Magazine*, May 15, 1983, p. 42.

[48] Gans's classic study was reissued in 1982 in an updated and expanded edition by the Free Press, and all references are to this edition.

A general review of the literature on the Italian-American family, which I have also drawn on for this section, is by Francis X. Femminella and Jill S. Quadagno, "The Italian American family," in Charles H. Mindell and Robert W. Haberstein (eds.), *Ethnic Families in America: Patterns and Variations* (New York: Elsevier, 1976).

[49] Sensitive accounts of some of the nuances of Italian-American family life are found in Gambino, *Blood of My Blood*, and in Elizabeth Stone, "It's still hard to grow up Italian," *The New York Times Magazine*, December 17, 1978, pp. 42-104.

[50] Gans, *The Urban Villagers*, pp. 36-41, Chapter 4.

[51] Greeley, *Why Can't They Be Like Us?*, pp. 77-78; Greeley, *The American Catholic*, pp. 191-94.

[52] Greeley, *Ethnicity*, pp. 45-46; and Femminella and Quadagno, "The Italian American family," p. 74. The figure pertains to marital status at the time of the interview and does not mean that only 2 percent had ever been divorced.

[53] Gans, *The Urban Villagers*, Chapter 3.

[54] Ibid., p. 59.

[55] Gambino, *Blood of My Blood*, pp. 129-30; on male reserve in the West End, see Gans, *The Urban Villagers*, p. 48.

[56] Femminella and Quadagno, "The Italian American family," pp. 75-76.

[57] No approval of crime is intended by this description. It is merely meant to emphasize that organized crime is not something alien or separate from society but integrally a part of it.

[58] This section leans heavily on the account by Humbert S. Nelli, *The Business of Crime: Italians and Syndicate Crime in the United States* (New York: Oxford University Press, 1976). The phrase "Americanization of the mobs" is attributed by Nelli to the underworld (p. 179).

[59] Ibid., Chapter 7.

[60] Leonard Katz, *Uncle Frank: The Biography of Frank Costello* (New York: Pocket Books, 1975), p. viii.

[61] Nelli, *The Business of Crime*, Chapters 6 and 7.

[62] Ibid., pp. 207-12.

[63] Ibid., Chapter 8.

[64] For skeptical reviews, see Dwight C. Smith, Jr., and Richard D. Alba, "Organized crime and American life," *Society*, 16, No. 3 (March/April, 1979), 32-38; Dwight C. Smith, Jr., *The Mafia Mystique* (New York: Basic Books, 1975); Joseph L. Albini, *The American Mafia: Genesis of a Legend* (New York: Appleton-Century-Crofts, 1971); Alan Block, *East Side-West Side: Organizing Crime in New York, 1930-1950* (Cardiff, Wales: University College Cardiff Press, 1980); and Nelli, *The Business of Crime.*

[65]Nelli, *The Business of Crime,* pp. 179-84; Block, *East Side-West Side,* pp. 3-9.

[66]Noel F. Busch, "Joe DiMaggio: Baseball's most sensational big-league star starts what should be his best year so far," *Life,* May 1, 1939, 62-69. © 1939, Times Inc. Reprinted with permission.

[67]Maury Allen, *Where Have You Gone, Joe DiMaggio? The Story of America's Last Hero* (New York: Dutton, 1975).

[68]For example, Nathan Glazer, *Affirmative Discrimination: Ethnic Inequality and Public Policy* (New York: Basic Books, 1975).

CHAPTER FIVE
THE DEMOGRAPHY
OF ITALIAN AMERICANS

In this and the succeeding chapter, we will give close scrutiny to the present place of the Italian group in American society, focusing especially on its distinctiveness. The broad issues concern the social mobility and assimilation of Italian Americans; these issues are pointed toward the question, Is Italian-American ethnicity destined to be a permanent feature of American life? This is the larger puzzle at stake in such specific questions as, Is the educational and occupational achievement of Italians different from that of other Americans? Do they retain ethnic cultural traits—in family-linked values, attitudes, and behaviors, for example? Do they maintain strong social ties to the group?

First, it is necessary to describe the kinds of data that can be brought to bear on such questions, to clarify the strengths and limitations of each type, and, even more important, the possible inconsistencies among them. Anyone who reads deeply in the literature on Italian Americans or any other white ethnic group will come away amazed at the apparent contradictions among different studies. Frequently, the contradictions are more superficial than real because they stem from subtle inconsistencies in research design and type of data, rather than in the social realities reflected or, perhaps better put, refracted through the research. One of the major inconsistencies, oddly enough, lies in the way the boundaries of an ethnic group are drawn by questions tapping ethnic identification. National ancestry is no longer as salient a social characteristic for white Americans as it was only half a century ago; and further complications are added by the fact that many Americans have more than one nationality in their family background. (In fact, according to a 1979 Census Bureau study, nearly half of Americans who reported specific national ancestry claimed ancestry from more than one group.)[1] Consequently, the precise way in which questions about ethnic background are posed and the manner in which the identifying information volunteered by individuals is handled (e.g., how are individuals with mixed ancestry classified?) can have a significant effect on the conclusions drawn from the research.

TYPES OF ETHNICITY DATA

One of the major data types used in ethnic research is *decennial census data*. As the name indicates, these data are taken from the surveys conducted every ten years with the American population by the Bureau of the Census. Census data provide the basis for studies of ethnic segregation and are frequently used in characterizing the educational and occupational achievements of ethnic groups.

Data from a decennial census survey have one enormous appeal: They provide enough members of an ancestry group for very detailed analysis. Tables from a census are sometimes based on a complete count of the entire American population or that of a very large area; and even tables constructed from census samples are generally based on huge samples that contain thousands of persons from a single ethnic group. As a result, one can look at the characteristics of interesting subgroups, such as Italian Americans in large cities born after 1945, with confidence that the numbers in the subgroups are sufficient to support the conclusions.

But this advantage is more than outweighed by some severe drawbacks. For one, the range of information collected by decennial censuses is very restricted. Censuses do not, for example, contain any direct questions about beliefs, attitudes, and values (and perhaps should not, since government prying into beliefs could potentially have a political character). Hence, census data do not permit any sensitive scrutiny of ethnic cultural persistence; their strength lies in the realm of standard demographic characteristics, such as occupation, marital status, and family size.

One restriction is worth singling out, although it is not critical for the study of Italian Americans. Census data contain no information about religion because government probes about religion would, in the eyes of many, violate the separation of church and state. Since Italians are a largely Catholic group, religious data are not essential to a social portrait of them. But religion is in general an essential ingredient in the social definition of many American ethnic groups, and consequently the lack of religious information in the census weakens the delineation of reference groups against which to compare Italian Americans. An obvious case in point is the quintessential American core group, so-called white Anglo-Saxon Protestants.

Another drawback has been crippling in the past. Before the 1980 census, the Census Bureau did not count the third and later generations of an ethnic group. Ethnic ancestry was determined by the places of birth of an individual and his or her parents. The Census Bureau counted in the Italian ancestry group only those persons who were born in Italy or had at least one parent born there. These first two generations in the United States constituted what was called the "foreign stock," and all others, regardless of ancestry, were placed in the catch-all category of native born of native-born parents. For the first half of this century, this limitation had little or no impact on findings concerning Italian Americans because the uncounted third generation was practically nonexistent, at least among adults. But this no longer held for the censuses of 1960 and 1970, when the number of third-generation Italian Americans who had reached maturity was growing and significant. Their absence from the census statistics for Italian Americans biased the results in the direction of lower apparent socioeconomic achievement and assimilation.

The 1980 census finally did ask for the first time a general question about ethnic ancestry (the question was not asked of everyone, but of an approximately 20 percent sample). Suitably, the question was a straightforward one about national ancestry, rather than ethnic identity; asking about the latter causes many persons to place themselves outside of the ethnic classification because they do not think of themselves, at least not most of the time, as belonging to an ethnic group. Another virtue of the census format was that it did not constrain answers to the question about ancestry by providing respondents with a predefined list of ethnic categories into which they had to fit their backgrounds; such lists force many persons with mixed ethnic ancestry to place themselves in a residual category (usually labeled "other") because a single-ancestry category doesn't seem quite right. The census in fact recorded mixed ancestry as such. The 1980 census will undoubtedly provide an important source of data for scholars of ethnicity for years to come, but for the purpose of constructing a portrait of Italians it suffers from an important drawback: the second and later generations cannot be distinguished from one another; only the immigrant generation is separately identifiable. (Oddly, this makes the 1980 census not comparable to any previous ones.)

Another kind of data collected by the Census Bureau is sometimes more useful than the decennial census. Every month, the Bureau conducts a Current Population Survey (CPS) to gather information about unemployment and work. The monthly survey is done on only a sample of households, not the whole population, but the sample is large enough to provide generous numbers for many subgroups. Occasionally, the survey asks questions about ethnic background, and later in this chapter, I will use data from a particularly valuable Current Population Survey, that of November, 1979. This survey employed the same ancestry question as the 1980 census;[2] and, in addition, it collected sufficient information to identify key generational groups. Nonetheless, the data from this survey, useful as they are, are still limited by the facts that religion is not recorded and that census surveys ask questions on a restricted range of topics.

A third source of data, public-opinion polls, is essential to the study of ethnicity. These polls do not follow a standard format because they are created by different survey organizations and conducted for varied purposes; nonetheless, they frequently inquire about ethnic background, religion, and much else besides. Of course, their questions about ethnic background must be scrutinized as to their merits, just as with census surveys. Public-opinion polls almost always ask for the standard demographic information, such as education and marital status; hence, they cover some of the same ground as the census surveys. But they also include questions tapping directly into cultural phenomena. Depending on the purposes of the survey, these might inquire about political identification, attitudes toward abortion, or the raising of children. Consequently, such surveys permit a more thorough examination of ethnic differences than is possible with census data.

One additional factor must be taken into account in assessing the value of a public-opinion poll for this purpose: namely, whether it employed a random sampling scheme or, because it was designed for the study of a specific ethnic group, whether it was based on a sampling strategy intended to be efficient in locating this group's members. Such strategies are used because the number of any group's members in a random sample of the national population is usually small. But the logic of these strategies usually is to look for concentrations of group members, and hence they inherently favor the less assimilated members of a group. This is true, for example, when samples are gathered in neighborhoods known to contain many Italian Americans because the residents tend to be persons with stronger group ties, or for much the same reason when a sample is taken from names supplied by leaders of Italian-American organizations.

Random samples are therefore preferable, but the difficulty of numbers still remains. The typical sample size of national surveys is between 1,500 and 2,000, and consequently, the representation of any single ethnic group is tiny, destroying confidence in conclusions about its characteristics. The typical survey sample contains fewer than 100 Italian Americans, and the sizes of many critical subgroups (Italian-American women, the third generation, etc.) are necessarily smaller. To overcome this impediment, several surveys must be combined to create a larger pool of ethnic respondents, and this is what I have done here.

The data used for the bulk of this and the next chapter are taken from the annual General Social Survey, carried out by the National Opinion Research Center (NORC), affiliated with the University of Chicago. The General Social Survey is, as its name implies, an omnibus survey, including a variety of topics within its compass. To attain a large sample of Italian Americans, I have combined the surveys from the years 1975-80.[3] The resulting statistical portrait should be interpreted as characteristic of Italian Americans in the late 1970s, although since gross change comes slowly for a large ethnic group, the portrait should remain reasonably accurate through the 1980s and perhaps even later.

WHO COUNTS AS AN ITALIAN AMERICAN?

That this question arises at all reflects the impact of rising intermarriage rates in the 1950s and 60s and the way in which the children of such marriages think about their ethnic background and consequently respond to inquiries about it. That the question can be given different answers—as, in fact, it can—results from the fact that surveys frame their ethnic inquiries in different ways, yielding different numbers of ethnic adherents.

One answer is provided by the 1980 census and the November, 1979, Current Population Survey, both of which asked for each member of a household, "What is . . . 's ancestry?" As noted before, responses were not constrained by a predefined list of categories, and multiple ancestry was recorded. A somewhat different answer is yielded by the General Social Survey. It too begins with a general question about ethnic background, "From what countries or part of the world did your ancestors come?" Again, the survey does not present any predetermined list of countries, and it is thus easier for the respondent to name more than one if he or she has mixed ancestry. But then the surveys part ways. The General Social Survey asks the respondent who cites more than one country, "Which of these countries do you feel closer to?" and the answer, if one is given, is recorded as the person's ancestry. No similar question is asked by the Census Bureau surveys. Obviously, then, the big difference between the survey types lies in the handling of mixed ancestry. Wherever possible, the General Social Survey singles out one nationality strand on the basis of a person's attachment to a single ethnic group, although the fact that he or she has other ancestry is also retained; the two Census Bureau surveys, on the other hand, treated the reported ethnic ingredients in a mixture as equal.[4]

The census surveys' definition of an ancestry group was more inclusive, and an apparently larger Italian-American group was the result. The Census Bureau estimated that in 1980 about 12 million persons in the United States claimed some Italian ancestry, and that they constituted 5.4 percent of the total population.[5] If the figures are limited to adults, defined as those 18 years of age or older, 8.5 million Americans were of Italian background, approximately 5.2 percent of adult Americans. The Italian group is a large ancestry group, but it falls far short of the sizes of the three largest, German, Irish, and English. In 1980, English and German origins each had approximately 50 million claimants, and Irish ancestry was cited by an estimated 40 million people.[6]

Italian Americans made up 4.7 percent of the combined samples from the General Social Survey, which is limited to adult Americans. Applying this percentage to the size of the adult American population yields an estimated 7.7 million Italian Americans; however, this figure should not be fixed on too rigidly, because even the size of the combined samples is not large enough to minimize statistical error. In any event, there is some discrepancy between the two methods of counting the group, and one reason is undoubtedly that not all individuals of partly Italian ancestry identify with it. Comparing the two estimates of the number of Italian-American adults implies that nonidentification among those of mixed ancestry may have reduced the group's potential size by 10 percent in the late 1970s (again, caution is warranted as a result of possible statistical imprecision). Looking at the discrepancy in another way—as a percentage of the entire part-Italian group—suggests, but does not prove, that a majority of individuals with mixed ancestry did identify as Italians.

Even if such a majority is real and persists, the discrepancy between the size of the population with at least some Italian ancestry and the number of persons who identify in some sense with the Italian-American group is bound to increase. The reason is that as a result of the increased intermarriage of the past few decades, the porportion of persons with mixed Italian ancestry is rising, and correspondingly, the proportion with solely Italian ancestry is shrinking. This is documented decisively by the relationship of ancestry type to age, presented in Table 5-1. The data are taken from the Current Population Survey and include all persons who reported any Italian ancestry. In older cohorts, persons with solely Italian ancestry substantially outnumber those of partly Italian ancestry, but the situation is reversed among the younger groups. Nearly 90 percent of the group aged 55 to 64 in 1979 was made of individuals of entirely Italian parentage, while individuals with such undivided ancestry were only 40 percent of the group aged 18 to 24 and sank to 20 percent of the group under 14.

These dramatic figures reveal that a tremendous swing in the nature of the Italian-ancestry group is fated to take place by the end of this century, as members of older cohorts, for the most part of unmixed ancestry, die and are replaced in the group by younger persons reaching maturity. The table depicts unambiguously the

TABLE 5-1 Type of Ancestry by Age among Persons of Italian Descent (1979)

	PERCENTAGE WITH MIXED ITALIAN ANCESTRY
All ages	48.0[a]
65 and over	5.9
55 to 64	11.4
45 to 54	18.5
35 to 44	36.1
25 to 34	48.1
18 to 24	60.5
14 to 17	71.3
5 to 13	77.8
Under 5	81.5

[a]The 1980 census estimate of the percentage of Italians with mixed ancestry is somewhat lower, 43.5 percent (see footnote 2).

SOURCE: November, 1979, Current Population Survey, reported in *Ancestry and Language in the United States: November 1979,* Current Population Reports, Special Studies, Series P-23, No. 116 (Washington, D.C.: U.S. Government Printing Office, 1982), Table 2.

concentration of mixed ancestry among those who were under 25 in 1979, but there is an even more startling way of making the same point. In the Current Population Survey, persons with only Italian ancestry made up two-thirds of the adult ancestry group, a comfortable majority.[7] But counting individuals of all ages, including children, they were a bare majority, 52 percent. In other words, by 1980, a scant century after the onset of mass Italian immigration, close to half of the entire ancestry group was composed of individuals who had one non-Italian parent.

The size of the emerging mixed-ancestry group sharpens the question of who should be counted as an Italian American. On the face of things, it makes little sense to include in the group individuals with mixed ancestry who do not identify themselves with the group. Their connection with the group is questionable; and in fact for some, Italian ancestry is just one element in a complex ethnic stew. For instance, the Census Bureau estimates from its 1980 figures that German-Irish-Italian ancestry (in alphabetic, not necessarily ethnic, order) is one of the most frequently named three-component ancestry combinations, possessed by close to a quarter million people.[8] Consequently, for most of this discussion, the Italian-American group is taken to include only individuals of wholly Italian parentage and those of mixed ancestry who feel closer to the Italian than to the other ethnic parts of their background. This requires reliance on the General Social Survey, since it, and not the census surveys, inquired about ethnic identification of respondents with mixed ethnic ancestry.

This narrowing of the group's definition does not, however, dispose of the issue of mixed ancestry and its significance. Among adult Italian Americans defined this way, nearly a quarter (23 percent, to be precise) have mixed ancestry; as Table 5-1 implies, this figure represents an increase from the recent past and will surely itself increase in the near future. Individuals with mixed ancestry who identify with an ethnic group hold a double-edged significance for it. On the one hand, the fact that they continue to identify with the group limits somewhat its losses through intermarriage. On the other hand, individuals whose parents are from different ethnic backgrounds (possibly also mixed) are unlikely to possess a group's cultural values to the same degree as those raised in a more homogeneous environment; and by virtue of the ultimate ambiguity of their own ancestry, they are unlikely to feel as strong an allegiance to any single group. In short, although individuals of mixed heritage may help to maintain the numerical strength of a group, they represent a potential dilution of ethnicity.[9]

A few words about religion are needed to close out the discussion. Religion is inextricably bound up with the definitions of many American ethnic groups. Irish Catholics, for example, must be distinguished from Irish Protestants, since these two groups entered the United States in different periods, settled in different places, and are distinguishable in a variety of ways, from politics to educational achievement.[10] Therefore, in defining groups to compare against Italian Americans, to chart the latter's shifting place, it is often desirable if not necessary to include religion (the religion in which a person was raised, in deference to the notion of ethnic *origins*, rather than current religion). But this seems undesirable for defining the Italian group, if only because this book concerns Italian Americans, whatever their religion. (Also, limiting the Italian group to persons raised as Catholics might bias the results a bit, by excluding some relatively acculturated Italian Americans who have been raised as Protestants.) In any event, the Italian-American group remains heavily Catholic. Over 90 percent of Italian Americans in the combined General Social Survey samples were raised as Catholics, and 80 percent called themselves Catholics at the time they were surveyed.

GENERATIONAL STRUCTURE

Even in the late 1970s, nearly a full century after the beginning of large-scale Italian immigration, most adult Italian Americans were still within living memory of the immigration experience. This is shown by Table 5-2, which presents selected demographic characteristics of the group. Almost half (precisely, 48 percent of the combined samples) belonged to the second generation, having had at least one immigrant parent. Another 10 percent were themselves immigrants. In other words, almost 60 percent belonged to the first two generations on American shores and were raised in Italy or an immigrant home.[11] In addition, one-third had at least one immigrant grandparent and were classified in the third generation. Only 7 percent had all American-born grandparents, putting them in the fourth or a later generation. By contrast, three-quarters of Protestants with ancestry from the British Isles (WASPs, in colloquial terms) belonged to the fourth and later generations, while under 10 percent were members of the earliest two. The contrast is strong even with Irish Catholics, whose ethnic presence is still visible in many American cities. In essence, the Irish are a generation ahead of the Italians: in the late 1970s, half belonged to the third generation, and a third belonged to later ones.

Change in this generational structure is imminent. As is true for ancestry type, generation is sharply related to birth cohort: those born recently are quite likely to belong to the third or a later generation, while those born earlier are quite unlikely. In fact, hardly any members of the third and later generations are to be found among the Italian Americans born before 1930 (these figures are not shown in the table). On the other hand, among the Italians born after World War II—limiting the generalization to those who were 18 or older by the late 1970s and are therefore represented in the data—more than three-quarters belonged to the third or a later generation. The fourth generation is small even in this recent cohort; only 16 percent belong to it. The transition underway, then, is from a predominantly second-generation group to a largely third-generation group. Consequently, it will remain true for the rest of this century that the bulk of adult Italian Americans are within living memory of immigration, having at least one immigrant grandparent.

Nonetheless, this shifting generational structure has many ramifications. The concentration of Italian Americans in the two earliest generations helps to explain why the group remains so visible on the American scene. Ethnic cultural insignia

TABLE 5-2   Selected Characteristics of Italian Americans in the Late 1970s (Restricted to Individuals Eighteen Years of Age and Older)

	ITALIANS	ALL AMERICANS
Generation		
First	10.6%	6.3%
Second	48.5%	13.6%
Third	33.8%	23.8%
Fourth or later	7.1%	56.3%
Birth cohort		
Before WW I	15.2%	17.9%
1914–29	25.0%	23.8%
1930–45	26.7%	27.2%
After WW II	33.0%	31.1%
Region		
New England	14.6%	4.3%
Middle Atlantic	44.3%	16.9%
Midwest	18.3%	28.8%
South	11.1%	33.1%
West	11.7%	17.0%
Size of place		
Within an SMSA with a large central city[a]	62.6%	42.9%
Central city	22.3%	18.7%
Suburbs	28.0%	16.2%
Other parts	12.3%	8.0%
Within an SMSA with a medium-sized central city[b]	20.6%	23.9%
Central city	10.0%	10.2%
Suburbs	6.9%	6.5%
Other parts	3.7%	7.2%
Small city[c]	2.9%	6.2%
Smaller places[d]	14.0%	27.0%

[a] SMSAs, or Standard Metropolitan Statistical Areas, are defined by the Bureau of the Census as large population agglomerations that form integrated social and economic communities. The specific areas that have received this designation are identified in the annual volumes of *Statistical Abstracts.*

A large central city is a city within such an area that contains a population of more than a quarter million.

[b] A medium-sized central city is one with a population in the range 50,000–250,000.

[c] A small city has a population in the range 10,000–49,999.

[d] Places with population under 10,000.

SOURCE: Tabulations from the NORC General Social Survey, 1975–80. Italian Americans are defined in the data as individuals who either are of wholly Italian ancestry or identify more closely with the Italian side of their ancestry in the event that they are of mixed parentage.

are likely to be prominent on individuals reared in the Old World or in immigrant homes; and these individuals are more likely than others to reside in ethnic neighborhoods, thereby creating the pockets of more intense ethnicity that can be found in many American cities. But the impending generational transition implies that this ethnic distinctiveness is likely to fade in the near future. Generally speaking, generational shifts are an important source of change among ethnic groups because each new generation represents a further step away from the point of immigration and toward accommodation with the host society. The transition from the second to the third generation is especially portentous: The third generation is the first not raised under the direct influence of the Old World, which it sees only through its grandparents. Consequently, its adherence to ethnic culture is likely to be thinner, shallower than that of its predecessors, although, paradoxically, because it feels more secure in its place in American society, it may be more confident in asserting its ethnic identity.

The changing generational composition of the group is implicated in the dramatic changes in mixed ancestry among Italians, as reported in Table 5-1. Intermarriage rates are usually higher, the later the generation; and the same is true for the proportion having mixed ancestry.[12] Even within the narrowly defined Italian-American group, mixed ancestry is strongly related to generational status. Only about 5 percent of the first two generations have mixed ancestry, but the proportion leaps to nearly 50 percent in the third and fourth generations. Consequently, as the generational structure shifts, the proportion of Italian Americans who have a non-Italian parent is bound to rise.

GEOGRAPHICAL DISTRIBUTION

Besides generation, another factor that remains conducive to ethnic solidarity and distinctiveness is geography. Italian Americans are heavily concentrated in just a few areas of the nation. According to Table 5-2, a little less than half (44 percent) reside in the Middle Atlantic states, New York, New Jersey, and Pennsylvania, states where Italians make up 12 percent of the population (in contrast to less than 5 percent nationwide). Fifteen percent of the group is in the New England states, where it makes up an even larger share, 16 percent, of the population. In addition, a substantial fraction, 18 percent, lives in the Midwest, but this is not really a region of concentration, since the group is only 3 percent of the population in these states. There are few Italians in the South, and somewhat more in the Western states, but the group is still underrepresented there.

Italian Americans remain urban dwellers, which they became when they first entered the United States, but they have now spread extensively into suburban areas. More than 80 percent of the group is found within the regions designated by the Bureau of the Census as "Standard Metropolitan Statistical Areas" (or SMSAs) that are centered on substantial-sized cities and their commuting areas—in comparison to only two-thirds of all Americans. Italian Americans are especially prevalent in large SMSAs, those containing central cities with more than a quarter million population. Over 62 percent live in such areas, in contrast to 43 percent of all Americans, but the Italians are no longer concentrated in the central cities themselves. Twenty-two percent are found in central cities with over a quarter million population, while 28 percent are found in their suburbs (another 12 percent are in other parts of these SMSAs). In fact, the density of the group in and around big cities is even more than these figures show. A finer breakdown reveals that 15 percent reside in the central cities of the 12 largest SMSAs, and over 20 percent are in their suburbs. At the other end of the spectrum of size of place, few Italian Americans are represented. Only 14 percent of the group reside in places with populations under 10,000—just half the concentration of all Americans, 27 percent of whom live in such places.

In sum, Italian Americans are located predominantly in the urban and suburban areas of the Northeast. A significant dilution of this presence does not appear near at hand. A comparison of the regional distribution of the second generation to that of the third and fourth reveals some decrease in the proportion living in the New England states but no change in the area of greatest concentration, the Middle Atlantic region. Even with the change, over half of the third and later generations are still in the Northeastern states. A similar pattern of slight shift is visible when Italians born after World War II are compared with older cohorts. No specific region is the major beneficiary, but as among other Americans, there appears to be some dispersal to the Southern and Western states. It is impossible to draw any conclusion about changes in the metropolitan concentration of the group, because there simply isn't any meaningful pattern by generation or cohort indicating change or firm stability.

The geographic concentration of the Italian group illustrates the impact of historical contingencies on American ethnic groups. A century after the beginnings of immigration, the regions in which the group is found in large numbers are the same regions in which immigrants first settled. To be sure, there has been plenty of movement within these broad zones. In large cities, the neighborhoods in which Italian Americans are presently found are not usually the same ones settled by their parents and grandparents. New York City's Little Italy provides an ironic example, because it is now increasingly occupied by Chinese Americans spreading out of Chinatown—even though the commercial streets are still occupied by Italian restaurants and stores, catering to tourists who nostalgically wish to visit an Italian immigrant enclave. In addition to movement within cities, there has been a considerable exodus to the suburbs. But the overall geographic distribution of the group does not resemble the distribution of all Americans.

The legacy of historical settlement patterns holds important consequences for ethnic solidarity. It makes possible substantial-sized ethnic communities, such as are found in many Northeastern cities (e.g., Brooklyn's Red Hook and Boston's North End). These pockets of more intense ethnicity allow individuals to submerge themselves in an ethnic world, reducing their need to accommodate to the larger society. As a result, ethnic communities tend to preserve distinctiveness, and they have an important symbolic function. For more assimilated Italian Americans, they stand as reminders of a recent ethnic past; and for non-Italians, they heighten sensitivity to ethnic differences. For both, then, ethnic communities help to keep ethnicity as a social and personal characteristic in the limelight.

But the Italian geographical concentration has another consequence that tends to counter this influence. All places in the United States are not equal: Most importantly, they have differed in the opportunities they have afforded for mobility. Some regions and cities have been economically more dynamic than others, and in this respect Italian Americans have been fortunately situated, since the urban areas of the Northeast have been among the most vibrant places for the better part of this century (although, to be sure, their luster has been tarnished recently). This means, in the terminology of the last chapter, that the structural mobility engendered by the changing socioeconomic substructure has been most readily available in these places, making them ethnically dynamic as well as economically so. As far as the Italians are concerned, this could be expected to lead to a diminution of their differences from other Americans.

SOCIAL MOBILITY

The issue of mobility remains in the foreground for the Italian group. As early chapters have emphasized, the ancestors of contemporary Italian Americans entered the United States as one of the most despised of European immigrant groups. Coming from the rural and backward Mezzogiorno, Italian immigrants typically took jobs at the very bottom of the labor force, in the ranks of unskilled labor, frequently using only the "peek and shuvil." They were suspicious of education, fearing its potential for disrupting the family system, and often prevented their children from going far in school. To many observers at the time of mass immigration, the Italian group seemed destined for the margins of the economic system, incapable of mobility or assimilation. The view of Italians as socially immobile has persisted into recent times, with some upgrading of imagery, even though there is evidence that they have been catching up with other Americans. According to the current iconography of ethnicity, Italians are the quintessential urban, working-class group. This portrait is found to some extent in the social science literature and is very widespread in the mass media. The obvious question is: Just where do Italians stand?

There are two cardinal indicators of social position. Education is one, because it plays a central role in an advanced industrial society such as our own, being the prime mechanism by which men and women qualify for places in the labor market. Education also has a prominent cultural role, instilling in students the values of standard American culture. In both respects, a fundamental distinction lies between higher education, at colleges and universities, and the preceding stages of the educational system. At present, a college education is usually required to qualify for the professional, technical, and managerial jobs situated in the upper reaches of the occupational system. College education generally has also a potent cultural influence. Colleges and universities often serve as intellectual "hothouses," in which students assimilate new and often critical ways of looking at the world, while dropping some of the traditional ways nurtured in their families and communities.

Occupation is the obvious second indicator. Occupation refers to the kind of work individuals do, whether they are lawyers or plumbers, for instance. Occupation is a key index because the work people do is important for its own sake, often forming a conspicuous element in their social identity and having a variety of subtle impacts on their lives, but also because occupation correlates strongly with income and other benefits that accrue from work, notably prestige. Numerous studies show that a consistent and stable prestige hierarchy attaches to occupations, and this provides one way of measuring occupational status.[13] In addition, two broad categories are useful for tracing changes among Italian Americans: upper white-collar occupations, which include the category of professional and technical occupations and that of managers; and blue-collar occupations, ranging from highly skilled craft occupations to those involving little or no skills and also including service jobs. Although the blue-collar category takes in a very wide spectrum of work, it is still pertinent because it encompasses the working-class occupations often viewed as the special niche of Italians.

Of course, it is essential to have a standard against which to compare Italian Americans in order to delineate cleanly their social position. There have been historical changes in levels of education and occupation—particularly a general uplift in the former—and if these are not taken into account, it is easy to mistake changes that leave the relative position of a group unchanged for changes that indicate more fundamental shifts. For this reason, a comparison of Italians with the amorphous category of all other Americans, a composite of many ethnic strands, would leave the true situation of the group uncertain. Consequently, I have chosen as a comparison group the paragon of the American core, Protestants with ancestry from the British Isles, or WASPs. They provide a demanding standard, since their educational and occupational achievement is higher than that of Americans on average. Nevertheless, one should not confuse this ethnic category with the stereotyped American elite; the poverty-stricken residents of Appalachia are mostly WASPs, just as some Wall Street bankers are. Nor is there any claim implied here that WASPs form a self-conscious ethnic group. Rather, Protestants who trace their ancestry to the British Isles are the prototype of what is *ethnically* American, and thus the comparison with them highlights not only the group's remarkable mobility since World War II, but also the erosion of Italian distinctiveness.

This mobility is not portrayed in the aggregate figures for the two "overall" groups shown in Table 5-3 and 5-4.[14] When Italian-American men and women of all ages and generations are combined, the group lags distinctly behind WASPs. Only a quarter of the Italian group have ever attended college, compared to more than 40 percent of Protestants of British ancestry. A mere 13 percent have attained the baccalaureate; over 20 percent of the group from the British Isles have earned that degree. There is also a marked gap at the upper end of the occupational spectrum. Over a third of the WASPs have professional, technical, and managerial occupations, while less than a quarter of the Italians do. The difference at the lower end, however, is not so great. A somewhat larger percentage of Italians are in blue-collar occupations, where they are concentrated in the middle of the range. Almost half the blue-collar Italians are found in the "operative" category (not shown separately in Table 5-4), which includes the jobs usually described as semi-skilled. About a quarter are in the highly skilled craft occupations, and another quarter are in the service category, which encompasses diverse sorts of jobs, although most are poorly paid and have little prestige. Finally, virtually no Italians are in the ranks of unskilled manual labor. That in itself represents a great change, since these were the jobs in which many immigrants, the parents and grandparents of present-day Italian Americans, began.

The tables also show some other ways of looking at these differences. Italian and British Americans differ in a number of ways that might be expected to give rise to educational and occupational differences between them. In comparison to the Italians, WASPs are concentrated in places that experienced less rapid growth over this century, such as rural areas and the South. But they also come on average from more advantaged families; their parents had better educations and better jobs. It is possible to adjust the ethnic differences in education and occupation for these background dissimilarities through the use of the statistical technique of regression analysis. The result can be interpreted as a comparison between members of the groups who have been set equal in terms of background variables. One column of each table presents such comparisons after adjustment for the region and size of place where an individual was raised and also where he or she currently resides. Age has also been added as a control here because it is related to both education and occupation. A second column presents comparisons after additional adjustment for social background, i.e., mother's and father's educations and father's occupation (mother's occupation is not available in these data). Because regression analysis is most effective on variables that are scales, education is treated in Table 5-3 as years in school (ranging from 0 to 20, the score for those with the most advanced graduate education), and occupation has been converted in Table 5-4 into an occupational prestige score (it stretches from 9, the score for bootblacks, to 82, that for physicians).[15]

The apparent gap between Italians and British Protestants is magnified by adjustment for region and urban-rural concentration. In Table 5-3 the Italian educational deficit of 1 year is nearly doubled by the adjustment, and in Table 5-4 the occupational prestige difference, under 4 points, is increased to 5.5. The precise meaning of the adjusted figures is that, by comparison with WASPs of the same age, raised and residing in the same places, Italian Americans are behind by nearly 2 years of education and nearly 6 points of occupational prestige. In other words, Italians appear even worse off when their concentration in the economically vigorous urban Northeast is taken into account. This same fact can also be put

TABLE 5-3 The Educational Attainment of Italian Americans in the Late 1970s (Restricted to Individuals Older than Twenty-Two)

	PERCENTAGE WITH SOME COLLEGE	PERCENTAGE WITH B.A. OR MORE	AVERAGE YEARS OF EDUCATION	DIFFERENCE FROM WASPS[a]	DIFFERENCE ADJUSTED FOR AGE, PLACE[b]	DIFFERENCE ADJUSTED ALSO FOR FAMILY BACKGROUND[c]
			BOTH SEXES			
Overall						
WASPs	42.4	21.7	12.6	—	—	—
Italians	27.6	12.6	11.6	-1.0*	-1.8*	-.4*
Ancestry type						
Wholly Italian	20.9	9.8	11.2	-1.4*	-2.1*	-.4*
Partly Italian	56.1	24.6	13.4	.8	-1.0*	-.1
Generation[d]						
First	19.0	9.5	9.0	-3.9*	-4.2*	-2.0*
Second	19.4	9.7	11.1	-1.7*	-2.1*	-.3
Third and fourth	41.7	20.0	13.4	.6	-.9*	-.1
Birth cohort						
Before WW I	7.5	3.8	8.6	-2.6*	-3.3*	-.4
1914–29	13.8	5.7	10.8	-1.7*	-2.3*	-.6
1930–45	33.3	14.0	12.7	-.5	-1.3*	.1
After WW II	52.9	26.5	13.5	.1	-.6	.1
			MEN ONLY			
Overall						
WASPs	48.5	25.8	12.9	—	—	—
Italians	43.9	18.0	12.4	-.5	-1.6*	-.3
Ancestry type						
Wholly Italian	35.8	13.8	11.9	-1.0*	-1.8*	-.3
Partly Italian	73.3	33.3	14.1	1.2	-.7	.2
Generation[d]						
First	33.3	11.1	10.3	-2.8*	-3.8*	-2.1*
Second	35.1	13.5	11.8	-1.3*	-1.6*	-.3
Third and fourth	57.1	28.6	14.0	.8	-.7	.1

Birth cohort					
Before WW I	10.0	5.0	9.2	−2.1*	−2.8*	.1
1914–29	27.9	11.6	11.6	−.9	−1.7*	−.1
1930–45	53.5	18.6	13.3	.3	−1.6*	−.1
After WW II	72.7	33.3	14.3	.1	.4	.2

WOMEN ONLY

Overall					
WASPs	37.3	18.5	12.4	—	—	
Italians	13.6	8.0	10.9	−1.5*	−2.1*	−.5*
Ancestry type					
Wholly Italian	8.9	6.7	10.6	−1.8*	−2.2*	−.5*
Partly Italian	37.0	14.8	12.6	.2	−1.5*	.7
Generation[d]					
First	8.3	8.3	7.9	−4.6*	−4.8*	−2.1*
Second	8.9	7.1	10.6	−2.0*	−2.4*	−.6
Third and fourth	28.1	12.5	12.9	.4	−1.1*	−.4
Birth cohort					
Before WW I	6.1	3.0	8.2	−2.9*	−3.5*	−.4
1914–29	0.0	0.0	10.0	−2.4*	−2.9*	−1.0*
1930–45	16.0	10.0	12.2	−.8	−1.3*	.1
After WW II	34.3	20.0	12.8	−.3	−.7	−.0

[a] In all cases but that of birth cohorts, the comparison is with the overall figure for British Protestants. In the case of birth cohorts, the comparison is with the average education of WASPs in the same cohort (the WASP figures by cohort, however, are not shown in the table to conserve space).

[b] The variables for which adjustments have been made include age, region where raised, current region, size of place where raised, current size of place.

[c] In addition to the age and place variables, adjustment has been made for father's and mother's educations and father's occupation.

[d] The generation variable is restricted to the survey years 1977–80, and for this reason the overall WASP figures used in calculating differences are slightly higher than those reported in the table.

NOTE: Asterisk (*) indicates statistical significance.

SOURCE: Tabulations from NORC General Social Survey, 1975–80.

TABLE 5-4 The Occupational Attainment of Italian Americans in the Late 1970s (Restricted to Individuals Older than Twenty-Two)

	PERCENTAGE HIGH WHITE COLLAR	PERCENTAGE BLUE COLLAR[a]	AVERAGE PRESTIGE	DIFFERENCE FROM WASPS[b]	DIFFERENCE ADJUSTED FOR AGE, PLACE[c]	DIFFERENCE ADJUSTED ALSO FOR FAMILY BACKGROUND[d]
			BOTH SEXES			
Overall						
WASPs	34.7	37.9	42.5	—	—	—
Italians	23.6	46.2	38.8	− 3.7*	− 5.5*	−1.1
Ancestry type						
Wholly Italian	20.6	49.4	38.0	− 4.5*	− 6.1*	−1.2
Partly Italian	36.4	32.7	42.0	− .5	− 2.8	− .2
Generation[e]						
First	20.0	65.0	34.3	− 9.0*	−11.0*	−5.3
Second	22.5	53.9	36.8	− 6.4*	− 8.0*	−3.0*
Third and fourth	28.8	39.0	42.5	− .7	− 2.6	− .4
Birth cohort						
Before WW I	11.8	66.7	33.5	− 9.1*	− 9.4*	−2.3
1914–29	18.1	51.8	36.5	− 5.3*	− 6.9*	−1.6
1930–45	33.7	33.7	42.6	− .5	− 2.4	2.3
After WW II	26.2	40.0	40.5	− 2.0	− 4.1*	−2.0
			MEN ONLY			
Overall						
WASPS	37.0	46.3	43.2	—	—	—
Italians	34.5	51.8	40.4	− 2.8*	− 4.8*	−1.2
Ancestry type						
Wholly Italian	31.2	55.0	39.4	− 3.9*	− 5.8*	−1.9
Partly Italian	46.7	40.0	44.1	.9	− 1.0	1.7
Generation[e]						
First	33.3	66.7	38.3	− 5.2	8.4	−4.5
Second	37.8	59.5	38.9	− 4.6*	− 5.9*	−2.1
Third and fourth	35.7	53.6	42.3	− 1.2	2.5	− .8

Birth cohort						
Before WW I	20.0	70.0	35.7	− 7.7*	− 6.5*	.2
1914–29	30.2	55.8	38.4	− 5.1*	− 6.3*	−2.4
1930–45	48.8	39.5	44.6	.3	3.2	.4
After WW II	30.3	51.5	40.3	.9	2.8	−1.0

WOMEN ONLY

Overall						
WASPS	32.6	30.1	41.8	—	—	—
Italians	13.4	40.9	37.3	− 4.5*	− 6.4*	−1.1
Ancestry type						
Wholly Italian	11.3	44.4	36.8	− 5.0*	− 6.6*	− .6
Partly Italian	24.0	24.0	39.5	2.3	5.4	−2.9
Generation[e]						
First	9.1	63.6	30.9	−12.0*	−13.9*	−5.2
Second	11.5	50.0	35.3	− 7.6*	− 9.9*	−4.1*
Third and fourth	22.6	25.8	42.7	.2	2.5	− .1
Birth cohort						
Before WW I	6.5	64.5	32.1	− 9.9*	−11.0*	−3.4
1914–29	5.0	47.5	34.5	− 5.8*	− 7.6*	− .9
1930–45	19.6	28.3	40.8	1.1	2.0	3.6
After WW II	21.9	28.1	40.7	2.9	5.0	−2.7

[a] Service occupations have been included in the blue-collar category.

[b] In all cases but that of birth cohorts, the comparison is with the overall figure for British Protestants. In the case of birth cohorts, the comparison is with the average occupation of WASPs in the same cohort (the WASP figures by cohort, however, are not shown in the table to conserve space).

[c] The variables for which adjustments have been made include age, region where raised, current region, size of place where raised, current size of place.

[d] In addition to the age and place variables, adjustment has been made for father's and mother's educations and father's occupation.

[e] The generation variable is restricted to the survey years 1977–80, and for this reason the overall WASP figures are slightly different from those reported in the table.

NOTE: Asterisk (*) indicates statistical significance.

SOURCE: Tabulations from NORC General Social Survey, 1975–80.

positively: Italians have gained some advantage from their geographical location and would perhaps have lower educational and occupational attainment had they settled in different places.

The gap is essentially explained by the next column of figures, which adds an adjustment for family background. Taking into account the education and occupation of their parents, Italians trail by less than half a year of education, a very small difference indeed. And the difference in occupational prestige is not, statistically speaking, "significant," which means that one cannot be sure that there is any difference at all. Even if it were statistically meaningful, however, it would still be quite small—merely 1 point, tiny by comparison with the range of the scale, over 70 points, and also by the measure of the variation of occupational prestige from one individual to another.[16] One can conclude that Italians lag behind WASPs chiefly because they had a lower starting point: Their parents had less education and less prestigious occupations, and they have been somewhat hindered as a result. This seemingly mundane conclusion contains an important implication, because it weakens the case for a powerful present-day ethnic factor, whether stemming from cultural handicaps or discrimination, that limits the attainments of Italians. That such influences operated in the past, and help to explain the lower educations and occupations of the parental generation, is made clear from the preceding chapters. But in the event that such influences were still at work, Italians should have lower attainment than could be expected from their family backgrounds, as for example do American Blacks because of discrimination.[17]

The Italian-WASP disparity is usefully decomposed by gender (see the second and third parts of these two tables), since inequality is much sharper for women than for men. In fact, the unadjusted overall figures show tremendous differences between British Protestant and Italian women. The latter are one-third as likely to have attended college, and one-half as likely to have graduated. The Italian women are also about a third as likely to be in the high white-collar occupations. By contrast, among the men, the overall percentages of college attendance are close, although British Protestants are somewhat more likely to have graduated. Moreover, the percentages of men from both groups who are found in high white-collar occupations are statistically indistinguishable, as are the percentages in blue-collar occupations. Differences among the men emerge after adjustment for geographical place, but the differences among the women after adjustment are even larger.

That the ethnic gap is wider among women would seem to hint at continuing cultural restraints on the achievements of Italian Americans, since the influence of the family ethos could be expected to be more of a hindrance and thus more visible for women than for men. But such a conclusion is not justified. What appears to be true is that the impact of family background is greater for women in general; this is sensible in terms of education, because poorer families may be more willing to devote their meager resources to an attempt to equalize educational opportunities for their sons, under the assumption that their educations hold great consequences for their futures, while treating the educations of their daughters as an unaffordable luxury.[18] And of course educational deficits generally mean occupational ones. Consequently, Italian-American women have suffered greater liabilities than the group's men as a result of the limited educations and occupations of their parents. It is worth recalling here that over half of adult Italian Americans in the late 1970s belonged to the first two generations, and thus had Old World or immigrant parents with very little education.

The overall disparities and unequal family backgrounds make the changes that have occurred among Italians all the more remarkable. To trace these, it is necessary to dissect the entire group into subgroups that reflect the alterations in life chances. This is done in Tables 5-3 and 5-4 in three different but interrelated ways: by distinguishing between those with wholly Italian ancestry and those with mixed background; between different generations; and between different birth cohorts.[19] The comparisons of these subgroups to WASPs all point to the same conclusion: that Italians are on the verge of catching up to core Americans. The Italian deficit is greatest among those of unmixed ancestry, the first and second generations, and individuals born before 1930. The deficit is sharply reduced or nonexistent among those of part-Italian background, the third and fourth generations, and persons born after 1930.

Consider the story in education, as indicated in Table 5-3 by the figures combined for both sexes, which summarize the basic pattern. The rate of college-going is only half as much among Italians of the first and second generations and those with unmixed ancestry as it is among British Protestants, but those in the third and fourth generations and individuals of part-Italian ancestry have caught up. Since these Italian subgroups have benefited from the group's concentration in places where educational attainment is higher, and since they are concentrated in the lower age range, where educational attainment is again higher, there are still differences from the WASP group after adjustments are made, but the disparities are much less for these subgroups than for the others.

The story is most incisively told by the changes across birth cohorts, since these reflect directly the historical variation in life chances. Here the script rises to the dramatic, because the Italian rate of college-going and the group's average years of education have accelerated rapidly across the decades. Very few Italians in the older cohorts went to college. For example, in the cohort born in the years 1914-29, between World War I and the close of mass immigration, under 15 percent went to college and under 6 percent graduated. The WASP rate of college-going for the same cohort (38 percent) was nearly three times higher, and the group's rate of college graduation (19 percent) was nearly four times higher (the WASP figures by cohort are not shown in Tables 5-3 and 5-4). Yet half the Italians born after World War II have gone to college, and a quarter have graduated. The figures for WASPs in the same cohort are nearly identical. The adjustment for place does not alter the conclusion that a convergence has occurred. It shows a wide difference in the oldest cohort that narrows rapidly and is essentially closed among those born after World War II.

Occupational movement has been less spectacular, but as shown in Table 5-4, it too reveals a rapid convergence, although parity with WASPs seems not yet quite

achieved. In the percentage placed in professional, technical, and managerial occupations and in average occupational prestige, the substantial gains made by Italians
with mixed ancestry, those in the third and fourth generations, and those born
after 1930 all point to a considerable contraction of inequality with WASPs. In
fact, for all but one of the critical subgroups, there are no significant differences
from WASPs after adjustment for place and age. The one clear discrepancy occurs
in the case of Italian Americans born after World War II, who stand 4 points lower
in occupational prestige than WASPs in the same cohort. (The seeming *decline* in
occupational prestige among Italians born after 1945 is not real, since most of the
members of this group were still quite young at the time of the surveys—the average
age was under 28—and the occupational position of many would rise in the future.)
But this difference should not overshadow the clear reduction in the occupational
gap indicated by the adjusted figures for type of ancestry, generations, and cohorts.

The educational and occupational figures for men and women suggest that
convergence has been more complete for Italian-American men than women.
Italian men who have mixed ancestry, belong to the third and fourth generations,
or were born after World War II are simply no different on average from WASP
men. In the case of men born after 1945, for example, a third of the Italians have
graduated from college, the same figure as found among British Protestants; 30
percent of the Italians have entered prestigious white-collar occupations, again the
same as among WASPs. Adjustment for place does not reveal any meaningful
differences.

Some differences appear to linger among the women, although it is impossible
to be certain of this because of the statistical limitations imposed by small numbers
of cases in some subgroups. To be sure, the progress made by Italian-American
women is clearly indicated by differences among the subgroups—for example,
college attendance is practically nil among the women born before 1930, but a
third of those born after World War II have gone (Table 5-3). Nonetheless, after
adjustment for place and age, women of partly Italian ancestry and female members
of the later generations remain behind WASP women by more than 1 year of education. That there are not significant occupational differences for the critical subgroups may be more a result of the small number of cases available than the absence
of real differences—at least this is what is demanded by a statistically conservative
reading of the large values obtained for the adjusted figures. The explanation again
appears to lie in family background: After adjustment for parental education and
occupation, only small and nonsignificant differences are found. But one must be
careful not to overstate the possible disadvantages for Italian-American women.
The educational and occupational achievements of WASP women are relatively
high; when the later generations and most recent cohort of Italian women are
compared to their peers among Protestant women of northern European background (exclusive of the British Isles), surely also an American core group, there
are no differences of even potential significance.

At this point, the Current Population Survey data may help to pin down
more decisively the extent of any remaining differences between Italian and British

Americans. The Current Population Survey has the already noted disadvantage that it fosters a too-inclusive definition of the Italian group (or, alternatively, a too restricted one, if the group is limited to individuals with two Italian parents); moreover, it does not contain the rich background data of the General Social Surveys, thus rendering statistical adjustments tenuous. But what it gives away in hese respects, it more than makes up for in the large number of individuals with Italian ancestry who were surveyed. This allows great confidence in comparisons, and makes a fine calibration of birth cohort possible. Table 5-5 focuses on three major indicators of college education and high occupational status among cohorts born after 1930—the cohorts for which the process of convergence really took hold. The combined whole- and part-Italian group is compared to British Americans in approximately five-year age intervals, separately for men and women.[20]

These unadjusted figures confirm that Italians have virtually closed the gap with WASPs, but they indicate also that the core group has been overtaken only in the most recent cohort, born after 1950. In a pattern that is somewhat inconsistent with that found in the General Social Survey data, the cohorts of Italian men born between the end of mass immigration and 1945 are definitely behind British men in higher educational attainment and, therefore, also in the percentages who pursue prestigious white-collar occupations. But the Italian participation in higher education increases among cohorts born after 1945, and it remains stable at a time when the core group's college-going and graduation decline. The mag-

TABLE 5-5   Educational and Occupational Attainments of Cohorts of Italian Americans Born after 1930 (Restricted to Individuals Older Than Twenty-two)

BIRTH COHORT	PERCENTAGE WITH SOME COLLEGE		PERCENTAGE WITH 4 YEARS OR MORE OF COLLEGE		PERCENTAGE HIGH WHITE COLLAR[a]	
	ITALIANS	WASPS	ITALIANS	WASPS	ITALIANS	WASPS
MEN ONLY						
1951–1956[b]	54.1	52.9	26.3	26.3	30.7	30.0
1946–1950	53.3	66.1	30.0	37.9	32.4	42.0
1941–1945	48.0	56.2	32.3	38.4	40.1	46.8
1936–1940	41.8	52.9	25.5	36.5	40.1	47.8
1931–1935	32.3	50.7	17.5	31.0	40.4	44.8
WOMEN ONLY						
1951–1956[b]	45.8	50.2	25.4	24.2	36.7	36.5
1946–1950	38.5	53.7	19.3	32.3	29.5	40.8
1941–1945	29.2	44.6	13.0	21.6	21.3	33.8
1936–1940	21.2	39.6	8.0	22.1	24.0	31.8
1931–1935	12.7	33.3	6.5	16.4	17.6	30.7

[a] This category includes professional, technical, and managerial occupations.

[b] This cohort is extended by 1 year to include 23-year-olds (as of 1979) and, thus, to effect comparability to preceding tables.

SOURCE: Tabulations from November, 1979, Current Population Survey.

nitude of the fall-off in graduation in the more recent cohort is of course over-
stated on account of its youth (its members range in age from 23 to 28, and some
will graduate later). But the drop in college attendance shows that the decline
is real; and, incidentally, it is found among white men as a whole. It is thus as a
result of their momentum that Italian men achieve parity in the cohort born after
1950, both in educational and occupational terms.

Even greater momentum toward parity is visible among Italian women. The
rates of college-going and graduation were very low among Italian women born
during the early 1930s, but both rates increased sharply with each new cohort.
WASP success in higher education also increased steadily over the early cohorts,
but once again educational attainment continues to climb among Italians at a time
when it levels off among WASPs. As a result, in the cohort born after 1950, Italian
women are just about equal to British women in educational attainment and, for
the very first time, in the percentage found in the upper range of the occupational
spectrum.

It is possible that statistical adjustments would change this picture somewhat
and occupational differences may open up as recent cohorts age, but clearly the big
story is the growing convergence of Italian-American men and women with American core groups in terms of social status.[21] Admittedly, one could still quibble with
the educational and occupational indicators used in the tables, because they over-
look some kinds of status differences. For instance, just because the quantity of
education is the same does not mean that the quality or the prestige is so, especially
at the level of higher education, since there are significant prestige differences
among America's colleges and universities. Hence, it could be argued that the mere
fact that young Italian-American men attend college at the same rate as young
WASP men does not demonstrate educational equality, because the Italians may be
concentrated in less prestigious or lower-quality colleges (this, of course, has not
been demonstrated). But no one has yet been able to demonstrate convincingly
that college quality makes a large or permanent difference in later achievement.
And years of educational attainment and occupational prestige have impressive
correlations with many other aspects of social standing. They do appear to capture
the prominent features of social position, even if some subtleties remain out of
reach.

In the aggregate, then, Italian Americans lag notably behind Protestants of
British ancestry, but this is because of the wide gap that exists for the first two
generations and older cohorts of Italians, and—presumably because they are more
steeped in whatever ethnic ethos remains—for those whose ancestry is derived
entirely from the group. Parity with WASPs has very nearly been obtained by the
third and later generations, those born after World War II, and individuals of part-
Italian ancestry.

The Italian-American trajectory confirms the importance of post-World War
II structural mobility, engendered by occupational shifts and the transformation of
higher education to a system of mass access. The fact of structural mobility helps

to resolve what might otherwise appear as a paradox in these findings. Since family background influences attainment, the lower positioning of Italian Americans at the start might seem to entail permanent disadvantage relative to British Americans, in which even gains by Italians would be matched by gains on the part of the core group. That the two groups did not remain frozen in relative inequality is attributable to the effects of structural transformations, which opened up the social structure and allowed Italians—and, it should be noted, other ethnics—to catch up. Thereby, structural mobility permitted a fundamental ethnic realignment to take place.

The aggregate gap with WASPs seems certain to close further in the near future. For one thing, the family backgrounds of Italian men and women reaching maturity during the remainder of this century will resemble those of WASPs because these men and women will be the children of the recent, and successful, cohorts. But, also, the group's demographic profile is undergoing a metamorphosis. And as the entire Italian-American group is more and more composed of persons with mixed-ancestry backgrounds, who belong to the third and later generations, and who were born in a period when blatant discrimination against Italians had all but ceased, differences with WASPs should dwindle and perhaps even disappear.

CONCLUSION

The demographic patterns reviewed in this chapter help to explain why Italian Americans stand out in the American perception as an intensely ethnic group. A full century after immigration began, a majority of the group belongs to the two earliest generations, and it remains densely concentrated in a few regions of the country, where it forms sizable portions of the population. The generational concentration means that most Italian-American adults have been reared under the immediate influence of the Old World or immigrant cultures. The place concentration implies the existence of substantial-sized ethnic communities, zones of more vivid ethnicity, which are highly visible because they are located in the largest metropolitan areas. Their presence is likely to affect more assimilated Italians, for whom they serve as tangible reminders of their own recent ethnic pasts, perhaps keeping some ethnic memories alive and making ethnicity itself a more salient social and personal characteristic. As long as Italians remain so compacted in the urban Northeast, these communities are never far away.

But underneath the ethnic surface, tremendous subterranean changes are taking place. One lies in the shift from the second to the third generation. Increasingly, the Italian group is composed of men and women who have not been raised in the shadow of the immigrant experience, but witness it only through their grandparents, if at all. Their exposure to the Old World or immigrant cultures, in other words, is from a distance. Equally significant for the attenuation of ethnicity is the demographic impact of rising intermarriage rates. A profound transformation is underway, as the proportion of the group of purely Italian parentage is shrinking rapidly and that of part-Italian background is expanding. This will result in a permanent metamorphosis of the group, since individuals of partly non-Italian ancestry have been raised not only in mixed homes but by and large outside the bosom of the ethnic community. They can be expected to show only tinges of ethnic cultural influences and also a less intense sense of ethnic identity.

A third fundamental change is the convergence between Italians and American core groups in terms of social status. In the aggregate, Italians still lag behind, but this is due to the legacy of historical disadvantages, reflected in the inferior educational and occupational position of older cohorts, the first and second generations, and those of Italian parentage on both sides. The third and fourth generations, those born after World War II, and those of mixed background have either caught up or are about to do so. The changes have been spectacular, especially in the realm of education, where the Mezzogiorno ethos would have seemed to doom Italians to inferiority for generations. Italian Americans have risen from ragpickers and ditchdiggers to virtual parity within three generations.

NOTES

[1]Specifically, 46 percent did, according to the U.S. Bureau of the Census, *Ancestry and Language in the United States: November 1979,* Current Population Reports, Special Studies, Series P-23, No. 116 (Washington, D.C.: U.S. Government Printing Office, 1982), p. 7.

[2]Interestingly, the November, 1979, CPS study and the 1980 census produced different estimates of the percentage of the population with mixed ancestry. Overall, according to the 1980 census, 37.0 percent of individuals who reported any ancestry claimed mixed ancestry, as opposed to 46.1 percent in the Current Population Survey (the difference was smaller among those of Italian ancestry, 43.5 versus 48.0). One reason for the differences may be that the CPS was conducted by face-to-face interviews, while the 1980 census was done by mailed questionnaires; a respondent being interviewed by another person may volunteer more complete information than one who is completing a form. Consequently, the CPS may be more believable on ancestry matters than the 1980 census, even though one would normally give greater credence to the decennial census because of its vastly larger sample.

For more information on the 1980 census and the comparison to the 1979 Current Population Survey, see U.S. Bureau of the Census, *1980 Census of the Population: Ancestry of the Population by State: 1980,* Supplementary Report PC80-S1-10 (Washington, D.C.: U.S. Government Printing Office, 1983).

[3]James Allan Davis, *General Social Surveys, 1972–1980* (machine-readable data file). Principal Investigator: James A. Davis; Associate Study Director: Tom W. Smith; Research Assistant: C. Bruce Stephenson. (Chicago: National Opinion Research Center, producer, 1980; Storrs, Conn.: Roper Public Opinion Research Center, University of Connecticut, distributor).

The surveys in the interval 1975–80 yield a combined sample of 7,459 persons for whom there is valid ethnic information. Of these, 350 are Italian Americans.

[4]To be precise, the General Social Survey records the occurrence of mixed ancestry but not the specific ingredients beyond the person's identity. This means, unfortunately, that persons with part-Italian ancestry who do not identify as Italian (i.e., who do not choose this identity over others in their background) cannot be located in the data. The census surveys, on the other hand, are also limited in one respect. They retained only the first two ancestries reported; additional ones were ignored (except for some special three-ancestry combinations).

[5]The precise estimate was 12,183,692 (*Ancestry of the Population,* p. 15).

[6]Ibid. These groups, it should be noted, overlap considerably.

[7]*Ancestry and Language,* p. 8.

[8]*Ancestry of the Population,* p. 6.

[9]See Richard D. Alba and Mitchell B. Chamlin, "A preliminary examination of ethnic identification among whites," *American Sociological Review,* 48, No. 2 (April, 1983), 240–47.

[10]See Andrew M. Greeley, *Ethnicity in the United States: A Preliminary Reconnaissance* (New York: John Wiley, 1974), especially Chapter 2. A major reason for the ethnic distinction between Irish Catholics and Protestants lies in European history. The Protestants generally are descendants of the so-called Scotch-Irish, people who migrated from Scotland to Ireland after English conquest of the island.

[11]These percentages may seem to contradict Figure 3–1, which shows the third and later generations to make up a substantial majority; but this is because the figure includes persons of all ages, not simply adults. The contrast illustrates the speed at which the generational composition of the group is changing.

[12]Richard D. Alba, "Social assimilation among American Catholic national-origin groups," *American Sociological Review,* 41, No. 6 (December, 1976), pp. 1037–40.

[13]A major study of occupational prestige is by Donald J. Treiman, *Occupational Prestige in Comparative Perspective* (New York: Academic Press, 1977).

[14]The analysis in this section has been restricted to individuals older than 22 in order to avoid the confounding presence of many persons with incomplete educations and temporary jobs, taken while in school.

[15]The regression analysis includes all white, not just Italians and WASPs, in order to establish more precisely the relations of occupation and education to the variables being controlled statistically. Nonwhites were excluded because there is good reason to believe that these relations are different for them.

[16]Individual-to-individual variation provides one of the best ways of grappling with the question of how large any specific difference is. The standard deviation can be used to measure such variation. The standard deviation of occupational prestige is 13.5 points, and 1 point is a small fraction of it. (By contrast, the standard deviation of education is 3.2 years.)

[17]The historical Black-white pattern is described by David L. Featherman and Robert M. Hauser, *Opportunity and Change* (New York: Academic Press, 1978), Chapter 6. They assert that some convergence has occurred in recent decades, but the claim is disputed by many.

[18]Karl L. Alexander and Bruce K. Eckland, "Sex differences in the educational attainment process," *American Sociological Review,* 39, No. 5 (October, 1974), 668–82.

[19]These views are interrelated because of the correlations among ancestry type, generation, and birth cohort. The Italian group in the General Social Survey data is too small to permit the three variables to be controlled at once.

[20]The Current Population Survey data do not, of course, contain information about religion; therefore, they necessitate a somewhat different definition of a group to be used as a standard of comparison. In this case, the British group has been taken to contain only individuals whose ancestry is entirely English, Scottish, Welsh (but not Irish), or combinations of these three.

The data also do not indicate whether the baccalaureate degree was earned. Four or more years of college has been assumed to be equivalent.

[21]Some readers may wonder what my analysis has added to the researches of Greeley and Lieberson, discussed in Chapter 4, who also traced ethnic progress by birth cohort. There are, in fact, numerous specific differences between this analysis and the two earlier ones. In comparison with one or the other (and sometimes both), this analysis adds: attention to mixed ancestry and to generations; separate analysis of women; a more refined standard of comparison, namely, British Protestants; more rigorous controls for background variables; and lastly, but very importantly, more current data.

There are a number of differences that emerge in the findings as a result. Two crucial ones are the more disadvantaged position of Italian-American women; and a later date for the attainment of parity with the American core.

CHAPTER SIX
ETHNICITY'S DIMMING: INDICES OF ASSIMILATION

Italians occupy a prominent niche in conventional imagery as representatives of what might be called "authentic" ethnicity. The standard portrait is of a group that has made the necessary cultural accommodations to American society while managing to retain its essential values, especially in the aura that suffuses the family. The family is viewed not only as an object of veneration but also as a magnet for personal allegiance and, consequently, as the continuing unit of communal solidarity. Loyalty to the family is presumed to be expressed in an unwillingness to move away, so that grandparents, parents, and grown children live within short distances from one another, perhaps even on the same block or in the same house, and visit one another frequently. The result, according to many, is vital ethnic neighborhoods that resist incursions by outsiders and refuse to disintegrate.

Just how valid is this portrait? In the previous chapter, we skirted the question when we examined such demographic facts as the regional and size-of-place concentrations of the Italian Americans and also the group's recent educational and occupational mobility. In this chapter, however, we confront it directly, taking up first the issue of acculturation and then that of social or structural assimilation, the large-scale entry of the group's members into socially intimate relations with other Americans.

ACCULTURATION

The persistence of ethnic culture cannot be judged by the resilience of its outward forms. These tend to slide away rather quickly, because they are incompatible with economic survival, once the group has moved beyond the nether regions of the occupational world. Forms of dress and personal habits, such as the Mezzogiorno custom of wearing garlic amulets as protection against the "evil eye,"[1] tend to be brought into conformity with American customs out of the need to get along with non-Italians on the job or in school. Even those outward manifestations that are central to cultural identity tend to weaken. Chapter 4 noted the virtual disappearance of Italian as a language of everyday use in later generations.

Cuisine provides the most tantalizing case. Despite what might seem to be the stubbornness of taste buds, it too tends to change across the generations, although not to disappear altogether. In his study of second-generation Italian Americans in Boston's West End, Herbert Gans observed that Italian cooking still prevailed but in a milder form than in the immigrant generation. Most families still ate only Italian food at home, often with pasta made in their own kitchens. But the food was less spicy than that of their parents, and the second generation purchased olive oil and wine at the store instead of preparing stronger homemade versions, as their parents had.[2] Gans's observations are brought up to date by a recent study of Italians living in and around Bridgeport, Connecticut, conducted by James Crispino. Crispino found that many later-generation Italian Americans prepared Italian dishes, but no longer very frequently. Well over half of the third and fourth generations knew how to prepare three or more Italian dishes (besides the obvious ones, pizza and spaghetti), but only a small percentage did so on a very regular basis. About 20 percent of the two later generations ate Italian food at home three or more times a week, compared to 60 percent of the first generation. The making of pasta at home was also subsiding. Only 15 percent of Italians with American-born grandparents continued the tradition, compared to over 40 percent of the immigrant generation.[3]

One reason why Italian-American cuisine persists with relative ease (compared to other outward cultural forms) lies in its acceptance by American tastes, but this same fact implies a diminished Italian distinctiveness in this respect. Italian-American foods have become American foods, to the point that many American cookbooks, such as the kitchen bible, *The Joy of Cooking,* feature Americanized versions of Italian dishes, ranging from lasagne to veal scallopini. In the last few years, a more authentic cuisine, albeit largely from northern Italy, has become popular, and Italian cookbooks can be found in many American homes, along with pasta makers, which have become fashionable kitchen accessories, at least in upper-middle-class homes. It is even possible that the percentage of non-Italians who know how to make three or more Italian dishes is not that different from the percentage among the later generations of Italians in Crispino's study. Among the outward manifestations of culture, cuisine is probably unique in the sense that its weakening among Italians and its acceptability in the wider society bring about a convergence, in which acculturation occurs as a two-way process of interaction between ethnic group and host society, rather than as a one-way imposition of the host culture on the new group.

If one is to find a surviving cultural distinctiveness among Italian Americans, it presumably lies not in the outward but the inner forms of culture–in the realm of values. Here, too, the group's social mobility holds potent implications that must be taken into account. The massive upward movement documented in the last chapter implies that the Italian-American family ethos could not have survived in its pristine form, since it is incompatible with mobility on such a scale. Ominous portents concerning education, and mobility generally, are raised by the southern Italian axioms that warn of *la via nuova,* "the new way," and admonish parents not to make their children better than themselves. The message is: Don't let your children go far; it will undermine their loyalty to the family. If this aspect of immigrant culture still held sway, the tremendous educational surge among those born after World War II would not have been possible. If an Italian-American ethos has survived, then, we should look for it in shadings and nuances coloring the family and family roles, in the importance accorded to the family, and in greater family cohesiveness.

Searching for Remnants of the Family Ethos

The family ethos brought by immigrants was a complex cultural system, with many interlocking elements. Such a system could not survive intact in a new and very different society, but some of its features might endure if suitably modified to fit the general outlines of American society and culture. Of those that lend themselves to such reinterpretation in an American environment, probably the most important is family solidarity, and especially solidarity in terms of a wide kinship network. One manifestation of this has been noted before: the peer group, a social circle of kin and family friends who socialize on a regular basis.[4] Another manifestation is loyalty to the family group, as expressed, for example, in a reluctance to move far away from it, or a willingness to live in the same neighborhood or even the same house as parents and siblings. Both of these traits have been claimed for contemporary Italian Americans.

A second general feature that lends itself to reinterpretation involves an attitude of protectiveness toward the family as an institution. Such a stance pervaded Mezzogiorno culture, ranging in expression from the many proverbs that warned of dangers to the family, to the safeguards for women in their role as vulnerable vessels of the family's honor. Within the range of contemporary American attitudes, protectiveness might be manifest in conservative attitudes on family matters and a rejection of some current-day American shifts in the family, such as more lenient divorce laws, legal availability of abortion, and more relaxed attitudes towards sexuality outside of marriage. We also might find a reverberation in a more general conservatism, a concern for the maintenance of traditional institutions and a disdain for social innovations. Indeed, the stereotypes of Italian Americans paint them as conservatives in general (e.g., on "law-and-order" issues), and also as conservatives on the specific issues that relate to the family as an institution.

Both types of conservatism correspond with broad currents in American culture and politics. For this reason, a lot of relevant data are available in the General Social Survey, which regularly inquires about issues such as divorce, abortion, and capital punishment. Some comparisons between Italians and WASPs on these matters are presented in Table 6-1; such comparisons test Italians' cultural convergence with the American core by comparing them with a group that is unmistakably a part of it. Our search for residues of the family ethos opens here.

Certainly, one issue on which such residues should be visible, if, in fact, the ethos continues to be vital, is abortion. This issue has stirred conflicting passions.

TABLE 6-1   Cultural Comparison between WASPs and Italian Americans (as of the Late 1970s)

	WASP MEAN	ITALIAN MEAN	DIFFERENCE	DIFFERENCE AFTER ADJUSTMENT[a]
Antiabortion scale	1.33	1.42	.09	.20*
Antifeminism scale	1.26	1.25	— .01	.08
Premarital sex is "always wrong"	34.5%	22.6%	−11.9*	1.3
Adultery is "always wrong"	69.8%	58.6%	−11.2*	— 3.5
Homosexual sex is "always wrong"	69.3%	60.4%	— 8.9*	— 4.7
Ever divorced or legally separated	25.7%	21.9%	— 3.8	— 4.4
Divorce should be "more difficult"	50.1%	41.3%	— 8.8*	— 3.1
Favor capital punishment	69.1%	70.2%	1.1	— 2.1
Reside in place where grew up	39.5%	53.2%	13.7*	6.6*
Parents living with grown children a "good idea"	29.4%	41.8%	12.4*	7.5*
Socialize with relatives weekly	33.8%	46.8%	13.0*	10.4*
Mistrust scale	1.10	1.27	.17*	.03
Scale of value put on self-direction for children	1.24	1.17	— .07	— .12
Young people "should be taught by their elders"	37.8%	53.0%	15.2*	19.8*
Value work that "gives a feeling of accomplishment"	57.1%	43.6%	−13.5*	— 6.5
Political party self-identification	3.88	3.27	— .61*	— .61*
Ideological self-identification	4.19	3.91	— .28*	— .11
Believe in a life after death	78.3%	58.4%	−19.9*	−10.4*

[a] Variables for which adjustment has been made include current region and size of place, those where respondent grew up, education and occupation of respondent and parents, age, and sex.

NOTE: Asterisk (*) indicates statistical significance.

SOURCE: Tabulations from the NORC General Social Survey, 1975-80.

Accordingly, American culture taken as a whole does not prescribe attitudes toward it but offers the leeway for liberal and conservative viewpoints to take shape. The General Social Survey solicits the respondent's opinion about whether a woman should be allowed to obtain a legal abortion under various circumstances. Among those presented are: "if she is married and does not want any more children"; "if the family has a very low income and cannot afford any more children"; and "if she is not married and does not want to marry the man."[5] These situations, in which a presumably healthy pregnancy has resulted from voluntary sexual activity, are the litmus test for abortion attitudes. Opinion about them is fairly evenly divided among Americans, according to the surveys. This is not true for such circumstances as a life-endangering or defective pregnancy, or one resulting from rape. In any of these situations, the great majority of Americans would permit a legal abortion.

In Table 6-1, Italian Americans in the aggregate are compared to Protestants with ancestry from the British Isles by means of a scale derived from responses to the litmus-test items. The scale is simply a count of the number of times the respondent would *not* permit an abortion, and hence can vary from 0 to 3, if the respondent would deny an abortion under each of the circumstances. According to the comparison, WASPs and Italians are statistically indistinguishable. The average for both groups is under 1.5 denials. This may seem very surprising in light of the fact that Italians are a heavily Catholic group, but in fact the stereotype that Catholics are overwhelmingly opposed to abortion is not correct. Catholics are really not very different from Protestants on the issue of legal abortion, although it should be noted that Italians are somewhat more liberal on this matter than other Catholic groups.

Of course, Italians are concentrated in the urban areas of the Northeast, where liberal opinions on abortion prevail, while WASPs are relatively more frequent in the South and rural locales, places where conservative opinions hold sway. This fact may make the groups appear more similar in the aggregate than their members are when located in the same place. On the other hand, Italians on average are less educated than WASPs, and this should predispose them to be more conservative (in general, highly educated people are more willing to allow legal abortions). Taking these and other factors[6] into account changes the comparison, but not very drastically. Italians do appear to be more conservative on abortion than WASPs who are comparable in terms of the factors that have been adjusted, but the difference is small. Measured by the scale, Italians would deny an abortion .2 more than WASPs.

Another area in which shifting American mores run afoul of conservative attitudes towards the family concerns the role of women. Increasingly, Americans no longer expect women to be chained to home and family responsibilities and their right to pursue careers is acknowledged. These changes contravene the family ethos, which places women at the center of family life, as its heart. The implications are displayed by the immigrant generation: Although immigrant women may have worked outside the home out of economic necessity, it seems clear that the immigrant preference was to keep women at home, if at all possible.[7] Attitudes about the place of women outside the home have been tapped by four questions asked by the General Social Survey in several of its years. The one that tests these attitudes most directly is, "Do you approve or disapprove of a married woman earning money in business or industry if she has a husband capable of supporting her?" But responses to all four questions are strongly interrelated,[8] and accordingly I have combined them into a scale, by counting the number of times a respondent expressed disapproval of women outside the home.

Here, too, there is no difference in the aggregate between WASPs and Italian Americans. For the most part, members of both groups do not condemn women outside the home, averaging a bit more than one disapproval in responding to the four questions. In this case, however, unlike that of abortion attitudes, adjustment for place, education, social background, and other factors, does not alter the comparison.

So far, the evidence for a distinctive conservatism on the part of Italian Americans seems measly, but what about the sexual revolution and the relaxation of prohibitions against sex outside of marriage? These touch on a deep well of concerns in the family ethos, which held the regulation of sexuality to be the cornerstone of family solidarity. In its fullest form, it mandated the virginity of unmarried women, requiring their strict chaperoning to assure this, and regarded adultery as an unexpungeable blot on a family's honor. The survival of these norms can be examined with the General Social Survey data. In several of its years, the survey has asked whether the respondent regards premarital sex and adultery as "always wrong." It has also asked about homosexual sex, and I have included this item here as well.[9]

On all these matters, Italian Americans are *more* liberal than WASPs. Premarital sex provides perhaps the most interesting case. A half century ago, Italians were divided over whether young women should be allowed to "associate with men"—date them, in contemporary language—before becoming engaged to them (see Chapter 3). But in the late 1970s, under a quarter of the group condemned premarital sex as always wrong (a third of WASPs did so). Two-thirds of Italian Americans chose the two mildest of the four categories, saying that premarital sex was "wrong only sometimes" or "not wrong at all." Needless to say, larger proportions of the Italians disapproved of adultery and homosexuality, but a difference in the liberal direction from WASPs remained. About 60 percent of the Italians found adultery and homosexuality to be always wrong, but about 70 percent of the British Protestant group expressed unqualified disapproval.

The key to the greater Italian permissiveness on sexual matters is their presence in the urban Northeast, where cosmopolitan tolerance is widespread. In this case, the liberalizing influence of the metropolis is not fully counterbalanced by the lower education of Italian Americans, because education is only weakly related to permissiveness. (Age, however, is strongly related; lenience is a preserve of the young.) In any event, after adjustment, there is not a statistically meaningful difference between the two groups. In other words, the apparent liberalism of

Italians does not result from an ethnic factor, but from the group's concentration in liberal places.

Divorce is the final area in which we can use the General Social Survey to look for reflections of protectiveness toward the family as an institution. A very high percentage of immigrants believed that divorce was never permissible (see Table 3-1), and some observers have been led by this facet of immigrant and Mezzogiorno culture to suggest that Italians are unlikely to get divorced.[10] However, this no longer appears to be true. According to the General Social Survey, over 20 percent of ever-married Italian Americans have been divorced or legally separated.[11] There is not a statistically meaningful difference between this percentage and that found among WASPs, but Italians are more likely to get divorced or legally separated than the members of some other groups, such as Irish Catholics, for whom the percentage hovers around 15 percent.

Further confounding any belief in the persistence of a conservative family ethos is the fact that Italians are not especially supportive of a tightening of divorce laws, to make divorce more difficult. Forty percent believe that divorce should be more difficult to obtain, but this percentage must be compared to the 50 percent of WASPs and most other white ethnic groups who believe this.[12] More than a third of Italians are willing to make divorce easier to obtain, while only a quarter of WASPs and most other whites are as lenient. Once again, the greater apparent liberalism of Italians does not result from a true ethnic factor but from the group's residential concentration. Once this is taken into account, it disappears.

As far as a more general conservatism is concerned, pursuit of differences from WASPs is not so critical, because such a conservatism is much less central to the notion of the Italian-American ethos than is the conservatism specific to the family. Still, one point is worth taking up because it is raised so persistently in the standard imagery of Italians: capital punishment. Italians are frequently portrayed as "law-and-order" conservatives, favoring extreme penalties for criminals, but there is little basis for such a stereotype. On the issue of capital punishment, the group holds opinions no different from those of WASPs and white Americans generally. About 70 percent of Italians and WASPs are in favor of capital punishment;[13] only Blacks and Irish Catholics show a noticeably lower rate of approval. The absence of a difference between Italians and WASPs is not affected by adjustments.

In sum, the evidence seems clear that the Italian concentrations in and around great metropolitan centers has helped to erode their traditional family conservatism, to the point that their views on social issues pertaining to the family are scarcely distinguishable from those of WASPs. When it comes to family solidarity, the evidence for family distinctiveness proves to be somewhat stronger, but the distinctiveness itself is far from extreme. In passing, it is worth noting something not presented in Table 6-1: Italians are not more satisfied with their families than anyone else. While over 60 percent of Italians pronounce themselves "very happy" with their marriage, 70 percent of WASPs do the same. Over 40 percent of Italians say they are satisfied "a very great deal" with their family life; the percentage among WASPs is the same.

But by indirect evidence, Italian Americans do appear to be more reluctant to move away from the family. An impressive 53 percent reside in the same place where they grew up, although the percentage of WASPs who do so is also high, 40 percent (see Table 6-1). Of course, these percentages do not indicate how many members of both groups remain in the same place because of strong family ties. Moreover, Italian Americans have grown up in the very urban magnets that attract others from their hometowns because they contain vast concentrations of occupational opportunities and also culture—New York City is the prototype and so Italian immobility has to be discounted somewhat; had Italians grown up primarily in small-town America, they might not be so reluctant to move away. In the aggregate, Italians also have less education and lower occupational status, and these factors too are associated with deeper geographic roots. When all these factors are taken into account,[14] Italians are only modestly more likely than WASPs to remain in the same place—by 7 percentage points. Since there may be other reasons for remaining in the place where one grew up, it seems apparent that a distinctive Italian reluctance to move away from the family must be minor in magnitude.

Family solidarity also seems mildly evident in the greater approval expressed by Italians of taking in older parents. Over 40 percent of the group think that parents and grown children sharing a home is generally a "good idea," while about the same percentage disagree and think it is a "bad idea."[15] But only 30 percent of WASPs think this a good idea, and over half think it a bad one. (Curiously, older people of all groups, Italians included, seem to think less of it than younger people, perhaps because they recognize its disadvantages for themselves.) Factors other than ethnicity explain part of the difference between the two groups in approval of the idea, but after adjustment a modest difference of 8 percentage points remains.

Lastly, the Italian pattern of socializing with relatives does remain, at least to some degree. Nearly half of Italian Americans socialize with family members weekly or more frequently, compared to only a third of WASPs.[16] This difference is not explained very much by background variables, as the tendency to socialize within the family is only modestly lower among the more highly educated, and this is counterbalanced for WASPs by the fact that it is modestly higher among those who live in smaller places. When education, place, and other variables are statistically controlled, Italians are still 10 percent more likely to socialize on a weekly basis with relatives. (This probably overstates the true difference since Italians are more likely to live where they grew up and hence near their relatives, a factor that is not controlled here.)

Thus, what remains of the family ethos is a mild version of family solidarity. Conservative attitudes with respect to the family have all but withered away; on questions of divorce, homosexuality, premarital sex, abortion, and nontraditional roles for women, Italian Americans are now as liberal—or as conservative, if one likes—as WASPs and other Americans. What remains is a slightly greater tendency to remain in the same place, greatly diluted from ancestral peasant rootedness, and a moderately greater willingness to live with and keep company with relatives.

Whether these can survive the high rates of social mobility (documented in the last chapter) and frequent ethnic intermarriage (to be discussed shortly) is a question that deserves an answer; but before answering it, it is worthwhile to look for remnants of an Italian-American ethos in a few other areas.

Some Other Cultural Elements

Closely related to the family ethos is suspiciousness toward strangers. This is just the other face of the coin of family solidarity, since in the Mezzogiorno strangers were viewed as having their own family interests uppermost in mind. This is the kernel of truth in Edward Banfield's notion of "amoral familism" applied to southern Italian society.[17] An attitude of mistrust stems also from *campanilismo*, the village-mindedness according to which the residents of neighboring villages were practically foreigners. That this attitude survived through the early decades in America is suggested by the frequent image of the Italian neighborhood as scarcely penetrable by strangers.[18]

Any vestiges of suspiciousness can be looked for in responses to three questions asked in several survey years. One was, "Do you think most people would try to take advantage of you if they got a chance, or would they try to be fair?"; and the other two were quite similar in wording.[19] A scale has been composed by counting the number of mistrustful responses an individual gave to the three questions. But according to the averages in Table 6-1, Italians are only slightly more untrusting than WASPs, and neither group is particularly so. WASPs averaged just a shade over one untrusting response to the three questions, while Italians averaged one and a quarter. Some groups are more suspicious of others than Italians and WASPs. Other Catholics from southern and eastern Europe averaged one and a half untrusting responses, and Hispanics averaged one and two-thirds (these figures are not shown in the table).

Little remains of these differences after adjustments are made. The attitude of suspicion declines sharply with education and also, but less sharply, with advancing occupational position. In addition, it is lower among individuals with relatively high social origins and those located in smaller and less anonymous places. Curiously, suspiciousness is also very high among young Americans from all ethnic groups, perhaps as a result of the political scandals and the general demystification of public life during the 1970s. Aside from age, all of these factors would tend to make Italians more mistrustful than WASPs, independently of any cultural force at work. When they are taken into account, there is no longer a perceptible difference between Italians and WASPs, or for that matter between Hispanics and WASPs. Only the other Catholics from southern and eastern Europe remain as distinctly more suspicious. Perhaps in this case, a cultural influence is present.

The expectation that children should conform to the authority of adults is another element in a presumed Italian-American ethos, and it too can be related to the circumstances of the family in southern Italian society. Childhood was short in the Mezzogiorno, and the transition to adulthood abrupt, as children were expected to take up adult roles in their early years and to make sacrifices for the sake of the family. Under these conditions, the expectation of obedience to parents was unqualified. Indeed, even in the early 1930s, few Italian Americans disagreed with the statement that "children owe absolute obedience to parents" (see Table 3-1); and in the 1950s, Herbert Gans observed that Italian-American parents expected their children to behave in conformity with adult wishes and commands and put their emphasis on outward behavior rather than their children's inner motives.[20]

The expectation of filial obedience could be expected to be reinforced by broad value clusters that have been found in American and other industrial societies. In insightful research, Melvin Kohn and his colleagues have demonstrated that parents seek to pass on to their children what they see as necessary for success in the adult world; which traits these are, however, depends on the parents' work experiences. Consequently, there are critical differences between working-class and middle-class parents, because of their different experiences with authority and autonomy. Reflecting their experiences of subordination on the job, working-class parents often seek to instill conformity to authority in their children, fearing that any display of independence will prove only to be a rebellious prelude to a slide into a lower class. Middle-class parents, on the other hand, tend to value self-direction for their children.

Kohn and his coworkers have found these differences by presenting parents with a list of possible traits for their children, such as "that a child is honest," and asking them which they felt were the three most and the three least desirable. Parents tend to respond as if they perceive an underlying dimension of self-direction versus conformity. Parents who value self-direction rate as desirable such traits as self-control and responsibility, while disparaging others, such as obedience to parents and neatness. Parents who value conformity rate the traits in reverse.[21]

Similar questions have been asked of respondents, both parents and nonparents, to the General Social Survey. I have combined responses into a simple index to capture the spirit of the value distinction, counting a +1 each time a respondent valued one of the traits associated with self-direction and also each time he or she disparaged one of those associated with conformity, and counting a -1 for the reverse, a valuing of a conformity trait or a disparaging of one of self-direction.[22] The resulting sum can vary from +6 to -6, and 0 represents a point midway between the opposite poles of self-direction and conformity.

There is no meaningful difference between Italians and WASPs on this scale. Both averaged a bit more than +1, leaning slightly toward self-direction. Adjustment for education and occupation, which are associated with greater value placed on self-direction, does not change the picture. There is also, incidentally, no difference between the two groups in preference for the one trait, obedience to parents, that stands out as particularly pivotal in descriptions of Mezzogiorno and immigrant cultures. Only a quarter of Italian Americans prized obedience as one of the three most desirable traits, as compared to 28 percent of WASPs. The difference is insignificant statistically.

Yet one question, asked in one year only, did seem to capture some cultural vestiges bearing on self-direction versus conformity. Respondents to the 1980 survey were asked whether young people should be "taught by their elders to do what is right" or "taught to think for themselves even though they may do something their elders disapprove of."[23] More than half of the Italians agreed with the alternative that would be favored in the Mezzogiorno—namely, that young people should be taught by their elders—but only 38 percent of the WASPs took this position. Adjustment for education and age, the two most important factors associated with responses to the question, as well as other variables, does not reduce the difference between the two groups but in fact increases it somewhat to 20 percent. This difference indicates that there may be some survivals of a conception of children held by the southern Italian and immigrant ancestors of present-day Italians, but the fact that such a distinctive conception is not consistently visible suggests that it survives more as a shading or nuance than as a discrete regimen of childrearing. This suggestion is buttressed by the fact that it is the WASP position that is relatively unusual in this instance. Of all the major ethnic groups examined, British Protestants had the lowest percentage expressing approval of the authority of elders. The Italian percentage is not that far from the percentage of all other Americans, 45 percent, who believe that young people should be taught by their elders to do what is right.

A final sort of attitude that reflects on the possible persistence of ethnic cultural elements and that can be examined from the survey data has to do with desirable traits in a job. In the harsh circumstances of southern Italy, the emphasis was very practical and such an emphasis carried over into the American setting, as immigrants entered the ranks of unskilled manual labor. If this endures, one would expect Italians to value the extrinsic features of a job, such as the salary and the spare time it affords, rather than its intrinsic features, the satisfaction and challenge of the work. Indeed, such values were observed in the West End by Herbert Gans, who found that the neighborhood's residents considered the ideal job to be "one that pays the most money for the least physical discomfort" and "demands no emotional involvement."[24]

The General Social Survey has asked respondents in some years what traits they value most in a job, including as possibilities such extrinsic features as high income, job security, and lots of spare time, and the intrinsic feature that the work is important and "gives a feeling of accomplishment."[25] The percentages who ranked this last feature as most important are tabulated in Table 6-1. Overall, Italian Americans are less likely to do so; only 44 percent did, compared to 57 percent of the WASPs. On closer inspection, however this difference turns out to have less to do with culture than with the American experiences of the groups. Neither a desire for high income nor one for a lot of spare time plays a role in creating the difference. The chief reason that Italians rate work satisfaction less highly than WASPs is that they rate job security more so. The preference for security is concentrated in the older cohorts of Italians and some other ethnic groups (such as other Catholics from southern and eastern Europe), probably because these groups were more vulnerable to unemployment and economic setback during the Depression of the 1930s and the bitter memory still lingers. A smaller part of the difference lies in the somewhat greater preference of young Italians for advancement possibilities, a preference that is certainly understandable for members of a socially mobile group. These explanations imply that the difference between the two groups in preference for work satisfaction is associated with the lower average occupational standing and social origins of Italians; and when these and other characteristics of Italians are taken into account, the group is no longer demonstrably different from WASPs.

The will-o-the-wisp quality to the cultural residues of an Italian-American ethos does not mean a complete absence of differences regarding some issues not central to the ethos, and to round out the discussion, I have included a few in Table 6-1.

One lies in the political party affiliations of the two groups, and here the continued impact of the early history of Italians in the United States is evident. Italians settled in many northeastern cities where Democratic political machines organized the immigrant vote, and their early political loyalties were to the Democratic Party (although some Italians joined the Republican Party out of a perception that Irish control of the machines blocked the group's political advances). But even today, the predominant loyalty of Italian Americans remains with the Democratic Party. The table shows the averages for Italians and WASPs on a scale of political self-identification that extends from 1 for strong Democrats to 7 for strong Republicans.[26] The average for the Protestant group falls in the middle of the scale, and the group is fairly evenly balanced between Republicans and Democrats. The Italians by contrast are inclined in the Democratic direction, and few call themselves Republicans (22 percent, compared to 41 percent of WASPs). Adjustment for background variables does not alter the difference between the two groups.

Moreover, the preference of Italians for the Democratic Party seems fairly resilient. An examination of the youngest Italians, whose social mobility might be expected to produce some switches to the Republicans, reveals little of such change. There is evidence of softening in a smaller percentage of "strong" Democrats and a greater percentage of Independents leaning in the Democratic direction, but the overall percentage who claim to be Democrat or to lean in that direction is no smaller than among older Italian Americans.

Underscoring the historical roots of the difference in party loyalties between the two groups is the fact that it is not matched by a difference in ideological self-perception. Table 6-1 also presents the averages for the two groups on a scale similar to that for political party, which in this case ranges from 1 for individuals who believe themselves to be extremely liberal to 7 for those who perceive themselves as extremely conservative. In the aggregate, there is a minor difference between Italians and WASPs, with the former a bit more liberal, but it is explained entirely by the background variables.

A final difference illustrates the oddities that can survive a process of massive acculturation, usually because of their lack of salience. The case in point is the relative lack of belief among Italian Americans in a life after death. According to the General Social Survey, just a bit more than half of the group professes this belief, compared to over three-quarters of WASPs.[27] The difference is reduced by taking into account such facts as that belief in an afterlife is more prevalent in the South and among individuals raised on farms, but it is not explained completely. Perhaps reflecting the continued alienation of some Italians from the Catholic Church, members of the group appear to be 10 percent less likely to believe in life after death than comparable WASPs and also than comparable Irish Catholics.

What is one to conclude about the existence of an Italian-American cultural ethos? Taken as a whole, the evidence suggests only mild differences between Italians and WASPs on matters that would be central to the presumed ethos. Italians display moderately greater family solidarity, but they are not more conservative on issues concerning the family—if anything, they are more liberal as a result of their concentration in more cosmopolitan places. Italians are a bit more mistrustful of others and also less likely to value the intrinsic rewards of work. But both of these differences are explained by the remaining distance between the two groups on demographic factors—particularly, education and occupation. Such an explanation implies that there is not a powerful ethnic factor at work and that the attitudinal differences will fade further as the socioeconomic gap closes in the coming decades. Finally, Italians do not appear different in their attitudes towards child-rearing, at least as these are revealed by the value placed on traits reflecting self-direction versus conformity to authority; but they are different on one question having to do with respect for the authority of elders. This is the one instance of a substantial difference between the two groups on a key element in the conventional portrait of a distinctive Italian ethos. Even here, however, the apparent confirmation of cultural distinctiveness is open to question, because it is WASPs who are comparatively unusual and Italians are simply not that different from Americans in general.

Whenever no more than minor differences are found in survey data, the interpretation of them is always open to a conservative gambit, a posture of leaning over backwards to acknowledge the ways in which the obvious conclusions may go wrong. There is, for one, always the possibility that questions in public-opinion polls fail to capture attitudinal subtleties. Accordingly, the paltriness of the differences between Italians and WASPs in the survey evidence does not eliminate the possibility of shadings and nuances in Italian-American attitudes on the family and other matters at the core of the ethnic culture's concerns. But these mild differences do remove the possibility of a sharply delineated Italian-American ethos that sets the group clearly apart from other Americans. Thus, differences there may be, but they are generally muted among the majority of Italian Americans, surviving in a more intense form if at all among a small minority. Even those differences that are not so modest, such as the persisting loyalty of the group to the Democratic Party, are contained within a narrow band of variation found among other Americans as well and hence do not set a seal of ethnic distinctiveness on Italians as a group. In sum, the evidence so far suggests the cultural integration of Italian

Americans into the larger society. This integration is revealed with even greater definitiveness by the evidence on intermarriage, to which we now turn.

STRUCTURAL ASSIMILATION

Social or structural assimilation refers to the occurrence of socially intimate relations, such as friendship and marriage, between members of an ethnic group and others, and it is without question the dimension of assimilation with the greatest portent for ethnic change. Milton Gordon has called it the "keystone of the arch of assimilation," conjecturing that "once structural assimilation has occurred, either simultaneously with or subsequent to acculturation, all of the other types of assimilation will naturally follow."[28] One basis for Gordon's widely accepted view is that ethnic distinctiveness, whether expressed in terms of culture, ethnic identity, or ethnic political interests that must be defended, can only be maintained by networks of ethnic group members, whose shared ethnicity is mutually supportive. Such networks are the true meaning of community, and once they disintegrate, the way is open to the rapid and full assimilation of the group.

Intermarriage serves as a cardinal indicator of social assimilation, for reasons both obvious and subtle. Because marriage is an enduring and intimate relationship, intermarriage tests the perceptions of a group, the willingness of Italians and non-Italians to accept each other in a long-lasting and exclusive relation. In the language of social scientists, the degree of intermarriage measures the social distance between Italians and others. Moreover, an intermarriage is not simply an isolated crossing of ethnic boundaries but has far wider ramifications. Marriage creates not just a single new relation but a host of them, as two sets of persons are joined as relatives. Other linkages are potential at the time of marriage: those between the newly married couple and their future children, who will be raised in an ethnically mixed family.

Finally, the occurrence of intermarriage indicates the existence of other relations that penetrate ethnic boundaries. Intermarriage stands as the measurable pinnacle of an invisible multitude of other ethnic intermixings—particularly at the level of acquaintanceships and friendships that lead to encounters resulting in marriages. And the general intermingling that precedes intermarriage generally persists into it: The personal networks of intermarried individuals tend to contain greater ethnic diversity than do those of individuals who marry within their own group.[29]

Even though intermarriage is a crucial indicator of the state of ethnicity, intermarriage data are hard to come by. Few public-opinion polls inquire about the ethnic origins of a respondent's spouse; the General Social Survey does not (except for religion, which we will come to shortly). This forces me to rely on the 1979 Current Population Survey, which, it should be recalled, has the disadvantage of a too inclusive Italian group. But since it makes little sense to treat persons of unmixed and mixed Italian ancestry as equivalent in their probability of out-marriage, the two ancestry types must be separated in an intermarriage table, and this overcomes some of the group-defining difficulty in these data. Table 6-2 shows the intermarriage patterns for Italian-American men and women, both in the aggregate and broken down by age and generational status.

Mention was made in Chapter 4 of the best data from the 1960s concerning the intermarriage of Italians. These showed that as of 1963-64, about 59 percent

TABLE 6-2   Marriage Patterns of Persons of Italian Ancestry (as of 1979)

ANCESTRY TYPE	PATTERNS OF HUSBANDS			PATTERNS OF WIVES		
	WIFE'S ANCESTRY TYPE			HUSBAND'S ANCESTRY TYPE		
	UN-MIXED ITALIAN	MIXED ITALIAN	NO ITALIAN	UN-MIXED ITALIAN	MIXED ITALIAN	NO ITALIAN
Overall						
Unmixed Italian	42.6%	5.3%	52.1%	48.4%	3.0%	48.6%
Mixed Italian	8.2%	12.6%	79.2%	12.8%	9.7%	77.5%
By age						
Under 30 years						
Unmixed Italian	21.1%	11.8%	67.1%	27.5%	4.5%	68.0%
Mixed Italian	5.0%	17.6%	77.5%	10.4%	11.1%	78.4%
30-39 years						
Unmixed Italian	30.4%	6.9%	62.7%	36.8%	6.9%	56.3%
Mixed Italian	8.9%	14.4%	76.7%	12.4%	10.6%	77.0%
40-49 years						
Unmixed Italian	34.9%	8.1%	57.0%	50.0%	1.3%	48.7%
Mixed Italian	8.9%	10.2%	81.0%	17.0%	5.2%	77.8%
50-59 years						
Unmixed Italian	50.6%	2.8%	46.6%	54.3%	1.0%	44.7%
Mixed Italian	8.8%	3.1%	88.2%	17.0%	7.8%	75.2%
60 years and older						
Unmixed Italian	59.6%	1.5%	38.9%	65.3%	2.1%	32.5%
Mixed Italian	14.9%	4.3%	80.8%	16.4%	6.9%	76.7%
By generation						
First generation						
Unmixed Italian	75.4%	2.7%	21.9%	82.3%	0.7%	16.9%
Mixed Italian	Number of cases too small			Number of cases too small		
Second generation						
Unmixed Italian	43.9%	4.6%	51.4%	50.4%	1.8%	47.8%
Mixed Italian	10.0%	8.2%	81.8%	17.0%	5.6%	77.4%
Third generation						
Unmixed Italian	25.2%	7.5%	67.3%	32.2%	5.7%	62.1%
Mixed Italian	8.2%	12.6%	79.2%	12.2%	10.3%	77.5%

NOTE: Percentages may not add to 100.0% because of rounding.

SOURCE: Tabulations from November, 1979, Current Population Survey.

of individuals with unmixed Italian ancestry chose spouses with the same unmixed background.[30] Comparing this fairly high rate of marriage within the group with the equivalent percentages from the 1979 survey, shown in Table 6-2 (43 percent among the men and 48 percent among the women), is one way of revealing the impact of steadily rising intermarriage rates: In a decade and a half, these aggregate rates have declined by more than 10 percent. Of course, it is not clear whether these rates measure the totality of in-group marriage, because it is not obvious whether marriages that join individuals of part-Italian and all-Italian ancestry (or two part-Italian individuals) should be classified as within or outside of the group. One earlier analysis treated these as intermarriages, on the grounds that they did reflect some degree of intermixing, but not everyone would be willing to accept such an argument. Hence, the intermarriage rate of Italian-American men of unmixed ancestry could be taken to be 57 or 52 percent, depending on how one classifies the ambiguous marriages, and that for women could be either 52 or 49 percent.

This ambiguity aside, the overall pattern of steadily rising intermarriage is clear. Among individuals with two Italian parents, a comfortable majority in the oldest cohort married within the group, but the rate of marriage to others with unmixed Italian ancestry declines inexorably with each new cohort. The trend of decreasing marriage within the group is not affected much when marriages to individuals with one Italian parent are counted as in-marriages. In the youngest cohort, which contains those who were under 30 in 1979, the rate of marriage outside the group ranges from 67 to almost 80 percent, depending on how one classifies the ambiguous marriages and whether one is talking about women or men.[31] The trend of increasing intermarriage with advancing generational status is also sharp; the rate of intermarriage in the third generation is almost as high as in the youngest cohort. The two patterns of change are of course interrelated because cohort and generation are correlated, meaning that membership in the third or a later generation is associated with recent birth. However, controlling for both age and generation at the same time does not alter the magnitude of change much (this analysis is not shown in the table). The intermarriage rate of the youngest cohort of the third and later generations is just a bit higher than that of the youngest cohort overall (among the men, 70 percent married someone with no Italian ancestry, and amont the women, 73 percent did so).

The marriage pattern of individuals with part-Italian ancestry reveals their general detachment from the Italian-American group. In each cohort, between 75 and 80 percent of these individuals typically take spouses without any Italian ancestry; the figures are similar in the second and third generations (for obvious reasons, there are few first-generation Italians with mixed backgrounds). Of course, it could be objected that the mixed ancestry group is too inclusive and that the rate of in-marriage would appear quite different if we could locate the part of it that identifies as Italian American. It is tempting when thinking along these lines to credit all the marriages between individuals with some Italian ancestry to this subgroup, which would suggest that its rate of in-marriage might be quite high. However, this sort of accounting would be misleading because some individuals who do not identify themselves as Italian Americans would still marry persons with Italian ancestry. Consequently, dividing up the mixed ancestry group would probably not dramatically affect the apparent rate of endogamy.

This line of reasoning raises as a question the "background" or "random" rate of in-group marriage—that is, the rate of in-marriage that would occur if individuals took no note of ethnic distinctions in choosing a mate. The answer to this question also bears on a point that is frequently made when rising rates of intermarriage are discussed: namely, that rates of endogamy remain well above the background rate, indicating the persistence of some ethnic solidarity. At first glance, this point seems obvious, given that Italians are only 5 percent of the national population (and presumably, only 5 percent should marry other Italians if marriages were contracted without regard for ethnicity). But this first glance overlooks the group's geographical concentration and thus the fact that it forms much higher proportions of the population in the areas where its members are heavily located. In Chapter 5, it was noted that almost 60 percent of Italians are found in the New England and Middle Atlantic states, and of course they are not randomly distributed throughout these regions. According to the 1980 census, Italian Americans are densest in just six states—Connecticut, Massachusetts, New Jersey, New York, Pennsylvania, and Rhode Island—where their proportion in the population ranges from 10 percent in Pennsylvania to nearly 20 percent in Rhode Island. Even putting matters in this way understates the density pertinent to the background rate of in-marriage, because Italian Americans are most clustered in the metropolitan and suburban areas of these states (to take an extreme case, the group is a quarter of Long Island's population). Moreover, nonwhites ought to be discounted in figuring density because the interracial marriage rate is tiny; nonwhites are not part of the same marriage pool with whites. As a rough estimate, then, a figure of about 15 percent as the background rate of marriage to individuals with some Italian ancestry is a reasonable guess. By this standard, the rate at which individuals with part-Italian ancestry marry others with some Italian ancestry is only moderately above what could be expected from chance;[32] but the rate for those with solely Italian ancestry is, even in the youngest cohort, distinctly greater than the background rate.

Nonetheless, by any standard, the current rates of intermarriage by Italian Americans, as revealed by the youngest cohort and the third generation, are high. This conclusion still leaves open the possibility that what are intermarriages from the point of view of national origin are in-marriages from another, namely that of religion. Such a possibility is suggested by one of the more famous theses about American ethnicity, the "Triple Melting Pot" theory, popularized by Will Herberg's book, *Protestant-Catholic-Jew,* in the 1950s.[33] Herberg advanced the argument that ethnicity based on religion was destined to become a permanent feature of American life. Rising rates of intermarriage across nationality lines but within religious boundaries would weaken ethnicity based on nationality while increasing the social importance of religious group memberships. In the case of Catholics, intermarriage would bring about a pan-Catholic group by submerging national cultural differences and giving rise to an undivided American Catholicism.

But it appears that the rising tide of intermarriage is sweeping across religious boundaries, just as it is those of national origin. This is evident from Table 6-3, derived from the General Social Survey, which inquires about the religious origins of both respondents and their spouses. The table is restricted to Italian Americans raised as Catholics (approximately 90 percent of the group), and overall, it shows only a modest rate of interreligious marriage, 33.3 percent. A sharp pattern of change is revealed, however, when the Catholic group is broken down by birth cohort, generation, and type of ancestry. Consider generation as an example. Eighty percent of second-generation Italian Catholics married other Catholics, but only half of the third and later generations have done so. Similarly, about half of the Italian Catholics born after World War II and of those with mixed ancestry have married non-Catholics, mostly Protestants.

The great increase in intermarriage necessarily implies accompanying changes in other relational patterns. An instance of this is residential segregation. Chapter 4 observed that the segregation of Italians still seemed substantial in 1970;[34] presumably, however, the "integration" of households through intermarriage means a decline of neighborhoods that are predominantly Italian. As noted in the earlier chapter, this may be hard to detect in conventional segregation indices, because they obscure changes across generations and birth cohorts; but fortunately another

TABLE 6-3   Marriage Patterns of Italian-American Catholics (as of the Late 1970s)

	RELIGION IN WHICH SPOUSE WAS RAISED		
	CATHOLIC	PROTESTANT	OTHER
Overall	66.7%	29.5%	3.8%
Ancestry type			
Wholly Italian	71.7%	25.0%	3.3%
Partly Italian	41.9%	51.6%	6.5%
Generation			
First	72.7%	18.2%	9.1%
Second	80.7%	14.0%	5.3%
Third or later	45.2%	54.8%	0.0%
Birth cohort			
Before WW I	85.0%	15.0%	0.0%
1914–29	72.1%	23.0%	4.9%
1930–45	66.2%	29.2%	4.6%
After WW II	48.6%	48.6%	2.7%

NOTE: Percentages may not add up to 100.0% because of rounding.

SOURCE: Tabulations from the NORC General Social Survey, 1975–80.

kind of evidence is handy. In his study of Bridgeport's Italian Americans, James Crispino asked about the ethnic compositions of respondents' current neighborhoods and of those in which they were raised. He found that, although 63 percent grew up in a neighborhood that was at least half Italian, only 16 percent lived in such an exclusively Italian area at the time of the study.[35]

The obvious conclusion, then, from the surge of marriage across national and religious lines is that the force of ethnicity is dissipating. Some writers have attempted to avoid this conclusion by an argument that a durable ethnicity does not require ethnic homogeneity in primary networks of socially intimate relations, but only the existence of so-called secondary networks of ties to ethnic organizations. According to this argument, even if individuals have many personal relations that cross ethnic boundaries, an ethnic part of them is maintained if they meet their ethnic peers in organizations dedicated to group concerns, such as the Italian-American Anti-Defamation League.[36] This argument accords well with the view, first espoused by Nathan Glazer and Daniel Patrick Moynihan, that in accommodating themselves to American society, ethnic groups have become chiefly political interest groups, protecting ethnic turf. And it gains impressionsitic evidence from the apparent rise since the 1960s of ethnic organizations reviving and defending group interests, whether these involve a preservation of ethnic culture, an assault on offensive stereotypes, legal aid for individuals who feel themselves to be the victims of discrimination, or political activities on behalf of the homeland.

In the case of the Italians and also those of many other groups, however plausible this scenario may seem initially, it runs afoul of the evidence once this rises above the impressionistic level. For example, the General Social Survey asks individuals what kinds of organizations they belong to; and included in the list of types that are specifically asked about are "nationality groups." Only 2.8 percent of Italian Americans responding to these surveys claimed to belong to such groups—a percentage, incidentally, no different from that found among all other Americans.[37] Moreover, just as with intermarriage, membership in ethnic organizations is a function of generation and birth cohort. In his Bridgeport study, Crispino noted "a tendency for older, earlier generation ethnics to belong to clubs which attract mainly Italians." The reason is a preference for "associating with others who are of the same class and ethnicity as they."[38]

In the case of Italians, the low rate of membership in ethnic organizations might seem to testify to the existence of an ethnic survival—a disinterest in the public, as opposed to the private, sphere, a vestige of the alienation from authority characteristic of the Mezzogiorno. Indeed, some observers claim a persisting difficulty on the part of Italian Americans in organizing themselves for effective communal action, a difficulty that they attribute to the constraints imposed by ethnic culture.[39] This seems unlikely, however, in light of the breakup of the family-centered culture, the presumed heart of any constraints. Far more likely is that this disinterest, additionally reflected in the tiny rate of membership in ethnic organizations, is just another confirmation of the running tide of assimilation and the consequent ebbing of ethnicity's salience.

ORGANIZED CRIME

The subject of assimilation cannot be left without touching on the issue of organized crime. The continuing prominence of Italians in crime might seem to signal a countervailing tendency to the general trend of assimilation, and it thus requires some consideration. For obvious reasons, any discussion of the present and future of Italians in crime cannot be as definitive as the preceding chapter and a half have been; the hard evidence is simply lacking.

Reflection on the relationship of ethnicity to organized crime suggests that the Italian prominence may remain for a while, seeming to outlive the weakening of Italian-American ethnicity through massive assimilation, before eventually succumbing to the same assimilatory forces. The reason is not any special ethnic vitality that sustains criminal networks but, rather, the exigencies of criminal careers. Once they are embarked upon, which generally happens early in life, individuals tend to remain in them. Consequently, criminal networks can be kept alive through a prolonged period by cohorts of men who became career criminals decades before, under very different conditions than prevail in the present.

The impact of assimilation, then, may not be visible for a while, until crime networks begin to fall apart because they have been unable for a long time to recruit significant numbers of young men for illicit occupations. In the case of the Italians, the general trends that have already been discussed would seem to imply a drying up of the conditions that promote recruitment. One change that obviously holds this implication is the spectacular improvement in the mobility chances for Italian Americans, reducing the likelihood that younger members of the group will opt for the highly risky route to success through crime. But just as importantly, the general cultural and social conditions in which crime networks emerge and flourish are dissipating among Italians.

One feature of organized crime that goes frequently overlooked is the problematic nature of criminal organization. Cooperation in crime, especially cooperation across years and decades, does not come easily. Criminals have good reason to suspect one another of duplicity and even to worry about being murdered at the hands of their "friends." And when in jeopardy, they cannot do what ordinary citizens can: resort to the police and the courts for protection of their rights. Hence, *trust* is the crucial problem to solve if criminal networks are to flourish; it is their essential mortar. This is one of the reasons why ethnicity is so important in organized crime, why crime groups tend to be drawn from people with similar ethnic origins: Criminals find it easier to trust someone who is like themselves than to trust someone who is ethnically different. One indication of this is that membership in Italian-American crime families has been generally restricted to men of southern Italian origins, whose parents were both Italian, and usually to those who married an Italian-American woman.[40]

In terms of meeting the problem of trust, the typical situation of an ethnic group during its early period of settlement provides the right conditions for criminal networks to emerge. Trust is facilitated by common origins; the more two individuals share in common and the further back in time their bond goes, the easier it will be for them to rely on each other in dangerous endeavors. Ethnic enclaves, then, are fertile soil for crime groups. Residential segregation facilitates the coming together of young men who are prospects for criminal careers (teenage gangs are a significant breeding ground for racketeers). Segregation also affords protection to embryonic criminal networks, because outsiders generally take little note of what takes place within ghettoes.

In the case of the Italians, the usual effects of these conditions were enhanced by the group's ethos and by the value placed on kinship. Because of the problematic nature of trust, cultures that stress the importance of kinship—especially kinship beyond the limited confines of the nuclear family—provide advantages in the establishment of stable criminal organization. Kinship provides an especially durable foundation for a criminal relationship, since strong sentiments reinforce the link and make betrayal difficult. In addition, extended kinship provides a relatively large pool of potential participants for illicit enterprise. The success of Italian Americans in organized crime can be traced in large part to the cultural emphasis on kinship (as opposed to the widely publicized aspects of a secret society). Crime "families"—the name is aptly chosen—are interlaced by connecting threads created out of kinship, including under this term kinship arising through marriage and the institution of godparentship.[41]

In both of these respects, the prevailing trend of assimilation, the mobility out of the ghetto and the waning of the family-centered ethos should largely dissolve the conditions conducive to the recruitment of Italian-American young men for crime. This expectation, moreover, seems consistent with what is known of the demographic facts of Cosa Nostra crime families. If it were true, we should expect to find that crime families were top-heavy with aged men, with little renewal produced by young men of talent entering their ranks. This is in turn supported by the little observable turnover at the top of Italian-American organized crime, the fact that many men in its leadership positions have occupied them for decades. It is also supported by more systematic evidence—specifically, by the results of Annelise Graebner Anderson's unique and detailed study of a crime family in an unnamed large city. Utilizing the records of federal law-enforcement agencies, Anderson found that in 1969 the median age of its 75 members was 60; none was under 35. She found a similar concentration in advanced ages in another crime group she studied.[42]

Anderson's meticulous research also debunks the mythology surrounding the great wealth assumed to be acquired by gangsters. Contrary to the popular belief that most racketeers are affluent, if not millionaires, she discovered that a majority of this crime family's members lived in modest circumstances—65 percent had annual incomes estimated at under $20,000 in 1969—and some were even indigent, with incomes under $5,000.[43] If this financial picture is true of other crime families as well, then it provides an additional reason to expect that few young Italian-American men would be eager for crime careers.

There is indirect evidence that, as a result of the drying up of recruitment, a process of debilitation has begun to set in. Starting around 1980, the FBI and other law-enforcement agencies began to enjoy great success in penetrating Italian-American crime families with informants and undercover agents, suggesting that a dearth of members has forced those who remain to rely on persons who are not well known to them. But the gradual dwindling of Italian-American crime families will not mean the disappearance of *American* organized crime. As was true in the past when Italians supplanted Irish and Jewish criminals, a process of ethnic succession is at work. As Italians depart from crime, criminal groups composed of Blacks, Chinese, Colombians, Cubans, and other Hispanics are rising to take their place. The rotation of ethnic groups through organized crime provides one of the strongest reasons for viewing this crime form as an American institution, through which groups pass along trajectories determined by aspects of their culture and place in the larger society. Organized crime, in the unsurpassed phrase of Daniel Bell, is "the queer ladder of mobility in American life."[44]

CONCLUSION

The evidence in this chapter demonstrates the great extent to which assimilation has penetrated the bastions of Italian-American ethnicity. Even in relation to the family, the moving spirit of the Italian-American ethos, the attitudes of contemporary Italian Americans are simply not very different from those of WASPs. In fact, in several respects, Italians are more liberal than the American core group as a result of their concentration in the urban Northeast—rather than more conservative, as the stereotype of the Italian ethos would lead one to expect. In the light of the great emphasis placed on female chastity among immigrant Italians, a pointed instance of this greater liberalism lies in the moral judgments about premarital and adulterous sex.

To be sure, there are some differences between the two groups in the direction of the supposed Italian-American ethos. Chiefly, these are to be found in the area of family solidarity. Italians are more likely to socialize with relatives and are less likely to move away from the place where they were born and raised, presumably because of their stronger attachment to their families. But in virtually all cases, these differences between Italians and British Protestants are no more than modest in size, and usually they are even less than modest once social background and other factors distinguishing the two groups are taken into account. In sum, the cultural coloration of Italian Americans is no longer the vibrant earthy hue of the Mezzogiorno that earlier in the century stood out in the eyes of Americans; as a result of powerful assimilatory forces, it has paled to a pastel swatch that is barely noticeable against the neutral American background.

The most significant evidence of the depth of the assimilation of Italian Americans, however, does not lie in the shallowness of any remaining cultural distinctiveness but in the current high rates of intermarriage—depending on how one defines an intermarriage, somewhere from two-thirds to four-fifths of young

Italian Americans intermarry. One reason why intermarriage is such a critical indicator of assimilation is that it measures the cultural and social distance between Italians and others; it betrays the extent to which individuals who know each other fairly well at the time of marriage feel that there may be an unbridgeable gap between them. This test is all the more significant in the Italian case, as a consequence of the supposed family-centered culture of the group. Because this carries implications for the relations created by marriage, Italians and those who consider marrying them should be sensitive to conflicting, culturally engendered expectations, such as those relevant to the roles of husbands and wives or the raising of children. The current high rates of Italian intermarriage indicate, then, that the family-centered culture has weakened and that the cultural gap has narrowed.

But intermarriage not only tests the extent of existing cultural differences; it ultimately alters them. It is part of a process by which further acculturation is accomplished. Those who intermarry are usually culturally alike at the start, but prolonged and intimate exposure to an ethnically different spouse tends to bring about further subtle adjustments, leading to even greater similarity. In the abstract, this can be a two-way process, but since Italian Americans represent a minority culture, the direction of their adjustment probably is for the most part away from any Italian ethos. But regardless of whether this adjustment is predominantly a one-direction or a two-direction process, the important point is that any residual Italian cultural distinctiveness is further diluted.

Colleen Leahy Johnson's study of kinship contact among Italian Americans in Syracuse, New York, illustrates the general principle. She compared in-married and out-married Italians to each other and to Protestants of non-Italian background in terms of the frequency of their contact with parents, siblings, and other relatives. Although contact with the relatives on the Italian side appeared dominant among the intermarried Italians in the sense that both spouses saw more of the Italian than of the non-Italian relatives, the frequency of contact was diminished; the intermarried group stood intermediate between the in-married Italians, the majority of whom had daily contact with parents and with siblings, and the Protestants, who had comparatively infrequent contact with their relatives.[45] Johnson's research implies that high rates of intermarriage are associated with further erosion of what Herbert Gans labeled as the "peer-group society" in the 1950s.

At this point, one may wonder whether a reawakening of interest in ethnicity, believed by many to have occurred in the 1970s, might reverse this seemingly inexorable tide of assimilation, which has been washing away ethnic distinctiveness like so many castles in the sand. The answer, I think, is no. The social assimilation epitomized by high rates of intermarriage does not appear to be reversible. Here, the theories of Peter Blau, described in Chapter 1, are pertinent.[46] As Blau emphasizes, intermarriage is to a very important degree a function of the size of a group. The smaller it is, the more difficult it is for an individual to find a suitable spouse within its boundaries and hence the greater is the probability of intermarriage. Blau's theory implies that high rates of ethnic intermarriage in the present guarantee high rates in the future because they deplete ethnic communities of a substantial part of the next generation, in effect reducing the size of the group. Like Humpty Dumpty, then, once intermarriage rates reach sufficiently high levels—and surely 70 to 80 percent is a high level—ethnic solidarity cannot be put back together again, even by all the king's horses and all the king's soldiers.

NOTES

[1] Leonard Covello, *The Social Background of the Italo-American School Child* (Totowa, N.J.: Rowman & Littlefield, 1972), p. 111.

[2] Herbert Gans, *The Urban Villagers: Group and Class in the Life of Italian Americans,* updated and expanded edition (New York: Free Press, 1982), p. 33.

[3] James A. Crispino, *The Assimilation of Ethnic Groups: The Italian Case* (Staten Island: Center for Migration Studies, 1980), pp. 48–50. Crispino's study in all probability overstates fidelity to Italian cooking. His study design is likely to have overselected individuals with a strong sense of Italian-American identity. Moreover, a fair number of individuals did not answer the cooking questions and are therefore not included in the percentages. As Crispino admits, this nonresponse may hide some persons who do not prepare or eat Italian food at home and thought their nonresponse would indicate this.

Despite these drawbacks, Crispino's study offers a reasonably comprehensive analysis of Italian-American ethnicity in an urban Northeastern area typical of those with many Italians, and his findings complement in many ways those presented in this chapter.

[4] See p. 93.

[5] The NORC General Social Survey is described by its codebook: James A. Davis, Tom W. Smith, and C. Bruce Stephenson, *General Social Surveys, 1972-1980: Cumulative Codebook* (Chicago: National Opinion Research Center, 1980). The exact wording of the abortion question is, "Please tell me whether or not *you* think it should be possible for a pregnant woman to obtain a *legal* abortion if . . . " The situations described in the text, along with several others, were then substituted for the "if" clause (*Cumulative Codebook,* pp. 143–44).

[6] The list of factors controlled includes regions and places of current residence and where raised; respondent's, father's, and mother's educations; respondent's and father's occupations; and respondent's age and sex. As in the previous chapter, the regression analyses on which adjustments are based are restricted to whites, since relationships may be different among nonwhites.

The list of factors remains the same throughout the chapter, except in one case, which is duly noted where it occurs in the text.

[7] See pp. 53–54.

[8] The other questions are, "Do you agree or disagree with this statement? Women should take care of running their homes and leave running the country up to men"; "If your party nominated a woman for President, would you vote for her if she were qualified for the job?" "Tell me if you agree or disagree with this statement: Most men are better suited emotionally for politics than are most women" (*Cumulative Codebook,* p. 142).

[9] The questions are worded, "There's been a lot of discussion about the way morals and attitudes about sex are changing in this country. If a man and a woman have sex relations before marriage, do you think it is always wrong, almost always wrong, wrong only sometimes, or not wrong at all?" "What is your opinion about a *married* person having sexual relations with someone *other* than the marriage partner—is it always wrong, almost always wrong, wrong only sometimes, or not wrong at all?" "What about sexual relations between two *adults* of the *same* sex—do you think it is always wrong, almost always wrong, wrong only sometimes, or not wrong at all?" (*Cumulative Codebook,* pp. 148–49).

[10] Francis X. Femminella and Jill S. Quadagno make this claim in their article, "The Italian American family," in Charles H. Mindell and Robert W. Haberstein (eds.), *Ethnic Families in America: Patterns and Variations* (New York: Elsevier, 1976), p. 74.

[11] Because of the survey's wording, the data do not permit a distinction between divorce and legal separation.

The large difference between the divorce rate here and the very low figure reported by Andrew Greeley and noted in Chapter 4 (p. 93) is due to the fact that Greeley reported the percentage of the group who were separated or divorced and not remarried at the time they were surveyed. The number presented here is the percent who have *ever* been divorced or legally separated. This is a more valid indicator of family stability.

[12] The question was "Should divorce in this country be easier or more difficult to obtain than it is now?" (*Cumulative Codebook*, p. 148).

[13] The question was worded, "Do you favor or oppose the death penalty for persons convicted of murder?" (*Cumulative Codebook*, p. 81).

[14] The list of factors taken into account has to be modified for this analysis. If the region and size of place of current residence are controlled, as is done elsewhere in this chapter, then in effect one is predicting geographic mobility from itself (since knowledge of regions and places of origin and of current residence amounts to knowledge of mobility). Consequently, the current region and type of place have been removed from the list, but those where the respondent was raised continue to be controlled.

[15] The question was worded, "As you know, many older people share a home with their grown children. Do you think this is generally a good idea or a bad idea?" (*Cumulative Codebook*, p. 125). The answers to this question do not indicate, of course, how many people would actually be willing to take in elderly parents; no doubt, the practice is less common than the general approval of it.

[16] The question asked specifically for the frequency with which the respondent spent "a social evening with relatives" (*Cumulative Codebook*, p. 122).

[17] Edward C. Banfield, *The Moral Basis of a Backward Society* (New York: Free Press, 1958).

[18] For example, Nathan Glazer and Daniel Patrick Moynihan assert: "'Free from strangers' is again the motif. Even today in Italian neighborhoods strangers are conspicuous. A non-Italian newcomer encounters a tight net of friendship and blood relation that binds the community excludes outsiders until they are found to be 'all right'" [*Beyond the Melting Pot*, second edition (Cambridge, Mass.: MIT Press, 1970), p. 189.]

[19] The other questions were, "Generally speaking, would you say that most people can be trusted or that you can't be too careful in dealing with people?" "Would you say that most of the time people try to be helpful, or that they are mostly just looking out for themselves?" (*Cumulative Codebook*, p. 103).

[20] See p. 94.

[21] Kohn's research is discussed in many places. One of the best is his book, *Class and Conformity: A Study in Values* (Homewood, Ill.: Dorsey Press, 1969).

[22] The questions in the General Social Survey read: "The qualities listed on this card may all be important, but which *three* would you say are the *most desirable* for a *child* to have? Which *one* of *these three* is the *most* desirable of all? All of the qualities listed on this card may be desirable, but could you tell me which *three* you consider *least important*? And which *one* of these three is *least important* of all?" The card referred to in the question contains the traits: (1) "that he has good manners," (2) "that he tries hard to succeed," (3) "that he is honest," (4) "that he is neat and clean," (5) "that he has good sense and sound judgment," (6) "that he has self-control," (7) "that he acts like a boy (she acts like a girl)," (8) "that he gets along well with other children," (9) "that he obeys his parents well," (10) "that he is responsible," (11) "that he is considerate of others," (12) "that he is interested in how and why things happen," (13) "that he is a good student" (*Cumulative Codebook*, pp. 109–12). Following Kohn and others, the fifth, sixth, and tenth through twelfth traits are taken as indicators of self-direction, while the first, fourth, ninth and thirteenth are used to represent conformity to authority.

It should be noted that the wording of the General Social Survey question is significantly different from that used by Kohn in his studies. The meaning of the difference is debated by James and Sonia Wright, on the one hand, and Kohn, on the other, in the *American Sociological Review*, 41, No. 3 (June, 1976), 527–48.

[23] *Cumulative Codebook,* p. 121.

[24] Gans, *The Urban Villagers,* p. 123.

[25] Respondents are asked: "Would you please look at this card and tell me which *one* thing on this list you would *most* prefer in a job? Which comes *next*? Which is the *third* most important? Which is the *fourth* most important?" The card contains the entries "high income," "no danger of being fired," "working hours are short, lots of free time," "chances for advancement," "work important and gives a feeling of accomplishment" (*Cumulative Codebook,* pp. 136–37).

[26] The other categories are, "Not very strong Democrat" (value = 2); "Independent, close to Democrat" (3), "Independent" (4), "Independent, close to Republican" (5), "Not very strong Republican" (6) (*Cumulative Codebook,* p. 66). (The values reported here have been increased by 1 from those in the codebook.)

[27] The question asked simply: "Do you believe there is a life after death?" (*Cumulative Codebook,* p. 90).

[28] Milton M. Gordon, *Assimilation in American Life: The Role of Race, Religion, and National Origins* (New York: Oxford University Press, 1964), p. 81.

[29] Richard D. Alba, "Social assimilation among American Catholic national-origin groups," *American Sociological Review,* 41, No. 6 (December, 1976), pp. 1040–44. For more on the significance of intermarriage, see Robert K. Merton, "Intermarriage and the social structure" in his *Sociological Ambivalence and Other Essays* (New York: Free Press, 1976).

[30] Alba, "Social assimilation," Table 1.

[31] The slightly higher rates of marriage to individuals with unmixed Italian ancestry that are found among women might seem to hint that loyalty to the group is weaker among men. Although this possibility seems tantalizing from the data, it is dubious. Women are more likely to be found at home and thus to be the respondents to the survey; and respondents, be they women or men, tend to give greater detail about their own ancestries than those of their spouses. Consequently, among men, the category of unmixed ancestry is more likely to contain some individuals who in fact have mixed parentage; and such persons are also more likely to be intermarried.

[32] A similar sort of numerical reasoning explains the rise in marriages to individuals with mixed Italian ancestry, which is obvious in the progression from older to younger cohorts in Table 6-2. There were few such individuals around in the older cohorts, and hence the rate of marriage to them could only be small. As their availability has increased, so too has entry into marriage with them. This is not a trivial point, because it diminishes the possibility of a change in preferences for such spouses.

[33] Will Herberg, *Protestant-Catholic-Jew* (New York: Doubleday, 1955).

[34] See pp. 86–89.

[35] Crispino, *Assimilation of Ethnic Groups,* pp. 89–93. Crispino also describes similar changes in friendship patterns (pp. 80–89).

[36] The argument is advanced by Charles C. Moskos, Jr., *Greek Americans: Struggle and Success* (Englewood Cliffs, N.J.: Prentice-Hall, 1980), p. 147.

[37] This percentage, it must be conceded, underestimates the rate of membership in ethnic organizations because some of the types covered under other categories of the same question, such as veterans' groups and fraternities, may have an ethnic character (the data do not allow these to be separated from those that are nonethnic). Nonetheless, if ethnic interests were really salient in the minds of Italian Americans and others, the rate of membership in avowedly ethnic organizations ought to be much higher.

[38] Crispino, *Assimilation of Ethnic Groups,* pp. 76, 78.

[39] Glazer and Moynihan, *Beyond the Melting Pot,* pp. 192–94.

[40] Donald R. Cressey, *Theft of the Nation: The Structure and Operations of Organized Crime in America* (New York: Harper & Row, 1969), p. 118.

[41] A summary statement on this point is by Dwight C. Smith, Jr., and Richard D. Alba, "Organized crime and American life," *Society,* 16, No. 3 (March/April, 1979), 32–38. A more

detailed account, including some of the best evidence on the workings of a crime family, is found in Francis A. J. Ianni with Elizabeth Reuss-Ianni, *A Family Business: Kinship and Social Control in Organized Crime* (New York: Russell Sage Foundation, 1972), especially Chapter 8.

[42] Annelise Graebner Anderson, *The Business of Organized Crime: A Cosa Nostra Family* (Stanford, Cal.: Hoover Institution Press, 1979), pp. 41–44.

[43] Anderson, *Business of Organized Crime,* pp. 105–7. That such modest financial circumstances are not uncommon is confirmed by the transcribed conversations of a New Jersey *capo,* Simone De Cavalcante, which were made public at his trial. These show De Cavalcante worring a lot about small amounts of money and even about unemployed crime family members.

[44] Daniel Bell, "Crime as an American way of life," in *The End of Ideology* (New York: Collier, 1961).

[45] Colleen Leahy Johnson, "Sibling solidarity: Its origin and functioning in Italian-American families," *Journal of Marriage and the Family,* 44, No. 2 (February, 1982), 155–67.

[46] See pp. 13–15.

CHAPTER SEVEN
INTO THE TWILIGHT
OF ETHNICITY

Italian Americans stand on the verge of the twilight of their ethnicity. "Twilight" appears an accurate metaphor for a stage when ethnic differences remain visible but only faintly so, when ethnic forms can be perceived only in vague outline. The twilight metaphor acknowledges that ethnicity has not entirely disappeared, and therefore, that the misguided optimism of the melting-pot ideology earlier in the century seems to have been ill-founded; but at the same time, it captures the reality that ethnicity is nonetheless steadily receding. The twilight metaphor also allows for the occasional flare-ups of ethnic feelings and conflicts that give the illusion that ethnicity is reviving, but are little more than flickers in the fading light.

The approach of this twilight is deceptive, for a fading glow remains from the intense ethnicity of the earlier part of this century. The processes leading to twilight have not affected all Italian Americans to the same degree, and anyone looking at the group in the aggregate for ethnic survivals can find them, but this is primarily because of the ethnicity attributable to its older members and earlier generations. Once the group is decomposed by generations or birth cohorts, the evidence on behalf of the looming twilight seems overwhelming. Despite the image in the American consciousness of an intense, family-centered Italian-American culture, the group's cultural distinctiveness has paled to a feeble version of its former self. Paralleling this change, the social boundary between Italians and other Americans has become easily permeable; intermarriage, an irrevocable indicator of change in social perceptions, takes place quite freely between later-generation and young Italians and those of other European ancestries. Acculturation and social assimilation have been fed by a surge in the educational and occupational attainment of Italians, which has brought cohorts born since World War II to the brink of parity with Protestants of British ancestry, the quintessential American core group.

As if to promise further assimilation, this profound transformation of the Italian-American group has taken place at a time when the fourth generation, the first generation without direct contact with the immigrant experience, is still small. But this generation will grow substantially in size during the rest of the century, and simultaneously, the first and second generations, whose members have been raised in the Old World or in the immigrant ghetto and thus bear the most intense ethnicity, will shrink. The fourth generation will be far more interspersed among other Americans than preceding generations have been, and its members will have mixed ethnic ancestry for the most part. Thus, ethnicity can be expected to become more muted still, completing a process that has brought a group that was considered to be unassimilable in the early 1900s to the point of full integration into American society, a scant century after the onset of its immigration.

THE IMPACT OF ETHNICITY'S TWILIGHT
ON AMERICANS OF EUROPEAN ANCESTRY

In a number of respects, events among the Italians seem to parallel those among other groups descended from European immigrants—although because of differences in their times of arrival, the specific situations that greeted them, and their occupational and cultural heritages, no two groups have followed exactly the same pathways to the twilight stage. Yet among almost all white ethnic groups, one can observe a progressive, if gradual, dampening of cultural distinctiveness. Their core values have been overwhelmed by a common American culture so that, even though cultural uniformity has not been the end result, the remaining differences among groups are so mild as to constitute neither a basis for group solidarity nor a barrier to intergroup contact. Stephen Steinberg makes this point effectively by observing that few who proclaim the vitality of ethnic cultures ask themselves about the quality and depth of what culture remains. But as Steinberg notes, much of the contemporary cultural manifestation of ethnic groups is confined to a symbolic plane that comes to life only occasionally and has little meaning for everyday existence. He offers the example of Scottish Americans who, with kilts and bagpipes, attended the International Gathering of the Clans for two weeks in 1977, but that of those Italian Americans who become ethnic only during infrequent visits to Little Italy or on Columbus Day would do equally as well. This is ethnicity as a leisure-time activity, rather than as a life-organizing force.[1]

Additionally, among almost all groups, one can see a spreading pattern of intermarriage, testimony to the trivial nature of remaining group differences and guarantee of additional assimilation. To take an example, the overall rate of inter-marriage for Irish Catholics was already at 70 percent by the mid-1960s, even though this rate included the marriages of older persons and those who belonged to early generations, many of whom had married thirty or forty years before. Three-quarters of Irish Catholics under 30 and of the group's third and fourth generations were then intermarrying. Of course, Irish Catholics were by the 1960s an old group on the American scene, their peak period of immigration having taken place in the mid-19th century, and their long residence could in principle explain this frequent intermarriage. To take a second example, this time of a group that immigrated around the turn of the century, the overall intermarriage rate for Polish Catholics was about 60 percent in the mid-1960s; at that time, two-thirds of the group's youngest members and of its third generation had intermarried.[2]

American Jews are probably the acid test of pervasive intermarriage, for their history of persecution in the Diaspora has made them acutely sensitive to the issue of intermarriage and group destiny. Historically, the rate of Jewish–Gentile inter-marriage in the United States has been quite low, at least in the aftermath of the massive influx of eastern European Jews (before that, the Jewish presence was small, and the intermarriage rate may have been correspondingly higher). Thus, one study of Jewish marriage patterns, conducted in the early 1970s, found the overall rate to be still quite low, around 9 percent, but among those who had mar-ried in the seven years preceding the study, a third had married non-Jews. Since then, other studies have documented this spurt in the frequency of marriage be-tween Jews and Gentiles.[3]

There has been considerable debate about the meaning and consequences of intermarriage of this magnitude for Judaism and Jewishness. Intermarriage does not have quite the same group-diminishing character for religious groups that it has for nationality groups. Because there is a strong norm of raising children within a religious heritage, formal or informal conversion of one spouse to the religious iden-tity of the other is a common outcome of interreligious marriage, one for which there is no counterpart for marriage across nationality lines. In the case of Jewish–Gentile intermarriage, studies suggest that Jewish identity is generally stronger and that conversion tends to occur in the Jewish direction, rather than the Gentile one. On net balance, then, the Jewish group may gain numerically, rather than lose, from intermarriage. Even if this is so, however, it does not detract from the funda-mental point that the sudden increase in intermarriage since the mid-1960s, occur-ring essentially among the post-World War II generation, indicates that the social boundary between Jews and Gentiles has been lowered significantly. As Stephen Steinberg puts it,

> Not only are youth of different ethnic backgrounds coming into more fre-quent contact in colleges and on the job, but since they increasingly share the same basic values and life-styles, they easily develop the kind of intimacy that leads to wedlock. In a word, the social and cultural constraints that once kept intermarriage at a minimum have all but dissolved.[4]

The twilight of ethnicity among white ethnic groups does not imply that their disappearance is imminent. This is a twilight that will not in the near future, and may never, turn into night. Several factors will preserve the ethnicity of European origins as a noticeable feature of the American landscape for the foreseeable future. To start with, there is the already acknowledged fact that ethnicity is still plainly visible among the members of earlier generations and older cohorts, who will remain numerous for some time to come. Also, even though the current of assimilation is running strong among later generations and the young, it does not carry everyone along with it. Some members of each ethnic group—and the number varies from group to group—retain a steadfast affiliation with the group and draw a fervent identity from it. Among the Italians, the number of such firm adherents is undoubtedly a minority among the youthful members of the third and fourth generations, and consequently their presence is not clearly registered in the survey data reviewed in Chapter 6. But in Northeastern cities, the concentration of Italian-American loyalists in neighborhoods with a definite ethnic character keeps alive the notion of an Italian-American ethnicity, even in the midst of widespread assimilation.

Renewed immigration, moreover, has imparted some new vitality to ethnicity. Large-scale immigration from Italy all but ceased after restrictive immigration legislation was enacted during the 1920s, but it has revived since 1965, when the immigration laws were revised to eliminate biased national-origin quotas. Since that time, about 20 thousand Italian immigrants on average have entered the United States annually. This volume is far below that which occurred in the peak years of immigration during the first decade and a half of this century, but it is enough to sustain and even to rebuild some Italian-American communities. And it provides a new population, admittedly small by comparison with the first half of the century, of first- and second-generation Italians to preserve something of the ethnic glaze on this one tile in the American mosaic.

However, even the virtual disappearance of ethnicity as a group-sustaining force would not mean an end to visible differences among ethnic categories in the near future, for ethnic contingencies will continue to reverberate for a while. Each group has its own peculiar history, its place and occupational concentrations, and these correlates of ethnicity will continue to exert some influence, even in the absence of ethnicity itself. One realm in which their impact is evident is that of elites, the men and women who shape national policies. Entry to an elite is in many respects a fortuitous process, with a heavy component of luck, but sponsorship also plays an important role, and consequently, social advantages such as wealth and coming from the right kind of family play their parts. Thus, even though national elites are no longer as WASP-dominated as they once were, the influence of ethnicity is still manifest. A few Italian Americans (e.g., Joseph Califano) have managed to break through, but the group remains quite underrepresented at this level.[5] Because networks of sponsorship tend to perpetuate the ethnic patterns of the past, elite levels register only slowly the ethnic changes at lower levels, and the Italian-American gap in representation is unlikely to close anytime soon.

That ethnic traces of European origins are still visible on the social facade of American society does not diminish the significance of the tremendous quieting of ethnicity as a social force among whites since World War II. Ethnic groups are no longer the confines within which most white Americans will spend a considerable portion of their lifetimes.

But this twilight of ethnicity among Americans of European ancestry is not matched by equal changes among most of America's racial minorities. Black Americans stand as the extreme case. Though their socioeconomic progress in recent decades has been debated, no informed observer claims that they have reached parity with whites. Unemployment among Blacks continues to run at much higher rates than among whites; and Black family income remains where it has been since the end of World War II, at roughly 60 percent of white family income. As persuasive as any other single fact in establishing that Blacks are not integrated into the economy on the same basis as whites is the lower returns they realize on so-called human capital investments, which presumably improve an individual's labor-market position: Black men, for example, receive lower income rewards for such factors as education and job experience by comparison with white men. It goes almost without saying, then, that racial boundaries remain salient. Residentially, Blacks are still extremely segregated from whites; and the incidence of Black-white intermarriage is tiny.[6]

The position of some other racial minorities is more ambiguous. Groups that, unlike Blacks, have been voluntary immigrants to the United States evidence developments like those among the white ethnics, though these are not as far along. For example, Japanese Americans, despite the bitter legacy of World War II internment, have been unusually successful in socioeconomic terms, with high rates of college attendance and occupational mobility. In tandem with this upward movement have come increases in intermarriage; it appears that over a third of third-generation Japanese Americans are marrying non-Japanese, usually whites.[7] In the near future, then, it may become appropriate to speak of an ethnic twilight among Japanese Americans and perhaps some Chinese Americans.

The picture for non-European immigrant groups is complicated by the large immigration that has sprung up since immigration laws were revised. The Immigration Act of 1965 repealed the high barriers that had blocked immigration from Asian countries (although it imposed for the first time an upper limit on immigration from the Western hemisphere). Asian, Latin American, and Caribbean countries have all contributed heavily to the resulting human flow. During the 1970s, for example, nearly 4 million immigrants arrived on American shores, but in great contrast to the past, only 730 thousand of them originated in European countries. About 1.4 million came from Asia, and 1.6 million from Latin America and the West Indies. Immigrants from Colombia, Cuba, India, Korea, Mexico, the Philippines, Taiwan and Hong Kong, Vietnam, and elsewhere are adding new pieces to the American ethnic mosaic.[8]

These new immigrants are beginning a stage of adjustment that European ethnics entered in the early years of this century. No doubt, in the future the term *ethnic* will become increasingly synonymous with ancestry from outside the European continent. Although ethnicity may be slipping into twilight for those whose immigrant forebears came from Europe, issues of ethnicity will remain intensely lit for American society.

EXPLAINING ETHNICITY'S TWILIGHT

The extent of Italian-American assimilation, a bare century after the onset of the group's mass entry into the United States, underlines the need for some explanation of the impending twilight. Few Americans witnessing the arrival of southern Italian immigrants earlier in this century would have predicted such an outcome. A fair number believed them to be racially inferior to the country's old-stock inhabitants, those with ancestral heritages derived from northern and western Europe. Almost everyone perceived them to be socially inferior to immigrants from most other parts of Europe. Coming from a rural and backward society that still felt the leaden hand of feudalism, Italian immigrants lacked industrial skills and appeared to have criminal proclivities; on both counts, they seemed incapable of assimilation to an urban, industrial society. Yet scarcely a hundred years later, their descendants stand on the threshold of educational and occupational parity with the American core, from whose members they are barely distinguishable in cultural terms and with whom they intermarry with considerable frequency. How could this have happened, and how could it have happened so quickly?

A traditional answer in ethnic writings comes in the form of a morality tale, which depicts a successful ethnic group's members as virtuous citizens who through ambition, hard work, and some of the "right stuff"—the cultural traits that make for success—overcome terrible odds and unfair hurdles placed in their way. No doubt there is some truth in these tales, and no one should underestimate the triumph against the odds in a story like that of Italians; but answers of this sort are nonetheless unsatisfactory. They are often used in support of a comforting view that unsuccessful groups fail through their own deficiencies; but in truth such morality tales do not tell us why some groups have been successful and others have not, since all groups have made strenuous efforts to break out of circles of discrimination. Moreover, if the right stuff were really as crucial as it is made out to be, then it is difficult to understand what has happened among the Italians. It is hard to see Mezzogiorno culture as other than an impediment to full integration in American society.

Sociological theory is also not much help here. There is not, in fact, a mature theory of ethnicity in industrial societies, in part because ethnicity was not an object of serious concern until fairly recently. But equally important as a bar to mature theory is the contingent nature of ethnicity itself. Ethnic phenomena depend for their development on the accretion of historical contingencies, and these vary substantially from group to group and society to society. From the standpoint of a familiar kind of sociological theorizing, which strives for generalizations that are independent of time and place, such contingencies appear as random events, or historical accidents, that disturb a fundamental uniformity. They are not, of course, really random, but they do prevent neat generalizations, which analyze ethnic developments in terms of a limited number of factors. Its contingent nature demands that ethnicity be considered in its historical context, and not merely by the light of universal theories.

To understand what has happened in the United States over the course of the 20th century, one must begin with some of the peculiarities of the earlier development of ethnicity on the new continent. Perhaps most important in this respect is the dispersal of ethnic groups through the territory of the United States, a result of the way in which the American population was built up by successive layers of immigration. In much of the world, ethnicity and geography strongly coincide, as regions of a country are largely homogeneous, dominated by the members of a single ethnic group. Yugoslavia offers an almost ideal illustration of this situation, which is conducive to a strict institutional separation among ethnic groups. School systems, workplaces, and communities are naturally ethnic preserves, and individuals spend, without any volition on their part, their lifetimes in an ethnic matrix. This is a genuine structural pluralism, one that has not generally obtained in the United States. To be sure, all groups have been more concentrated in some areas than in others, but with a few notable exceptions, such as the 19th-century German concentration in the Midwest, this has not meant ethnic homogeneity. Generally speaking, the largest territorial unit of homogeneity in the United States has been the urban neighborhood or the small town, neither of which is large enough for a group to sustain its own full complement of institutions. As a result, ethnic groups have had to butt up against one another in many institutional arenas, and the necessity of cross-ethnic contact has degraded "ethnic purity."

A second feature rooted in the great ethnic diversity of the United States is relevant here also. I take as a reasonable, if not self-evident, assumption that groups seek to preserve their power and privilege and that, to do this, they attempt to erect and maintain rigid social boundaries, buttressed by cultural and other distinctions. This assumption applies specifically to the old-stock Americans descended from the 17th- and 18th-century settlers who formed the ethnic core of the new nation. Under many circumstances, the natural desire to preserve advantages would keep ethnicity as a prominent social feature; but a preservation of dominance in its original ethnic form was made virtually impossible, on the one hand, by the massive immigration of the 19th and early 20th centuries, which was not only numerically overwhelming but added a host of new groups to the ethnic spectrum, and on the other hand, by the rise and evolution of industrial society.[9] As the economic foundations shifted to a largely manufacturing order and then to an increasingly managerial one, advancing industrialization demanded a certain type of labor force: one that did not need repressive discipline but had the capacity for self-discipline; that was sufficiently integrated to permit a ready communication of technical skills from one individual to another; and that offered not only a wide base of recruitment for managerial positions, but also a sizable number of individuals able to cooperate effectively in a large bureaucratic context. In short, what was needed was the assimilation of some subordinate ethnic groups to make a majority group without salient internal divisions; those outside the protection of the dominant culture could amount to no more than a minority of the population.

This assimilation was promoted by a profound transformation of the occupational structure, a key manifestation of advancing industrialization. As we saw in Chapter 4, the middle and upper rungs of the occupational hierarchy expanded enormously over the course of the century, while the bottom contracted, thus generating what is often called "structural mobility," an intergenerational movement across status boundaries that is necessary to fill labor needs. Had the distribution of slots throughout the occupational spectrum remained stagnant, the ethnic outcomes in American society might have been very different. Under such circumstances, upward mobility on any appreciable scale for Italians and other disparaged groups would have had to be balanced by substantial downward mobility on the part of members of the ethnic core. Clearly, then, it would have been in the interests of dominant groups to enforce a distinctly marked social boundary between themselves and other white ethnics to retain their privileged position.

The importance of this sustained, structurally engendered mobility lay, in other words, in its non-zero-sum character. In the manner of a vacuum, structural mobility forced some upward movement on the part of then-disadvantaged ethnics, and this had two pivotal consequences. It added to the likelihood that a gradual assimilation would be accepted by many ethnics, who, cognizant of the distance they had moved beyond their parents, came to identify themselves primarily as "middle-class" Americans. Also, by virtue of its bringing members of different groups shoulder to shoulder in equal-status contact, first at the workplace and then in the suburb, this structurally induced mobility broke down preexisting social boundaries between ethnics and the core and also among the ethnics themselves. These assimilatory outcomes were promoted additionally by a development accompanying the transformation of the occupational structure: the emergence of mass higher education. Higher education extends a sense of equality among its participants through an experience that is viewed as a sharp alteration in status and is sanctified by the selectivity of colleges and universities.

The dispersal of ethnic groups and the exigencies of the advancing industrial order help to explain the dimming of ethnicity among many American groups, but they are far from sufficient by themselves. In particular, since they imply a structural weakness for all groups, they do not provide any clues for solving the great puzzle in the sociology of American ethnicity: Why has the boundary of assimilation enclosed the groups descended from European immigrants in what approximates a "melting pot," while excluding minorities of color, especially Black, Hispanic, and Native Americans?

Since the needs of the industrial order did not require the assimilation of all groups, and since the exclusion of some from the emerging melting pot was compatible (at least on the surface) with the continued existence of jobs at the bottom of the occupational ladder, it might seem as if the emergence of race as the overriding difference could be explained in conventional fashion. Namely, the groups that were assimilated were racially similar to the core and, given their origins on the European continent, not that distant from it culturally; the groups that were excluded were racially identifiable and were from culturally exotic parts of the world, at least to European eyes. While there is much that is true in this observation, it is too pat in many respects, as I have tried to suggest through the example of the Italians. It assumes that the perception of ethnic differences was hard and fast, while in fact it was fluid and fairly amorphous. It assumes that the ultimate boundaries were not problematic, whereas the evolution of ethnicity was far from clear earlier in the century and responded to accumulating historical contingencies.

Some pivotal contingencies lay in the accidents of time and place. By and large, white ethnic groups were in the right places at the right times to take advantage of structural mobility, for this massive occupational shift did not happen everywhere at once. During the better part of this century, its effects were concentrated in the Northeast and Midwest, especially in their cities—precisely the places where the largest numbers of ethnics from the 19th and early 20th century immigrations were found. At the same time, other minorities were confined to peripheral areas: Black Americans were mostly located in the stagnant rural economy of the South; Hispanics in rural areas of the Southwest and Puerto Rico; and Native Americans on reservations, generally in the otherwise empty parts of Western states. To be sure, this placement at the margins was not entirely accidental. In the case of Blacks, Stephen Steinberg shows that a variety of devices were used to hold them in the South in quasi-servitude after the Civil War, because their labor was critical to the economy of cotton.[10] They did begin to move northward in large numbers during World War I, when labor shortages arose as a result of the interruption of immigration, and the migration to northern cities continued in the following decades. But the largest numbers came following World War II, and by then the die had been cast—white ethnics were positioned to take advantage of the choicest openings from future structural shifts.[11] The trek northward was also not as much help to non-European minorities because the points of entry into mobility channels changed over time. Early in the century, when impoverished European peasants flooded American cities, many unskilled jobs were available, enabling groups from rural Europe to gain a toehold in an urban labor market. But by mid-century, when rural Black migrants and also Hispanics were coming *en masse,* this was no longer true.[12]

These implications of the sequencing of ethnic arrivals are summarized in the concept of the *ethnic queue.* The concept presumes that groups derive advantages from early arrival. They are able to establish occupational niches, which give them an economic base and provide the leverage for future generations to leapfrog over their immigrant forebears. Later-arriving groups enter a labor market where many of the better positions are already reserved for the members of earlier, now more privileged groups. Hence, they find themselves confined, at least initially, to the least desirable jobs. By taking these, moreover, they contribute in an odd way to the mobility of earlier groups because they release them from the necessity of filling these bottom spots. In imagery appropriate for the notion of a queue, later arrivals "push" their predecessors up the occupational ladder. By implication, white ethnic groups were advantaged by the additional fact that they were not the last mass arrivals in American cities.[13]

Another set of contingencies flows from the sequence of group arrivals. Ironically, white ethnics ultimately benefited from the closing of the gates on mass immigration during the 1920s, which was directed at the time against them. A continuing influx of European immigrants would have continuously renewed ethnic cultures and sentiments, retarding if not altogether preventing the assimilation of the descendants of the immigrants. The shutting off of the immigrant flow made clear to the second and third generations that their futures lay in the new society. The turning off of the human spigot meant that these later generations among the Italians, coming to maturity in the 1930s and 1940s, would see the immigrant and Old World cultures as identified with an aging generation; the contrast between the old and the young sharpened the sense that accommodation to the manners and mores of the host society was desirable, even inevitable. Moreover, in accordance with a sociological axiom that prejudice and discrimination directed against a group increase as the flow of its members into an area does, the end of mass immigration made possible a gradual abating of antagonism toward the new immigrants and their descendants. It was, in other words, a precondition for their acceptability to other Americans.[14]

It could be argued that the ending of mass immigration had some benefits for minorities of color, too. The fact that fresh European arrivals were no longer available for filling many labor needs provided the opening for minorities to migrate to urban, industrial areas. But at the same time, the fact that prolonged and massive Black migration to Northern cities basically followed the era of mass European immigration, rather than coinciding with it, had repercussions that redounded to the further advantage of white ethnic groups. The influx of Blacks, which began during World War I and continued through the 1960s, aroused public consciousness of race, submerging to a degree that of nationality and reducing the salience of ethnic differences among whites. In this sense, Blacks drew off some of the antagonism that might have attached to European groups, thereby making other Americans more willing to accept the white ethnics.[15]

World War II crystallized the evolving advantages of white ethnics. The war acted as a catalyst, precipitating then-latent patterns in favor of whites into a manifest form. The wartime unity, somewhat self-consciously promoted on behalf of the war effort, clearly embraced the white ethnic groups; it was far more ambiguous, if not hostile, with respect to nonwhites. Italians, Jews, Poles, even Americans of German ancestry, all served in regular units of the armed forces, intermixed with other Americans. Blacks, however, served in all-Black units, which generally were not allowed frontline responsibilities until late in the war. And in one of the most infamous racist episodes in 20th-century America, Japanese Americans on the West Coast were interned and their property was confiscated.

Ultimately, the War had the effect of drawing the white ethnic groups into the magic circle of full citizenship, a result of a complicated interplay of factors. One was what Swedish sociologist Gunnar Myrdal has called the "American Creed," the belief in equality of opportunity for all individuals regardless of their origins. The Creed, it could be said, is as much honored in the breach as in the observance,[16] but it provided a culturally sanctioned rationale for an opening to disadvantaged ethnic groups. Timing, nonetheless, was again crucial. World War I had unleashed a prolonged and intense hysteria, prompted by the large number of immigrants from enemy nations. In 1917, when America entered the war, it was still in the throes of mass immigration. Not only had the era of mass immigration ended by the Second World War, but second and later generations predominated among the young men from European ancestry groups, the ones from these groups who would do the fighting.

But when all is said and done, the emerging gap between white ethnic groups and racial minorities did not simply result from structural forces and historical contingencies, but it derived also from the special burdens borne by Blacks and some others. These arose from an interaction between race and the manner by which groups entered American society. Racial groups stood out in a way that most European ancestry groups did not, and they were especially disparaged by ethnocentric images of "civilization," which elevated European groups while placing many non-European groups, particularly Afro-Americans and American Indians, into a "savage" pale. They were also denigrated by the continuing heritage derived from their incorporation by conquest and enslavement into the American nation. This was true in the most awful manner for Blacks, who could not easily shake off the stereotypes imposed on them, the legacy of more than two centuries of slavery. In short, a distinction must be made among groups according to their mode of entry. Groups that came as voluntary immigrants—and this includes Chinese and Japanese Americans—have had advantages that have eluded groups introduced by force. Notable among the latter are Blacks, Native Americans, and many Hispanics.[17]

Put simply, immigrant groups have had greater latitude to determine where they settle and what occupations they pursue. Even though white ethnics and racial minorities have been greatly despised in the past by American core groups, the racial groups have been more so and have suffered from unique barriers placed in the way of their progress. Consider, just as one example, the discrimination against Blacks by labor unions. Until the 1930s, and in some cases until much later, many labor unions either excluded Blacks from membership through constitutional provision or tacit agreement or, if they did not exclude Blacks altogether, placed them in segregated locals with fewer employment privileges. Even in cases where national unions were supportive of Black membership, individual locals frequently excluded them. Exclusion from union membership effectively barred Blacks from many occupations, ranging from airline pilot to pipefitter, and from numerous places of employment. No such consistent pattern existed in the case of Italians and other disparaged European groups. It was no doubt true in the early decades of this century that many native-born American workers were reluctant to work alongside Italians and other immigrants, and probably the immigrants were excluded from some unions. But such exclusions, if they existed, never became part of the institutional fabric as they did for Blacks. And the exclusion from union membership is not merely an isolated fact. It testifies to a larger set of attitudes that confronted Blacks and other minorities in places of employment. As a result, in the critical early decades of this century, white ethnics were able to open up a considerable lead over urban minorities in the dynamic manufacturing sector, a catapult for subsequent mobility.[18] And the example of institutional barriers in employment could be repeated in other areas as well, such as politics, residential segregation, and intermarriage.

At its root, the process that has brought Italians and other white ethnic groups to the verge of a twilight stage involves a realignment of ethnic boundaries. Such boundaries govern the degree to which groups encounter one another in situations conducive to close social relationships and their willingness to accept one another in such social intimacy. The mechanisms of the boundary shift involving white ethnics can be decomposed into two factors, broadly construed. The first was a structural transformation that made possible an upgrading of the social positions of recently arrived European groups; it is here that structural mobility and the somewhat fortuitous settlement of white ethnics in the most dynamic places play their part. Changes in the structural underpinnings made the older boundaries fluid; new boundaries were crystallized into permanent form by the second factor, which was cultural. It amounted to a redefinition of where white ethnics stood in the ethnic spectrum of American society, of their social distance from the core; and it is in this respect that events such as World War II take on their fullest significance. The reduction in social distance among all white groups led to a massive intermingling among them, i.e., structural assimilation, and this in turn has produced the ethnic twilight.

This analysis makes clear the problematic nature of boundary shifts in general. The shift that incorporated the white ethnic groups occurred on a mass scale and included numerous groups. But a number of interlocking processes and events were necessary to bring it about; the absence of any one could have set it back or shunted it in a different direction. From this vantage, the assimilation of white ethnic groups does not seem to have been inevitable, and there is no guarantee that boundaries will move further to include other groups in the future.

In conclusion, what stands out by implication in this account is the relative insignificance of cultural differences among ethnic groups compared to large-scale and impersonal forces such as structural mobility. This is a crucial point in the case of the Italians, given the evident limitations of Mezzogiorno culture in an urban, industrial society. It is obvious from earlier chapters that the family-centered ethos did have an impact, especially on the first two generations. But culture is malleable, and signs of change were already visible with the emergence of the second generation. The culture of the group continued to change as its position did. The story of the Italian Americans thus testifies to endless creativity of human beings, who fashion culture in order to help make sense of the world they know and are capable of reworking it in response to changes in their surroundings.

WHAT HAPPENED TO THE RESURGENCE OF ETHNICITY?

If the argument that ethnicity is entering a twilight stage among American whites is correct, and the evidence on its behalf seems undeniable, then this prompts a question: What happened to the widely proclaimed ethnic revival?

It seems at first sight a paradox that the notion of an ethnic revival came to the fore at the very moment when mobility and assimilation were really taking hold, but in fact the paradox is the explanation: The apparent resurgence of ethnicity was a product of ethnicity's receding. It was not so much that ethnicity was suddenly more vital after 1960, when the revival began to be proclaimed, as that it had previously been much less visible. In the earlier period, ethnicity could be described as a matter of patterns of daily life carried on in the relative seclusion of ethnic communities; since the ethnics were overwhelmingly working-class or lower-middle-class, ethnicity lacked public figures to give it visibility. But with accelerating speed after World War II, the prevailing winds of assimilation carried many ethnics into positions of prominence in American life, in the arts, in the academic world, and in politics, and thereby increased consciousness of ethnicity among upper-middle-class Americans—who previously might have dismissed it as a transient phenomenon of little consequence for their world.

The trends in the academic world, from which many of the writers concerned with ethnicity come, exemplify this process. The Jewish breakthrough into college and university faculties came a little before the popularity of the ethnic revival, as part of the post–World War II expansion of higher education. Catholic penetration developed more slowly, but Catholics began to reach parity during the 1960s.[19] It was only around 1960 that a critical mass of ethnic faculty developed at elite universities, one that was numerically strong enough to voice its own concerns and to serve as spokespersons for the previously unrepresented ethnics.

The experiences of many ethnics on their way added urgency to their need to speak out about ethnicity. Here there is something at work that could be described as a "beachhead" phenomenon. The first waves of a group's members to enter an arena of prestige and privilege generally meet with resistance to their presence and stumble across residues of prejudice against their group. And even if the antagonism is mild, the sense that they have entered a sphere where there are few others like themselves will have the same effect: to make them more conscious of their origins and resentful of what are perceived to be unfair hurdles placed in their way.[20] This phenomenon, however, is likely to be most intense for this initial cohort, subsiding among later cohorts as more ethnics reach these spheres and their presence becomes customary, rather than exceptional.

The tenor of the time at which they began to write added legitimacy to their concerns. The 1960s were a period of intense preoccupation with racial inequalities. Attention was focused on the exclusion of Blacks and other minorities from the American social contract, in which full participation in the social and material cornucopia seemed to be granted in return for assimilation to the majority culture. Racial minorities, it was held, were barred from complete assimilation by virtue of their ineradicable visibility. In such an intellectual atmosphere, it was natural to ask whether there were other groups that were kept to some degree from complete parity, and indeed it became quickly obvious that Italians, Jews, Poles, and others, were not yet accorded their full measure of admission to relatively elite strata. Ethnic differences attained the status of a moral currency, a way of making claims on the larger society, and this state of affairs waxed as the public debate over affirmative action for minority groups grew during the 1970s.[21]

By this argument, the supposed ethnic resurgence existed more in the eyes of its beholders than it did in any strengthening of ethnic sentiments, communities, and cultures. According to the evidence presented in Chapters 5 and 6, the assimilatory trajectory of groups like the Italians continued apace during the 1960s and 1970s, the decades of the proclaimed revival. Above all, the cresting of assimilation is reflected clearly in the steady rise in intermarriage among the two youngest cohorts (in Table 6-2), who married in this period.

But to demonstrate that a true revival did not take place is not to deny the very real contribution made by the renewed attention to ethnicity. What the ethnic writers did, and also what the ethnics themselves did, was to expand the definition of what is American. Before the massive assimilation of the post–World War II generation, the path of assimilation lay straight and narrow. There was one model of what an American looked like, one mold into which the ethnic had to fit, often at great personal cost, a lopping off of the past and a part of oneself. A recent memoir by Paul Cowan, *An Orphan in History,* speaks to the efforts many ethnics made. Cowan's family was originally Jewish, but his father changed the family name from "Cohen" to "Cowan" on his way up the social ladder. The assimilation his parents desired led them to cut themselves and their children off from the ethnic past. Ignoring Jewish rituals, they celebrated Christmas and Easter and kept Cowan and his siblings from meeting the part of the family that remained embarrassingly ethnic.[22]

Paul Cowan's father achieved great success at a time when ethnics were a small minority in the upper strata of American society. This numerical fact meant that he and others had to accept mobility on the terms laid down by dominant groups. But the massive penetration of these strata by ethnics in recent years creates a very different numerical situation, in which such drastic assimilation is no longer necessary, in which persons of ethnic origins can retain traces of these and still be mobile. The ethnic writers have played an important part in changing the terms of mobility and assimilation. They have been the voices of upwardly aspiring Americans of Irish, Italian, Jewish, Polish, and other backgrounds, providing a rationale that allows members of these groups to be successful without rejecting their names, their families, and their memories. In this sense, a kind of pluralism has been attained. It is not the often proclaimed cultural pluralism, in which ethnic groups provide the fundamental matrix for social life, but rather a pluralism at the margins, in which small ethnic flourishes, minor variations in life-style, are accepted into the American core. It is finally all right to be a little ethnic.

THE MELTING POT AT LAST?

Perhaps what has made the full import of the massive mobility and assimilation of the ethnics hard to see clearly is a limited vision of the melting pot. According to a common view, the melting pot would boil everything down to a gray, homogeneous slag; everyone would look and act the same. This view left many unprepared to recognize the melting pot coming into being—in which ethnic differences among whites will have receded but not altogether disappeared, while posing at the same time no serious hurdle to widespread interethnic contact.

There is even room for ethnic identity in a muted form in this melting pot. As Herbert Gans has observed, many mobile ethnics attempt to maintain some psychological connection with their origins, as a way of retaining some ethnic "spice" in their identity. But such a link must be compatible with their integration into middle-class society; in particular, it must not prevent them from mixing freely with others of different backgrounds. Hence this ethnic identity must be intermittent and undemanding in nature; for this reason, it focuses on symbols of ethnic cultures rather than the cultures themselves, and it tends to be expressed in leisure-time activities rather than in the fabric for everyday life. There is a wide latitude of expression available for this sort of "symbolic ethnicity," as Gans labels it. It can take the form of curiosity about the immigrant experience, often viewed nostalgically as a bittersweet authenticity in which the too assimilated third- or fourth-generation ethnic American cannot share, or it can be expressed by participation in a political movement with ethnic themes, perhaps concerned with the homeland or the group's standing in American society. Or it can be cast in the form of small details: objects in the home that have an ethnic meaning; occasional participation in ritual; or fondness for an ethnic cuisine.[23] But whether being Italian American is expressed in terms of a liking for opera or for homemade pasta, it is the individual who decides; generally, the decisions of one will not be those of another. In his study of Bridgeport, Connecticut, James Crispino asked his respondents about their support for various forms of Italian-American cultural and ethnic identity. There was little agreement among them, except for one thing: Close to 90 percent concurred that it was not all right to change one's name to sound less Italian.[24] Identity that is this diverse is unlikely to sustain ethnic-group cohesion.

Symbolic ethnicity is vastly different from the ethnicity of the past, which was a taken-for-granted part of everyday life, communal and at the same time imposed on the individual by the very fact of being born into the group. The ethnicity that survives in the melting pot is private and voluntary. The depth of change is profound: In less than a century, from the high point of mass immigration just before World War I, the ethnicity of white Americans has moved from the status of an irrevocable fact of birth to an ingredient of lifestyle. The ethnics and their children and grandchildren will not have to forget their ancestors as they step off into ethnicity's twilight.

NOTES

[1] Stephen Steinberg, *The Ethnic Myth: Race, Ethnicity, and Class in America* (Boston: Beacon Press, 1981), pp. 59–63.

[2] Richard D. Alba, "Social assimilation among American Catholic national-origin groups," *American Sociological Review,* 41, No. 6 (December, 1976), 1030–46.

[3] Fred Massarik and Alvin Chenkin, "United States National Jewish Population Study," *The American Jewish Yearbook* 74 (1973), 264–306. For a general review of Jewish intermarriage, see Bernard Farber and Leonard Gordon, "Accounting for Jewish intermarriage: An assessment of national and community studies," *Contemporary Jewry,* 6, No. 1 (Spring/Summer, 1982), 47–75.

[4] Steinberg, *The Ethnic Myth,* p. 70.

[5] Richard D. Alba and Gwen Moore, "Ethnicity in the American elite," *American Sociological Review,* 47, No. 3 (June, 1982), 373–83.

[6] Reynolds Farley, "Trends in racial inequalities: Have the gains of the 1960s disappeared in the 1970s?" *American Sociological Review,* 42, No. 2 (April, 1977), 189–208; Robert Hill, *The Illusion of Black Progress* (Washington, D.C.: National Urban League, 1978); David M. Heer, "Intermarriage," in *Harvard Encyclopedia of American Ethnic Groups,* ed. Stephen Thernstrom, Ann Orlov, and Oscar Handlin (Cambridge, Mass.: Harvard University Press, 1980).

[7] Darrel Montero, "The Japanese Americans: Changing patterns of assimilation over three generations," *American Sociological Review,* 46, No. 6 (December, 1981), 829–39; Eric Woodrum, "An assessment of Japanese American assimilation, pluralism, and subordination," *American Journal of Sociology,* 87, No. 1 (July, 1981), 157–69.

[8] Richard Polenberg, *One Nation Divisible: Class, Race, and Ethnicity in the United States Since 1938* (New York: Viking, 1980), pp. 202–7; U.S. Bureau of the Census, *Statistical Abstract of the United States: 1981* (Washington, D.C.: U.S. Government Printing Office, 1981), p. 88.

[9] It is of course possible for a numerical minority to maintain its dominance against a number of larger contending groups, as the example of South Africa demonstrates, but only under very special conditions; in the case of South Africa, the primacy of mining in its economic base meant that it did not require the kind of labor force that developed in the United States. See George M. Frederickson, *White Supremacy: A Comparative Study in American and South African History* (New York: Oxford University Press, 1981), Chapter 5.

[10] Steinberg, *The Ethnic Myth,* Chapter 7.

[11] Steinberg summarizes Black migration to the North in *The Ethnic Myth,* pp. 204–5.

[12] Robert Blauner, *Racial Oppression in America* (New York: Harper & Row, 1972), p. 64.

[13] The queuing notion is discussed in some detail by Stanley Lieberson, *A Piece of the Pie: Blacks and White Immigrants Since 1880* (Berkeley: University of California Press, 1980), pp. 377–81.

[14] Lieberson, *A Piece of the Pie,* p. 380.

[15] Ibid.

[16] Gunnar Myrdal, *An American Dilemma* (New York: Harper and Brothers, 1944); Robert K. Merton, "Discrimination and the American creed," in R. M. MacIver (ed.), *Discrimination and National Welfare* (New York: Harper & Brothers, 1948).

[17] The distinction between immigrant groups and so-called colonized minorities (i.e., those introduced by force), is developed extensively by Blauner, *Racial Oppression in America,* Chapter 2. The distinction is somewhat open to question with respect to Hispanics, and appears most justified in application to Puerto Ricans and the Mexican Americans of the Southwest.

[18] Herman D. Bloch, *The Circle of Discrimination: An Economic and Social Study of the Black Man in New York* (New York: New York University Press, 1969), Chapter 6; Lieberson, *A Piece of the Pie,* Chapter 11.

[19] Steinberg, *The Ethnic Myth,* pp. 145–48; also, Stephen Steinberg, *The Academic Melting Pot: Catholics and Jews in American Higher Education* (New York: McGraw-Hill, 1974), Chapter 5.

[20] The example of Andrew Greeley, one of the foremost of the ethnic writers, makes clear the connection between an interest in ethnicity and a perception of continued discrimination against ethnics. Greeley, of Irish Catholic ancestry and a priest, has frequently spoken out against what he perceives to be the anti-Catholic bigotry in the academic world.

[21] Many of the ethnic writers were ambivalent about or downright hostile to affirmative action, precisely because it seemed to overlook what they perceived as the still unfavorable position of white ethnics. See, for example, Nathan Glazer, *Affirmative Discrimination: Ethnic Inequality and Public Policy* (New York: Basic Books, 1975).

[22] Paul Cowan, *An Orphan in History: Retrieving a Jewish Legacy* (New York: Doubleday, 1982).

[23] Herbert J. Gans, "Symbolic ethnicity: The future of ethnic groups and cultures in America," *Ethnic and Racial Studies,* 2, No. 1 (January, 1979), 1–20.

[24] James A. Crispino, *The Assimilation of Ethnic Groups: The Italian Case* (Staten Island: Center for Migration Studies, 1980), pp. 54–63.

INDEX